THE WORKS OF
WILLIAM COLLINS

THE WORKS OF
William Collins

EDITED BY

RICHARD WENDORF

AND

CHARLES RYSKAMP

OXFORD
AT THE CLARENDON PRESS
1979

Oxford University Press, Walton Street, Oxford OX2 6DP

OXFORD LONDON GLASGOW
NEW YORK TORONTO MELBOURNE WELLINGTON
KUALA LUMPUR SINGAPORE HONG KONG TOKYO
DELHI BOMBAY CALCUTTA MADRAS KARACHI
NAIROBI DAR ES SALAAM CAPE TOWN

Published in the United States by
Oxford University Press, New York

© *Oxford University Press 1979*

British Library Cataloguing in Publication Data
Collins, William, b. 1721
   The works of William Collins. – (Oxford English
   texts)
   I. Wendorf, Richard   II. Ryskamp, Charles
   III. Series
   821'.5 PR3350 78–40758
   ISBN 0–19–812749–9

Printed in Great Britain
at the University Press, Oxford
by Eric Buckley
Printer to the University

ACKNOWLEDGEMENTS

IT is a pleasure to acknowledge the many debts we have incurred in the course of preparing this edition. For financial assistance we wish to thank the Folger Shakespeare Library for a Folger Library Fellowship and the Mrs Giles Whiting Foundation for a Whiting Fellowship in the Humanities. A grant from the American Philosophical Society allowed additional research in England to be completed. The preparation of the final typescript was greatly assisted by grants from Princeton and Northwestern Universities.

For permission to reproduce manuscript materials in this edition we are indebted to Mrs Donald F. Hyde; the late James Osborn; Colonel A. E. Cameron of Aldouri Castle, Inverness-shire; the British Library; and the President and Fellows of Trinity College, Oxford. For permission to examine books in private collections we are grateful to Mrs Hyde, Mr Osborn, Robert H. Taylor, Herman F. Liebert, John Sparrow, and Lord Rothschild.

We also wish to thank the following institutions for the use of their collections: Princeton University; Northwestern University; the Beinecke Library, Yale University; Harvard University; the Folger Shakespeare Library; the Library of Congress; Chapin Library, Williams College; the Newberry Library; the New York Public Library; the British Library; the Bodleian Library; the Victoria and Albert Museum; Cambridge University; Trinity College, Oxford; Worcester College, Oxford; Magdalen College, Oxford; and Trinity College, Cambridge. For assistance in providing information about their holdings we are indebted to the Boston Public Library; the Henry E. Huntington Library; the William Andrews Clark Memorial Library, University of California, Los Angeles; Rice University; and Texas Christian University.

Lawrence Lipking and John Baird both read the entire manuscript; their generous and judicious advice has in fact made this a work by several hands. We also wish to thank Professor Baird for providing a translation of Collins's 'Oratio ad Portas'. We are particularly grateful to James E. Tierney for sharing his knowledge of Robert Dodsley and the *Museum* with us, and to Mary Margaret Stewart for imparting discoveries made in her current work on Collins's life. For their generous assistance in providing information about Collins at Winchester College, we are indebted to J. M. G. Blakiston and to Paul Yeats-Edwards, the present Fellows' Librarian. For considerable help in the use of the recently acquired Harding Collection at the New Bodleian Library, we wish to thank Peter Ward Jones. For assistance in verifying the text we wish to thank Verlyn Klinkenborg and, for additional help in preparing the edition, Leonard Barkan, Thomas Blanding, William Brennan, Joseph Greenberg, Traugott Lawler, Herbert L. Sussman, Scott Westrem, and Pamela White. Also deserving of repeated thanks are Helen S. Wright (and, at a later date, Mary Dell Onley), whose diligence and accuracy in typing this work have made them important collaborators as well.

Northwestern University   RICHARD WENDORF

The Pierpont Morgan Library and   CHARLES RYSKAMP
Princeton University

CONTENTS

ABBREVIATIONS

All books issued before 1900 are understood to have been published in London unless otherwise noted. All quotations from Greek and Latin authors are from the Loeb Classical Library.

I. EDITIONS OF COLLINS'S POETRY

Odes
: *Odes on Several Descriptive and Allegoric Subjects*. 1747 (published December 1746).

Collection
: *A Collection of Poems by Several Hands*. Ed. Robert Dodsley. 6 vols. 1748–58. For bibliographical information concerning *Collection 1758a* and *1758b*, see William B. Todd, 'Concurrent Printing: An Analysis of Dodsley's *Collection of Poems by Several Hands*', *PBSA*, 46 (1952), 45–57.

Union
: *The Union: Or Select Scots and English Poems*. Ed. Thomas Warton. Edinburgh [Oxford], 1753 (rpt. 1759). The 1753 edn. exists in two states, with variants; see D. Nichol Smith, 'Thomas Warton's Miscellany: *The Union*', *RES*, 19 (1943), 263–75.

Poetical Calendar
: *Poetical Calendar*. Ed. Francis Fawkes and William Woty. 12 vols. (vols. xi–xii). 1763.

Langhorne
: *The Poetical Works of Mr. William Collins. With Memoirs of the Author; and Observations on His Genius and Writings*. Ed. John Langhorne. 1765 (rpt. 1771, 1776, 1781). The Yale University Library (Osborn Collection) copy of the 1781 edn. has valuable annotations by William Hymers. A pirated edn. of 1765 contains variants of no textual authority, which have not been recorded here (see Iolo A. Williams, *Points in Eighteenth-Century Verse* (London: Constable, 1934), pp. 71–2).

Pearch
: *A Collection of Poems in Two Volumes. By Several Hands*. Ed. George Pearch. 1768.

Dobson
: *The Poetical Works of William Collins*. Philadelphia: Thomas Dobson, 1788.

Strutt
: *Poems*. Ed. Benjamin Strutt. Colchester, 1796.

Barbauld
: *The Poetical Works of Mr. William Collins. With a Prefatory Essay*. Ed. Mrs A. L. Barbauld. 1797 (rpt. 1802).

Chalmers   *The Works of the English Poets.* Ed. Alexander Chalmers. 21 vols. (vol. xiii). 1810.

Dyce   *The Poetical Works of William Collins.* Ed. Alexander Dyce (with additional notes by John Mitford). 1827.

Crowe   *The Poems of William Collins.* Ed. William Crowe. Bath, 1828.

Brydges   *The Poetical Works of William Collins.* Ed. Sir Egerton Brydges (with a 'Memoir' by Sir Harris Nicolas). 1830 (rpt. 1853).

Miller   *The Poetical Works of James Beattie, LL.D. and William Collins.* Ed. Thomas Miller. 1846.

Gilfillan   *The Poetical Works of Goldsmith, Collins, and T. Warton.* Ed. George Gilfillan. Edinburgh, 1854.

Thomas   *The Poetical Works of William Collins.* Ed. W. Moy Thomas. 1858 (rpt. 1866, 1894, 1904).

Bronson   *The Poems of William Collins.* Ed. W. C. Bronson. Boston, 1898.

Stone   *The Poems of William Collins.* Ed. Christopher Stone. London: Frowde, 1907.

Poole   *The Poetical Works of Gray and Collins.* Ed. Christopher Stone and A. L. Poole. London: Oxford Univ. Press, 1917 (rev. 1927, 1937 by Frederick Page). Reissued 1977, ed. Roger Lonsdale.

Blunden   *The Poems of William Collins.* Ed. Edmund Blunden. London: Etchells and Macdonald, 1929.

Cunningham   *William Collins: Drafts & Fragments of Verse.* Ed. J. S. Cunningham. Oxford: Clarendon Press, 1956.

Johnston   *Selected Poems of Thomas Gray and William Collins.* Ed. Arthur Johnston. London: Arnold, 1967.

Lonsdale   *The Poems of Thomas Gray, William Collins and Oliver Goldsmith.* Ed. Roger Lonsdale. London: Longman, 1969.

II. OTHER WORKS

ECS   *Eighteenth-Century Studies.*
ELH   *English Literary History.*
GM   *Gentleman's Magazine.*
HLQ   *Huntington Library Quarterly.*
MLN   *Modern Language Notes.*
MP   *Modern Philology.*

NQ	*Notes and Queries.*
OED	*New* [Oxford] *English Dictionary.*
PBSA	*Papers of the Bibliographical Society of America.*
PMLA	*Publications of the Modern Language Association.*
PQ	*Philological Quarterly.*
RES	*Review of English Studies.*
SB	*Studies in Bibliography.*
SEL	*Studies in English Literature 1500–1900.*
SP	*Studies in Philology.*
TLS	*Times Literary Supplement.*

Ainsworth   Ainsworth, Edward G., Jr. *Poor Collins: His Life, His Art, and His Influence.* Ithaca: Cornell Univ. Press, 1937.

Boswell   Boswell, James. *The Life of Samuel Johnson.* Ed. G. B. Hill, rev. L. F. Powell. 6 vols. Oxford: Clarendon Press, 1934–50 (2nd edn., 1964).

Carver   Carver, P. L. 'Notes on the Life of William Collins.' *NQ*, 177 (Aug.–Oct. 1939), 128–32, 146–50, 167–71, 182–5, 201–4, 220–3, 240–3, 258–61, 272–4. Expanded in *The Life of a Poet: A Biographical Sketch of William Collins.* London: Sidgwick and Jackson, 1967.

Dict.   Johnson, Samuel. *A Dictionary of the English Language.* 2 vols. 1755.

Dryden   *The Poems of John Dryden.* Ed. James Kinsley. 4 vols. Oxford: Clarendon Press, 1958.

Foxon   Foxon, D. F. *English Verse 1701–1750: A Catalogue of Separately Printed Poems with Notes on Contemporary Collected Editions.* 2 vols. Cambridge: Cambridge Univ. Press, 1975.

Garrod   Garrod, H. W. *Collins.* Oxford: Clarendon Press, 1928.

Gray   *Correspondence of Thomas Gray.* Ed. Paget Toynbee and Leonard Whibley. 3 vols. Oxford: Clarendon Press, 1935. Reissued with corrections and additions by H. W. Starr, 1971.

Johnson   *The Yale Edition of the Works of Samuel Johnson.* Ed. E. L. McAdam, Jr., *et al.* 11 vols. New Haven: Yale Univ. Press, 1958– .

Lives   Johnson, Samuel. *Lives of the English Poets.* Ed. G. B. Hill. 3 vols. Oxford: Clarendon Press, 1905.

Milton   *The Poetical Works of John Milton.* Ed. Helen Darbishire. 2 vols. Oxford: Clarendon Press, 1952–5.

Museum	*The Museum: Or, The Literary and Historical Register.* Ed. Mark Akenside. 3 vols. 1746–7.
Nichols	Nichols, John. *Literary Anecdotes of the Eighteenth Century.* 9 vols. 1812–15.
Pope	*The Twickenham Edition of Alexander Pope.* Ed. John Butt *et al.* 11 vols. London: Methuen; New Haven: Yale Univ. Press, 1939–69.
Reaper	*The Reaper,* No. 26. *York Chronicle,* 16 Feb. 1797. Rpt. in Nathan Drake, *The Gleaner: A Series of Periodical Essays; Selected and Arranged from Scarce or Neglected Volumes,* 1811, iv. 474–84.
Rothschild	*The Rothschild Library: A Catalogue of the Collection of Eighteenth-Century Printed Books and Manuscripts Formed by Lord Rothschild.* 2 vols. Cambridge: Cambridge Univ. Press, 1954 (rpt. Dawsons, 1969).
Salmon	Salmon, Thomas. *Modern History: Or, The Present State Of All Nations.* 31 vols. 1725–38 (3rd edn., 3 vols., 1739).
Shakespeare	*The Riverside Shakespeare.* Ed. G. B. Evans *et al.* 2 vols. Boston: Houghton Mifflin, 1974.
Sigworth	Sigworth, Oliver F. *William Collins.* New York: Twayne, 1965.
Spectator	Addison, Joseph, *et al. The Spectator.* Ed. Donald F. Bond. 5 vols. Oxford: Clarendon Press, 1965.
Spenser	*The Poetical Works of Edmund Spenser.* Ed. J. C. Smith and E. de Selincourt. 3 vols. Oxford: Clarendon Press, 1909–10.
Spingarn	*Critical Essays of the Seventeenth Century.* Ed. J. E. Spingarn. 3 vols. Oxford: Clarendon Press, 1908–9.
Straus	Straus, Ralph. *Robert Dodsley: Poet, Publisher and Playwright.* London: John Lane, 1910.
Thomson	Thomson, James. *Poetical Works.* Ed. J. L. Robertson. London: Oxford Univ. Press, 1908.
Tinker	*The Tinker Library: A Bibliographical Catalogue of the Books and Manuscripts collected by Chauncey Brewster Tinker.* Ed. Robert F. Metzdorf. New Haven: Yale Univ. Library, 1959.
Waller	Waller, Edmund. *Works.* Ed. Elijah Fenton. 1729.
Watson	Dryden, John. *Of Dramatic Poesy and Other Critical Essays.* Ed. George Watson. 2 vols. London: Dent; New York: Dutton, 1962.

Williams   Williams, Iolo A. *Seven XVIIIth Century Bibliographies.*
                  London: Dulau, 1924.

Woodhouse   Woodhouse, A. S. P. 'Collins and the Creative Imagina-
                  tion: A Study in the Critical Background of his Odes
                  (1746).' *Studies in English by Members of University College
                  Toronto.* Ed. M. W. Wallace. Toronto: Univ. of Toronto
                  Press, 1931, pp. 59–130.

CHRONOLOGY

1721   25 December. Collins born to Elizabeth (aged 39) and William Collins (47) in Chichester, where his father, a hatter, has twice been mayor of the town. His sisters are Elizabeth (16) and Anne (15).

1725–33   Probably educated at the Prebendal School, Chichester.

1733   30 September. His father dies at Chichester.

1734   23 February. Admitted a Scholar to Winchester College, where his fellow students are Joseph Warton, William Whitehead, James Hampton, and John Mulso.

1739   His first published poems ('To Miss Aurelia C——r' and 'Sonnet') appear above pseudonyms in the *Gentleman's Magazine* (January and October). According to Joseph Warton, he has already begun writing the *Persian Eclogues*.

1740   Placed first on the roll of Scholars for New College (Warton is second, Mulso third), but no vacancy occurs. (Samuel Johnson later calls this 'the original misfortune of his life'.)

22 March. Matriculates at Queen's College, Oxford, but does not go up to Oxford until Michaelmas Term.

1741   29 July. Elected to a Demyship at Magdalen College, Oxford, where his cousin William Payne is a Fellow. His friends Joseph Warton, John Mulso, and Gilbert White are at Oriel.

1742   January. *Persian Eclogues* published by J. Roberts.

1743   18 November. Graduates B.A.

December. *Verses Humbly Address'd to Sir Thomas Hanmer* published by Mary Cooper. (Collins dates the poem '*Oxford, Dec. 3.*'). He may also have planned his edition of the *Galeomyomachia* before leaving Oxford.

1744   Probably arrives in London early in the year: the antiquarian William Oldys appears to refer to him and his 'Subscription' in a letter of 22 February; his *Epistle* is advertised on 6 April.

9 May. *An Epistle: Address'd to Sir Thomas Hanmer*, the first poem to carry his name, published by Dodsley and Cooper (includes his 'Song from Shakespear's *Cymbelyne*').

3 July. His mother dies at Chichester; her will, leaving property to her three children, not proved until 12 August 1745.

18 July. Mulso's letter to Gilbert White describes Collins as 'entirely an Author' and mentions his 'Subscriptions', apparently related to the planned *History of the Revival of Learning*.

17 September. A letter of Lt.-Col. Edmund Martin, Collins's uncle, indicates that he has applied for a living to the Duke of Richmond and has been offered a curacy at Birdham, which John Hardham (a tobacconist, and under-treasurer of Drury Lane Theatre) persuades him to reject.

8 October. Mulso writes to White that Collins is now his neighbour (at Miss Bundy's lodgings, at the corner of King's Square Court, Soho).

December. In the October–December issue of *A Literary Journal* (Dublin), his *Review of the Advancement of Learning, from 1300 to 1521* (*The History of the Revival of Learning*) is erroneously advertised as 'published in London'.

1745   White describes him as 'spending his time in all the dissipation of Ranelagh, Vauxhall, and the playhouses'. He plans to write tragedies, begins a translation of Aristotle's *Poetics* (with a commentary), and is engaged by Manby to write lives for the *Biographia Britannica* (which remain 'in embryo'). His friends now include Johnson, Garrick, Quin, Armstrong, and Foote.

11 May. Battle of Fontenoy and death of Capt. Charles Ross. Presumably writes his 'Ode, to a Lady' by the end of the month.

7 September. Mulso writes to White that Collins 'has been some Time return'd from Flanders', where he probably visited his uncle Col. Martin for advice about his career. Mulso also notes that Collins returned 'in order to put on ye Gown as I hear, & get a chaplaincy in a Regiment'.

1746   17 January. Battle of Falkirk, in which the English forces are defeated by the Young Pretender, apparently prompts Collins to write his 'Ode, Written in the beginning of the Year 1746'.

5 March. Will of his uncle, Charles Collins, proved, which leaves him property in Chichester. Collins raises money on this property on 10 April, and sells it on 30 May.

16 April. Battle of Culloden.

23 April. Letter from John Gilbert Cooper to Dodsley describes Collins as 'that wandering Knight'.

May (probably 20–2). Meets Joseph Warton at the Guildford Races, where they read each other's odes, resolve to 'join our forces, and to publish them immediately'.

28 May. Mulso mentions Collins's encounter with a bailiff at Miss

Bundy's. According to Johnson, who describes the same or a similar scrape, Collins escapes into the country (to Chichester).

7 June. His 'Ode, to a Lady' printed in Dodsley's *Museum* (edited by Akenside).

1 August. Mulso writes that he has received a letter from Collins in Antwerp in which Collins reports that he has travelled through Holland and is setting out for the army, presumably to meet his uncle once again.

4 December. Dodsley publishes Joseph Warton's *Odes on Various Subjects* separately, and issues a second edition on 9 January.

20 December. Andrew Millar publishes Collins's *Odes on Several Descriptive and Allegoric Subjects* (dated 1747). Later (possibly after his inheritance in 1749) Collins bought back the remaining copies and 'resigned [them] to the flames'.

1747   Now living in Richmond, where his friends include James Thomson.

1 May. Collins and his sisters sell their father's house in Chichester.

10–17 November. Writes to John Gilbert Cooper about their projected *Clarendon Review*, which is never published.

1748   7 April. Johnson, in his preface to Dodsley's *Preceptor*, refers to a new commentary on the *Poetics* as soon to be published. By this time, however, Collins appears to have abandoned this project.

27 August. Thomson dies at Richmond.

December. 'Ode, Written in the beginning of the Year 1746', 'Ode, to a Lady', and 'Ode to Evening' reprinted in Dodsley's *Collection* (2nd edn.).

1749   19 April. Col. Martin dies, leaving Collins an inheritance believed to be as much as £2,000.

June. *Ode Occasion'd by the Death of Mr. Thomson* published by Manby and Cox.

October. 'A Song from Shakespear's *Cymbelyne*' reprinted in the *Gentleman's Magazine*.

1750   January (and possibly December 1749). Writes 'Ode to a Friend on His Return &c' and presents it to John Home; it is published in 1788 as *An Ode on the Popular Superstitions of the Highlands of Scotland*.

Thomas Warton reports that he often saw Collins in London at this time

('This was before his illness'), and that he was still planning *The History of the Revival of Learning* and *The Clarendon Review*.

February–March. Two journals announce the imminent publication of *An Epistle to the Editor of Fairfax his Translation of Tasso's Jerusalem*, but the poem is not published (though advertised) by Manby and Cox.

2 July. William Hayes's musical setting of 'The Passions' performed at the Oxford Encaenia; the poem is printed as a pamphlet at Oxford and later at Winchester.

21 October. Elizabeth Collins marries Lieut. Nathaniel Tanner.

8 November. Collins writes to William Hayes from Chichester, asks for a copy of the Oxford pamphlet, and mentions both 'a more perfect Copy' of 'The Passions' and a new ode on 'the Music of the Græcian Theatre'.

1751   'About Easter'. Thomas Warton reports that Collins is seriously ill (and considers himself to be dying).

9 June. Collins writes to Warton from Chichester, where he now seems to be in good health.

1751–4   Ragsdale reports that Collins travels to France and Bath in 'hopes his health might be restored'. Johnson visits him in Islington following his return from France.

1753   May. Thomas Warton's *The Union*, published in Oxford, reprints the 'Ode to Evening' and *An Ode Occasion'd by the Death of Mr. Thomson*.

1754   According to Ragsdale, Collins's sister Anne removes him from MacDonald's madhouse in Chelsea to Chichester, where he is visited by the Wartons in September and presents them with several poetical fragments. His sister Elizabeth dies in June.

November. Visits Oxford 'for change of air and amusement', where he is seen, in a deplorable state, by Thomas Warton and Gilbert White.

1755   28 January. Marriage licence issued to Anne Collins and Lieut. Hugh Sempill; after his death (1762) she later marries Thomas Durnford, Rector of Bramdean and Vicar of Harting.

March. *An Epistle: Addrest to Sir Thomas Hanmer* and 'A Song from Shakespear's *Cymbelyne*' reprinted in Dodsley's *Collection* (vol. iv).

1756   Joseph Warton alludes to Collins's continued interest in *The History of the Revival of Learning* in his *Essay on . . . Pope*.

April. Johnson writes to Thomas Warton that Collins has not answered his letter.

1757 *Oriental Eclogues* published by J. Payne (advertised in January–February).

1759 According to Thomas Warton, Collins continues to talk of literary subjects 'not many months before his death'.

12 June. Collins dies at Chichester and is buried in St. Andrew's Church three days later.

INTRODUCTION

'THE time has surely come', H. O. White wrote in 1928, '. . . for a definitive edition of Collins, with an introduction and notes, bringing within the covers of one volume the fruits of recent researches in the poet's life and work.'[1] In the fifty years since White's plea, a number of new or revised editions of the works of William Collins have appeared, and yet none of these offers the definitive critical text and apparatus that are justified by the textual difficulties in Collins's poems and by Collins's assured stature as a major eighteenth-century English poet. The present critical edition is thus an attempt to provide an old-spelling text with full reference to manuscripts and early printings which will fulfil the needs of Collins's modern readers.

In preparing this edition, we have drawn upon a considerable amount of work which has already been devoted to Collins, especially in previous editions of his poetry. Two nineteenth-century editions deserve particular attention: that by Alexander Dyce (1827), which carefully collates the texts and traces much of the information we now have relating to Collins and his work; and that by Walter Bronson (1898), which presents an accurate text, variant readings, and an early attempt to provide full annotation. Until recently Bronson's edition has not been seriously challenged. Christopher Stone's edition (1907) does not give variant readings, nor can its editorial decisions always withstand close scrutiny. Stone's and Austin Lane Poole's revised edition (1937) gives more variant readings, but is still incomplete and too often inaccurate. It fails to provide reasons for choosing one text rather than another (the text of the *Persian Eclogues*, for example), and ignores the problems involved in the formulation of the Collins canon. Stone's and Poole's edition has recently been superseded by the *Poetical Works* of Gray and Collins, edited by Roger Lonsdale (1977). Lonsdale provides a fuller textual commentary than Stone and Poole (and texts of the Drafts and Fragments), but the edition

[1] 'The Text of Collins', *TLS* (5 Apr. 1928), p. 257.

does not supply a full textual apparatus. Lonsdale's text is more accurate than Stone's and Poole's, but some errors (especially in accidentals) remain, and the text of the *Persian Eclogues* does not uniformly follow its copy-text. Edmund Blunden's handsome edition (1929) includes a rather uneven commentary and is ultimately undermined by its numerous unsubstantiated attributions of poems to Collins. Arthur Johnston's edition (1967) offers a usually reliable text and valuable notes, but includes only a selection of poems. Roger Lonsdale's Longman edition (1969) is both more ambitious and exacting than its predecessors, and has been of great value to us at every turn. Lonsdale has collected pertinent bibliographical, biographical, historical (and even recent critical) information which has a bearing on the text, and has contributed important discussions and commentary on many poems, especially the Drafts and Fragments. He has succeeded admirably in modernizing Collins's text, and yet the principle of modernization has prevented the establishment of a full critical edition of Collins's works, and hence also of a complete textual commentary.

Textual problems in the Collins canon, one scholar has remarked, are either simple or unsolvable.[1] The present work is offered in the belief that there is ample justification for a new edition which will provide a thorough textual discussion of even the most simple decisions as well as a careful re-examination of those problems which have vexed all of Collins's editors. This edition thus differs from previous efforts (Lonsdale's, most notably) not only in its focus on the establishment of a text faithful to the contemporary texts which Collins 'intended', but in substantive changes as well. The most visible changes will be found in the texts of *Oriental Eclogues* and 'Ode, to a Lady', and in the inclusion of 'To Miss Aurelia C——r' among Collins's works. Manuscripts of Collins's letter to Cooper, his 'Ode to a Friend on his Return &c', and the Drafts and Fragments have been re-examined and presented in more complete form. These manuscripts are not fair copies, however, and thus it has not been possible to reconcile all discrepancies in spacing and capitalization with full confidence. It has been possible, on the other hand, to determine more clearly Dodsley's role in the presentation of texts

---

[1] Sigworth, p. 87.

of poems included in his own collections, especially in the presentation of accidentals; for a full discussion, see Richard Wendorf, 'Robert Dodsley as Editor', *SB*, 31 (1978), 235–48. To the traditional collection of Collins's poems have been added texts of his two surviving letters (one with a new source), the text of his 'Oratio ad Portas' (with a translation), and a discussion of lost letters, lost poems, unfinished projects, and poems and essays doubtfully attributed to Collins. In the discussion of each poem, moreover, an attempt has been made to supply the reader with the information necessary for an understanding of each textual decision, be it simple or an effort to penetrate the 'unsolvable'.

THE BIOGRAPHICAL PROBLEM

If certain textual problems within the Collins canon are in fact unsolvable, they are so primarily because—as each of Collins's editors, biographers, and critics has lamented—we have such a small amount of material concerning the poet and his work. Little is known, for instance, about Collins's first years in London, the years in which (as Johnson's 'Life' and several of the Drafts and Fragments suggest) he struggled in vain to find patronage for his work. Similarly, little is known about Collins's friendship with Joseph Warton, even though Joseph and his brother Thomas are two of our most important sources of information concerning Collins. But clearly the largest gap in our knowledge of his career comprises the years following 1749–50 in which Collins, now no longer publishing his poetry, was thought to be mad. Collins's apparent madness has produced serious problems for his biographers and critics, and, as our head-note to the *Oriental Eclogues* points out, for the textual scholar as well. The following discussion, which endeavours to gather all the relevant facts together for the first time, is an attempt to clarify our portrait of Collins during these shadowy years.[1]

An indication of the scarcity of material concerning Collins's last years can be seen in the efforts of Collins's first scholarly editor,

---

[1] For a discussion of the critical implications, and of the fictions issuing from Collins's illness, see Richard Wendorf, '"Poor Collins" Reconsidered', *HLQ*, 42 (1979), 91–116.

Alexander Dyce, to obtain anecdotes about the poet. Dyce wrote to Henry Mackenzie, the ageing 'man of feeling', who was a close associate of the dramatist John Home, to whom Collins inscribed his 'Ode to a Friend' ('Ode on the Popular Superstitions of the Highlands of Scotland'). Dyce received this reply in 1826:

In the present state of my health, writing is not an easy matter to me; but I am anxious not to delay acknowledging your letter on the subject of your proposed edition of Collins. It would gratify me if I could contribute to it; but I do not recollect hearing any anecdotes from Mr. Home, or having any communication with him or any one else, regarding Collins, the close of whose life made the subject rather a distressing one.[1]

Mackenzie's experience seems not to have been unique. Clearly Collins's madness has been, to some extent, the reason for our vague knowledge of his last years: either his seclusion isolated him from those who would normally have seen him and perhaps have written about him, or the possibility of madness itself became a cause for reticence. John Ragsdale, who preserved many facts about his friend's life in London, was forced to bring his account to a hasty close: 'I never saw him after his sister had removed him from M'Donald's mad-house at Chelsea to Chichester, where he soon sunk into a deplorable state of idiotism, which, when I was told, shocked me exceedingly; and even now the remembrance of a man, for whom I had a particular friendship, and in whose company I have passed so many pleasant, happy hours, gives me a severe shock.'[2] Collins did have friends who saw or heard more of him during his last years, however, and it is to these men—Samuel Johnson, Gilbert White, and Joseph and Thomas Warton—that we are indebted for the few fragments which form the following sketch of those sad years.

Collins's illness was thought to have begun shortly after the death of his uncle, Colonel Martin, in 1749. In 'Some Account of the Life and Writings of Mr. William Collins', published in the *Poetical Calendar* in 1763, James Hampton wrote that Collins's uncle left him a considerable fortune, 'which however he did not

---

[1] *The Reminiscences of Alexander Dyce*, ed. Richard Schrader (Columbus, Ohio: Ohio State Univ. Press, 1972), p. 233. [2] *The Reaper*, No. 26.

live long to enjoy, for he fell into a nervous disorder, which continued, with but short intervals, till his death, which happened in 1756. and with which disorder his head and intellects were at times affected'.[1] Johnson, who added a character sketch to Hampton's account, remembered the latter part of Collins's life 'with pity and sadness': the poet 'languished some years under that depression of mind which enchains the faculties without destroying them, and leaves reason the knowledge of right, without the power of pursuing it'. With these clouds gathering on his intellect, Collins sought relief in travel through France 'but found himself constrained to yield to his malady, and returned: he was for some time confined in a house of lunatics, and afterwards retired to the care of his sister in Colchester, where death at last came to his relief'.

Hampton's and Johnson's account is not entirely satisfactory, even as a rough outline of these years. Their mistaking both Collins's date and place of death indicates just how out of touch the biographers were with their subject, and this is corroborated by Johnson's letters in the mid-1750s, as we shall see. Johnson's short character of the poet proved, moreover, to be both enigmatic and highly influential. 'His morals were pure, and his opinions pious', Johnson began; but, in a characteristic turn, he pointed out that 'in a long continuance of poverty, and long habits of dissipation, it cannot be expected that any character should be exactly uniform'. Johnson does not have the 'temerity to affirm' that 'this man, wise and virtuous as he was, passed always unentangled through the snares of life', but he does claim 'that at least he preserved the source of action unpolluted', and that his faults stemmed from 'casual temptation' and not from his principles, which remained unshaken. What Johnson seems to be saying is that his friend was a good and virtuous man, but, as Johnson's contemporaries who had witnessed Collins's frustrations and anxieties in the late 1740s and early 1750s would have known, he was also human. Biographers in Johnson's footsteps, eager to discover clues to Collins's character (and thus to elucidate his later illness) have pounced on the poet's indolence and 'dissipation'.

[1] *Poetical Calendar*, xii. 109.

'Now what is Johnson telling us, or, more interestingly, what is he concealing?' a scholar has recently asked; 'What were the "long habits of dissipation"?'[1] But, as Birkbeck Hill's footnote points out in his edition of the *Lives*, Collins's 'dissipation' was defined in Johnson's dictionary as simply 'a scattered habit of attention'.[2] At this time the word did not mean 'a dissolute mode of living', as later biographers have often assumed.

The anecdote with which Johnson closes his narrative indicates that he did see Collins at least once during the years 1750–4; more important, it chronicles an encounter which demonstrates Collins's apparent health and lucidity at this time:

After his return from France, the writer of this character paid him a visit at Islington, where he was waiting for his sister, whom he had directed to meet him: there was then nothing of disorder discernable in his mind by any but himself, but he had then withdrawn from study, and travelled with no other book than an English testament, such as children carry to the school; when his friend took it into his hand, out of curiosity to see what companion a man of letters had chosen, 'I have but one book,' says Collins, 'but that is the best.'[3]

The other information we have concerning these years (1750–4) suggests that if Collins was in fact ill at this time his illness was, as Johnson said, most easily discernible to the poet himself. In 1750, for example, we know that Collins had not yet 'withdrawn from study', that he was still, according to Thomas Warton who visited him in London, planning his *History of the Revival of Learning*. In the spring of this year the publishers Manby and Cox advertised his 'Epistle to the Editor of Fairfax his Translation of Tasso's Jerusalem'.[4] In July 'The Passions' was performed at the Oxford Encaenia, and in November Collins wrote to William Hayes, who had set the poetry to music, informing him that he had both a revised version of the poem and an ode on 'the Music of the

---

[1] Sigworth, p. 55.

[2] *Lives*, iii. 338 n. (this is also pointed out by P. M. Spacks in her review of Sigworth's book, *PQ*, 45 (1966), 548). The word was often associated with diversion or amusement; cf. Boswell's journals of 1763–4.

[3] *Poetical Calendar*, xii. 112.

[4] See the discussion under Lost Poems, pp. 200–1, below.

Græcian Theatre'.[1] There is no evidence of any early sign of mental illness in connection with this apparent activity. Thomas Warton wrote that he

often saw Collins in London in 1750—This was before his illness. He then told me of his intended History of the *Revival of Learning*, and proposed a scheme of a *Review*, to be called the *Clarendon Review*, and to be printed at the University Press, under the conduct and authority of the University.[2]

The first specific evidence we have of Collins's illness dates from 1751. According to Thomas Warton,

About Easter, the next year, I was in London; when being given over, and supposed to be dying, he desired to see me, that he might take his last leave of me: But he grew better, and in the summer he sent me a letter on some private business, which I have now by me, dated Chichester, June 9th, 1751, written in a fine hand, and without the least symptom of a disordered or debilitated understanding.[3]

What Warton tells us here of Collins's illness and recovery suggests that the poet's ailment was both physical and severe, although it may also have produced symptoms of a disordered understanding. After June 1751, however, Collins seems (unfortunately) to have dropped out of Warton's sight until 1754, and it is during this period that Collins presumably travelled in France. Johnson's account of Collins's travels is substantiated by John Ragsdale. Ragsdale insisted (in 1793) that 'There are so few of his intimates now living, that I believe I am the only one who can give a true account of his family and connections. The principal part of what I write is from my own knowledge, or what I have heard from his nearest relations.'[4] Ragsdale did not see Collins after he was removed from the madhouse in Chelsea, nor was he positive of the date of Collins's death, but he does state that when Collins's 'health and faculties began to decline he went to France, and afterwards to Bath, in hopes his health might be restored, but without success'.[5]

Presumably Collins's travels to France and Bath lasted at least

[1] See p. 89, below.   [2] *The Reaper*, No. 26.
[3] Ibid. Collins's letter has not survived.   [4] Ibid.   [5] Ibid.

until 1753, for it was in the following year that he was confined in MacDonald's madhouse (how long we do not know) before being escorted home to Chichester by his sister Anne. We know that Johnson, who saw Collins in Islington after his stay in France, was out of touch with him by 8 March 1754, when he wrote to Thomas Warton:

But how little can we venture to exult in any intellectual powers or literary attainments, when we consider the condition of poor Collins. I knew him a few years ago full of hopes and full of projects, versed in many languages, high in fancy, and strong in retention. This busy and forcible mind is now under the government of those who lately would not have been able to comprehend the least and most narrow of its designs. What do you hear of him? are there hopes of his recovery? or is he to pass the remainder of his life in misery and degradation? perhaps with complete consciousness of his calamity.[1]

Johnson's statement that Collins's mind was now 'under the government' of others suggests that the poet was, at this time, still confined in an institution.

We do not know if Johnson's questions elicited a reply from Warton, but Warton did see Collins twice that year. By September Collins seems to have been sufficiently improved for Thomas and his brother Joseph to visit him in Chichester. Thomas relates that he was then living in the cathedral cloisters with his sister: 'The first day he was in high spirits at intervals, but exerted himself so much that he could not see us the second.'[2] But on that first day Collins showed his friends both an 'Ode to Mr. John Hume, on his leaving England for Scotland' and 'another Ode, of two or three-four-lined Stanzas, called The Bell of Arragon'. This first poem, the 'Superstitions Ode', was written much earlier—in 1749 or 1750— and the second poem has not survived, but it is significant to note Collins's interest at this time in showing these poems to his friends. Joseph Warton also had 'a few fragments of some other Odes, but too loose and imperfect for publication, yet containing traces of high imagery'.[3] Apparently these are the poems preserved in the

---

[1] *The Letters of Samuel Johnson*, ed. R. W. Chapman (Oxford: Clarendon Press, 1952), i. 53. Hereafter cited as Chapman. [2] *The Reaper*, No. 26. [3] Ibid.

Warton papers at Trinity College, Oxford, and they too may have been presented to the Wartons at this time. We do know that a revised copy of the *Persian Eclogues* (to be retitled *Oriental Eclogues*) was given to the two brothers, presumably also at this meeting in Chichester.

Thomas Warton saw Collins again in November. 'In 1754,' Warton wrote, 'he came to Oxford, for change of air and amusement, where he staid a month; I saw him frequently, but he was so weak and low, that he could not bear conversation. Once he walked from his lodgings, opposite Christ Church, to Trinity College, but supported by his servant.'[1] Warton's account is supplemented by Gilbert White's remembrance of Collins at Oxford, 'under Merton wall, in a very affecting situation, struggling, and conveyed by force, in the arms of two or three men, towards the parish of St. Clement, in which was a house that took in such unhappy objects'.[2] Collins was at this time, Warton added, 'labouring under the most deplorable langour of body, and dejection of mind'.[3]

After 1754 mention of Collins becomes even scarcer. He was apparently a witness to David Mallet's will in 1755, but nothing is known of their friendship, even before this period.[4] Johnson, who had written to Warton about their friend in December 1754— 'Poor dear Collins—Let me know whether you think it would give him pleasure if I should write to him. I have often been near his state, and therefore have it in great commiseration'—sent an even gloomier letter to Warton in April 1756:

What becomes of poor dear Collins? I wrote him a letter which he never answered. I suppose writing is very troublesome to him. That man is no common loss. The moralists all talk of the uncertainty of fortune, and the transitoriness of beauty; but it is yet more dreadful to consider that the powers of the mind are equally liable to change,

---

[1] Ibid.

[2] *GM*, 51 (Jan. 1781), 11.

[3] Boswell, i. 276 n. Boswell appends this note to one of Johnson's letters, dated 28 Nov. 1754. Corroboration of this date is supplied by Mary Margaret Stewart, who points out that Gilbert White remained in Oxford from 14 Oct. until 15 Nov. 1754; see his account-book, reproduced in *The Natural History and Antiquities of Selborne, in the County of Southampton*, ed. Thomas Bell (1877), ii. 344–5.

[4] David Mallet, *Ballads and Songs*, ed. Frederick Dinsdale (1857), p. 54.

that understanding may make its appearance and depart, that it may blaze and expire.[1]

James Hampton in fact thought that Collins died in 1756, and even Johnson seemed unsure of the date of his death.[2] But Joseph Warton, who apparently stayed in touch with his friend, seems as late as 1756 to have expected Collins to finish his *History of the Revival of Learning*. In his *Essay on the Writings and Genius of Pope*, published in that year, Warton writes: 'Concerning the particular encouragement given by Leo X. to polite literature, and the fine arts, I forbear to enlarge; because a friend of mine is at present engaged in writing, THE HISTORY OF THE AGE OF LEO X.'[3] Collins's project, James Hampton wrote, was a 'history of the revival of learning in Italy, under the pontificates of Julius II. and Leo X.'[4]

In 1757 Collins's revised *Oriental Eclogues* was published by J. Payne, although Collins's responsibility for this edition is a subject of some dispute. Thomas Warton, however, in his *History of English Poetry*, suggests in his references to Collins's extensive antiquarian library that the poet had kept his collection of early books, and that he was willing to talk of literary subjects 'not many months before his death'. Speaking of Skelton's '*Nigramansir*', Warton writes that

My lamented friend Mr. William Collins, whose ODES will be remembered while any taste for true poetry remains, shewed me this piece at Chichester, not many months before his death: and he pointed it out as a very rare and valuable curiosity. He intended to

[1] Chapman, i. 60, 90.

[2] Johnson's 'Life of Collins' adopts the 1756 date, but Johnson himself never specified an exact date for Collins's death. In his edition of *The Lives of the Poets* (Oxford: Oxford Univ. Press, 1971), p. 366, J. P. Hardy has reconstructed the process by which this error entered Johnson's 'Life'. Hampton's original 'Account' 'had simply read ". . . where death at last came to his relief". For the change the printer John Nichols was responsible, who wrote at the foot of a state of proof-sheets for this Life: "There is no mention when Mr. Collins died. It was in 1756 at Chichester." The misdating of Collins's death was therefore an error made by Nichols and not (as has been assumed) by Johnson.' But Hampton's 'Account' does include the mistaken date, and thus it seems likely that Nichols drew upon this source for his information. The proof-sheets Hardy refers to are in the Forster Collection of the Victoria and Albert Museum (Forster 298-48-D-56, 57).

[3] 5th edn. (1806), i. 182.   [4] *Poetical Calendar*, xii. 109.

write the HISTORY OF THE RESTORATION OF LEARNING UNDER LEO THE TENTH, and with a view to that design, had collected many scarce books.[1]

It is clear that in these final years Collins, retired to the cloisters and nursed by his sister, was less and less capable of vigorous activity. The two remaining accounts of his retirement make it evident, however, that even at this late date Collins was capable of entirely lucid intervals. Thomas Warton, who wrote to Chichester for information concerning Collins's last years, supplied this account:

In illustration to what Dr. Johnson has related, that during his last malady, he was a great reader of the Bible: I am favored with the following anecdote from the Rev. Mr. Shenton, vicar of St. Andrews at Chichester, by whom Collins was buried. 'Walking in my vicarial garden one Sunday evening during Mr. Collins's last illness, I heard a female (the servant I suppose) reading the Bible in his chamber. Mr. Collins had been accustomed to rave much, and make great moanings, but while she was reading, or rather attempting to read, he was not only silent, but attentive likewise, correcting her mistakes, which indeed were very frequent, through the whole of the twenty-seventh chapter of Genesis.'[2]

In a previous letter Shenton had told Warton: 'D[r] Smyth Rector of S[t.] Giles in the Fields can probably furnish you with some Anecdotes about M[r] Collins, as I know he was very conversant with him about the time his Health & Senses began to fail.'[3]

[1] Rev. edn. (1824), iii. 185 n. Warton also speaks of Collins's 'memory failing in his last calamitous indisposition' (iv. 309). We cannot be certain that Warton knew when Collins actually died, however, and thus it is possible that he actually meant to indicate their meetings in 1754. In a letter to Thomas Percy dated 1762, Warton specified that he had seen a book 'about eight years ago [i.e. 1754] in the hands of a gentleman quite of your own Cast, M[r] Collins of Chichester, who died soon afterwards' (*The Correspondence of Thomas Percy and Richard Farmer*, ed. Cleanth Brooks (Baton Rouge, La.: Louisiana State Univ. Press, 1946), pp. 45–6). On the other hand, Thomas mentioned in his *History* that many of Collins's scarce books 'fell into my hands at his death' (iii. 185 n.), and this suggests that Warton would have known that Collins died in 1759. Joseph's statement in the *Essay* indicates that one or both of the Wartons remained in touch with Collins after 1754.

[2] *The Reaper*, No. 26; Shenton's letter is BL Add. MS. 42561, f. 129. For other accounts of these final years in Chichester, which are apparently indebted to Langhorne and Boswell, see Alexander Hay, *The History of Chichester* (Chichester, 1804), p. 528, and James Dallaway, *A History of the Western Division of the County of Sussex* (1815–30), i. 185.   [3] BL Add. MS. 42561, f. 127.

The other story which survives from this period also suggests the kind of painful lucidity which Johnson had noted: 'is he to pass the remainder of his life in misery and degradation? perhaps with complete consciousness of his calamity.' William Smith, Treasurer of the Ordnance, who had been a fellow of the same chamber at Winchester as Collins, visited his friend in Chichester 'twelve or fourteen years' after they had left the college. When Collins saw his old friend he exclaimed, 'Smith, do you remember my Dream!' Smith apparently remembered it well:

[Collins had been] 'observed one morning to be particularly depressed and melancholy. Being pressed to disclose the cause, he at last said it was in consequence of a dream: for this he was laughed at, but desired to tell what it was; he said, he dreamed that he was walking in the fields where there was a lofty tree; that he climbed it, and when he had nearly reached the top, a great branch, upon which he had got, failed with him, and let him fall to the ground. This account caused more ridicule; and he was asked how he could possibly be affected by this common consequence of a school-boy adventure, when he did not pretend, even in imagination and sleep, to have received any hurt, he replied, that the Tree was the Tree of Poetry.'[1]

Collins died in 1759, eight long years after his first illness and premonition of death.

What are we to make of these few biographical fragments? Dr. Daniel H. Fuller, writing an opinion for Bronson's edition of 1898, believed that 'the causes of his mental derangement may be found, without doubt, in these congenital characteristics, in the stress of poverty and worry, and perhaps in his dissipation and intemperance.'[2] According to Fuller, Collins's chief congenital characteristic was his want of stability of character and seriousness of purpose; his disorder was less of the intellectual faculties than of his emotional nature. Fuller defined his insanity as a form of melancholia 'characterized by periods of great mental pain and wild

---

[1] Crowe, pp. ix–xi. Crowe claims that Smith repeated this story to Dr. Busby of Winchester College, who in turn retold it to an intimate friend of Crowe's. Smith's story is possibly apocryphal, and the date of their meeting difficult to establish. Although traditionally considered a late occurrence in Collins's life, Smith's visit could have been made as early as 1753–4, when Collins first retired to Chichester.

[2] Bronson, p. xxvi.

agitation, with more composed intervals in which the patient exhibits much self-control and mental clearness. It is probable that the poet's debilitated physical condition during his last years was due to his mental disease.' While Fuller saw Collins's malady rooted within, the outcome of congenital characteristics, Collins's recent biographer has described it as a violent encounter with an overwhelming external force. P. L. Carver, in *The Life of a Poet*, speculates that Collins was engulfed in a sudden flood of emotion: 'I know that I shall be on delicate ground if I mention the Methodist Revival, and the possibility that Collins had been infected by that influence with *le délire biblique*.'[1] Carver is indeed on delicate ground: there is no evidence, besides a strained reading of Johnson's and Warton's memoirs, to sustain such speculation.

A recent medical opinion, which takes a closer and more balanced view of the evidence, finds Collins a manic-depressive. Dr. W. B. Ober finds it 'reasonable to assign Collins' feelings of inadequacy as a major cause of his depression. Whether this emotional state was superimposed on some unknown (at this date unknowable) constitutional predisposition or organic factor is a matter of idle speculation.'[2] What Ober neglects to examine, however, is the possibility that Collins's mental distress was either the result of a physical disease or even mistaken for what was actually physical, and not mental, illness. The poet's debilitated physical condition during his last years, Fuller wrote, 'was due to his mental disease', but there is a possibility that this was simply the other way round. 'I would guess from the little evidence we have', Oliver Sigworth argues, 'that Collins was intermittently in very great pain, from what cause we cannot now say, but occasionally of such excruciating severity as to cause him to cry out and act irrationally.'[3] Collins's first illness, in 1751, does sound like a serious physical collapse, severe enough to convince Collins that he was soon to die; Shenton points to the time 'his Health & Senses began to fail'. Surely the possibility of a physical cause should not be ruled out, especially in light of the continuing research today into the nature

[1] p. 174.
[2] 'Madness and Poetry: A Note on Collins, Cowper, and Smart', *Bulletin of the New York Academy of Medicine*, 2nd ser., 46, No. 4 (Apr. 1970), 213.
[3] Sigworth, p. 53.

of mental disease. 'When the chemical and physiological basis of madness becomes clearer,' Matthew Hodgart has written, 'a number of phantoms will disappear, and the lives of the mad poets, quite a few of whom lived in the eighteenth century, will have to be reconsidered.'[1]

The work on Swift by Lord Brain and Irvin Ehrenpreis and on George III by Macalpine and Hunter is an indication of how myths of insanity become devalued, and it is difficult to see why Collins should be exempted from this process.[2] Johnson, in revising his early sketch for the 'Life of Collins' in 1781, qualified his discussion of Collins's illness with this assertion: 'His disorder was not alienation of mind, but general laxity and feebleness, a deficiency rather of his vital than intellectual powers. What he spoke wanted neither judgement nor spirit; but a few minutes exhausted him, so that he was forced to rest upon the couch, till a short cessation restored his powers, and he was again able to talk with his former vigour.'[3] Johnson's account is indebted to the Wartons, and they, like Gilbert White, saw Collins at his worst.

What remains most certain about Collins's madness is that the little evidence we possess does not support any single explanation. The facts which have been assembled here, however, should clear away certain persistent misconceptions. We can no longer believe the common assertion that Collins died in 1759 'having long been completely insane'.[4] In the first place, the longevity of Collins's illness is uncertain. We know that he was healthy in 1750, and that he recovered from his illness of the following year. He seems to have travelled in search of health in 1752 and 1753 (and, as Johnson suggests, have sought it unsuccessfully in the bottle as well),[5] but the first certain signs of any mental troubles are his

---

[1] *TLS* (28 Mar. 1975), p. 328.

[2] See Walter Russell Brain, 'The Illness of Dean Swift', *Irish Journal of Medical Science*, 6th ser., 320–1 (1952), 337–45; Ehrenpreis, *The Personality of Jonathan Swift* (Cambridge, Mass.: Harvard Univ. Press, 1958), ch. 6; and Ida Macalpine and Richard Hunter, *George III and the Mad-Business* (London: Allen Lane, 1969).

[3] *Lives*, iii. 340.   [4] Williams, p. 102.

[5] See *Lives*, iii. 340–1: 'The approaches of this dreadful malady he began to feel soon after his uncle's death, and, with the usual weakness of men so diseased, eagerly snatched that temporary relief with which the table and the bottle flatter and seduce.' Collins's drinking seems here to be a result of his illness, not a cause. Cf. Chapman, i. 59 (a letter from Johnson to Thomas Warton, 21 Dec. 1754): 'I had

stay in an asylum and retirement to Chichester in 1754. We may also conclude that, despite the occasional severity of his ailment, he was not 'completely' insane. The evidence clearly points to a disorder of intermittent character. Shenton speaks of Collins's 'last illness', which indicates that his disease was apparently remittent. We know that Collins was writing poetry as late as 1750, that he revised his eclogues sometime before 1754, that he was eager to show his uncollected and unfinished poetry to friends, and that his major project, the *History of the Revival of Learning*, was never despaired of by the Wartons. Collins's abilities (and perhaps his interests) seem to have changed during this last decade, but despite these changes, Thomas Warton informs us, he maintained his literary interests, even within a few months of his death.[1]

THE PRESENT EDITION

'The ideal of textual criticism', James Thorpe has stated, 'is to present the text which the author intended.'[2] This is an admirable ideal, but one which is persistently difficult to achieve in practice. It does not necessarily accommodate inconsistency of intention in the composition of a poem or poems, nor is the final intention always demonstrable: a poem, as Valéry pointed out, 'is never finished; it is only abandoned'. Similarly, intentions must be evinced by evidence, and evidence (in the case of Collins) rarely exists. Manuscripts survive for only twelve of his poems, none of which was published during the author's lifetime. And no proof-sheets or printer's copy exist for any of Collins's published poetry. Determining the author's intentions in substantive matters (as well as in the shadowy realm of accidentals) is thus a difficult venture in which a considerable measure of uncertainty necessarily prevails. Nevertheless, so far as is possible, this edition attempts

---

lately the favour of a Letter from your Brother with some account of poor Collins for whom I am much concerned: I have a notion that by very great temperance or more properly abstinence he might yet recover.'

[1] For the textual implications of these conclusions, see the head-note to *Oriental Eclogues*.

[2] *The Principles of Textual Criticism* (San Marino: The Huntington Library, 1972), p. 50.

to provide critical texts of the poems as Collins seems to have intended them to appear.

Because the poems have separate textual histories, the copy-text for each has been individually determined. The copy-text is reproduced *literatim* with the following exceptions: (i) authorial revisions are incorporated in the copy-text and made to conform to the style of the text in which they appear; (ii) long 's' has been silently modernized in both manuscript and printed texts; (iii) similarly, superior characters written above a full point ('M$^r_.$') have been silently altered ('M$^{r.}$'); (iv) printers' conventions which affect the indentation of a stanza or the first few words of a poem have been silently modified to match the rest of the poem; (v) similarly, irregularities which appear to have had their origin in the printing house (spacing between words or between lines in a poem, an inverted or otherwise misplaced apostrophe or comma, etc.) have also been silently modified. On the other hand, no attempt has been made to modify inconsistencies in accidentals (including the printing of italics and the dash) within individual poems or among poems in a collection, like the *Odes*. In general, all substantive variants occurring in editions published within Collins's lifetime (and in later editions of importance) have been included in the textual notes. Variants in accidentals are also recorded for those editions where it is at least possible that Collins was responsible for changes in accidentals (see the individual head-notes for details). Suggested emendations of the text are discussed in the commentary; none has been adopted within the present edition. Titles cited at the head of each poem are quoted *literatim* from the copy-text or, for the sake of clarity, from a revised edition in the case of *Oriental Eclogues* and *An Epistle: Addrest to Sir Thomas Hanmer*. In the head-notes, however, all titles are standardized. All poems have been arranged chronologically (so far as can be determined) with the exception of those also printed in the *Odes*, for which the scheme of Collins's collection has been preserved. Line numbers have been added in fives to all poems.

Collins's Drafts and Fragments (unfinished poems in manuscript) have been presented here as 'potential versions' of Collins's poetry. Each of the eleven fragments is treated, in James Thorpe's words, as a text 'presented for study purposes or for tentative consideration rather than as if it were a literary work comparable in status to the "actual" works of the author'.[1] These poems are thus printed apart from Collins's other works. The 'Ode to a Friend on his Return &c' (the 'Superstitions Ode'), however, which has long been read in 'final' published form, has for convenience been included among Collins's finished works. Deletions in manuscripts, and words which have been cancelled by other words written over them, are recorded in the textual notes. Where one word has been written above another, and neither deleted, the original word is given in the text and the suggested reading noted in the apparatus. A word is described as 'cancelling' another word where one word is written over another or where one word is expanded or otherwise altered to replace the original reading. Measurements of manuscripts are given in centimetres (height by width).

The commentary is designed to provide information essential to a reading of each poem. No attempt has been made to supply a full descriptive bibliography of Collins's texts, but the format and history of each separate publication are recorded in the individual head-notes, as well as relevant biographical and historical information. Although previous editors have paid considerable attention to parallel passages which Collins may have drawn upon, only Collins's major literary debts have been recorded here. The annotation is intended to provide a commentary on Collins's historical and contemporary allusions, glosses on particular usage, and comparisons with Collins's other poems. The reader who wishes to pursue verbal allusions in Collins's poetry should consult the editions of Dyce, Bronson, or Lonsdale (who offers the fullest compilation of Collins's possible borrowings). These comparisons have been considered of limited value in the present edition, which is designed to determine (and thus draw critical attention to) Collins's own texts, not to suggest other texts to which that of Collins may (or may not) be related. Verbal echoes are recorded, however, when they assist in the dating of a poem.

[1] Ibid., p. 187.

POEMS

To Miss Aurelia C——r, *on her Weeping at her Sister's Wedding.*

Cease, fair *Aurelia*, cease to mourn;
　　Lament not *Hannah*'s happy state;
You may be happy in your turn,
　　And seize the treasure you regret.
With *Love* united *Hymen* stands,   5
　　And softly whispers to your charms,
"Meet but your lover in my bands,
　　"You'll find your sister in his arms.

1–4, 5–8. *Divided into stanzas in Poetical Calendar*

SONNET.

When *Phœbe* form'd a wanton smile,
　　My soul! it reach'd not here!
Strange, that thy peace, thou trembler, flies
　　Before a rising tear!

From midst the drops, my love is born,   5
　　That o'er those eyelids rove:
Thus issued from a teeming wave
　　The fabled queen of love.

ORIENTAL ECLOGUES.

Written originally for the
ENTERTAINMENT
OF THE
LADIES of TAURIS.
And now translated.

—— *Ubi primus equis Oriens adflavit anhelis.* VIRG. GEORG. Lib. I.

THE
PREFACE.

It is with the Writings of Mankind, in some Measure, as with their Complexions or their Dress, each Nation hath a Peculiarity in all these, to distinguish it from the rest of the World.

   The Gravity of the Spaniard, *and the Levity of the* Frenchman, *are*
5 *as evident in all their Productions as in their Persons themselves; and the Stile of my Countrymen is as naturally Strong and Nervous, as that of an* Arabian *or Persian is rich and figurative.*

   There is an Elegancy and Wildness of Thought which recommends all their Compositions; and our Genius's are as much too cold for the Entertain-
10 *ment of such Sentiments, as our Climate is for their Fruits and Spices. If any of these Beauties are to be found in the following* Eclogues, *I hope my Reader will consider them as an Argument of their being Original. I received them at the Hands of a Merchant, who had made it his Business to enrich himself with the Learning, as well as the Silks and Carpets of the*

Title. PERSIAN / ECLOGUES. / Written originally for the / ENTERTAINMENT / OF THE / Ladies of *TAURIS*. / And now first translated, *&c.* 1742   *Motto.* *Quod si non hîc tantas fructus ostenderetur, & si ex his studiis delectatis sola peteretur; tamen, ut opinor, hanc animi remissionem humanissimam ac liberalissimam judicaretis.* CIC. pro Arch. Poeta. 1742 *In Dyce 1742 this motto is deleted, and the following quotation substituted in Collins's hand:* —Quos primus equis Oriens afflavit anhelis. Virg. *Also deleted is another version of this motto in Collins's hand:* Equis Oriens afflavit anhelis.
   Preface. Omitted in Poetical Calendar, Langhorne, Pearch   2 *Dress*,] dress; 1757
6 *Stile*] style 1757   14 *himself*] 'self' *is catchword and omitted in the text of* 1742

Persians. *The little Information I could gather concerning their Author,* 15
was, That his Name was Abdallah, *and that he was a Native of* Tauris.

It was in that City that he died of a Distemper fatal in those Parts,
whilst he was engag'd in celebrating the Victories of his favourite Monarch,
the Great Abbas.* *As to the* Eclogues *themselves, they give a very just*
View of the Miseries, and Inconveniences, as well as the Felicities that 20
attend one of the finest Countries in the East.

The Time of Writing them was probably in the Beginning of Sha Sultan
Hosseyn's *Reign, the Successor of* Sefi *or* Solyman *the Second.*

Whatever Defects, as, I doubt not, there will be many, fall under the
Reader's Observation, I hope his Candour will incline him to make the 25
following Reflection:

That the Works of Orientals *contain many Peculiarities, and that thro'*
Defect of Language few European *Translators can do them Justice.*

ECLOGUE the FIRST.

SELIM; *or, the Shepherd's Moral.*

SCENE, *a Valley near* Bagdat.

TIME, *the* MORNING.

Ye *Persian* Maids, attend your Poet's Lays,
And hear how Shepherds pass their golden Days:
Not all are blest, whom Fortune's Hand sustains
With Wealth in Courts, nor all that haunt the Plains:
Well may your Hearts believe the Truths I tell,   5
'Tis Virtue makes the Bliss, where'er we dwell.

---

* *In the* Persian *Tongue,* Abbas *signifieth "the Father of the People."*

---

16 Abdallah] Mahamed *1742,* ABDALLAH *1757*   19 n. *Included in 1757 only:*
IN the Persian tongue, ABBAS signifieth "the father of the people."   20 *Miseries,*]
miseries *1757   Inconveniences] Inconveniencies 1742,* inconveniences *1757 Felicities*]
felicities, *1757*   22 *of Writing] of the Writing 1742,* of writing *1757*
26 *Reflection] Reflections 1742,* reflection *1757*   27 Orientals] Orientials *1757*
(*misprint ?*)   *that*] that, *1757   thro'*] through *1757*   28 *Language*] language,
1757

2 Days:] days. *1757*   5 tell,] tell; *1757*

Thus *Selim* sung; by sacred Truth inspir'd;
Nor Praise, but such as Truth bestow'd, desir'd:
Wise in himself, his meaning Songs convey'd
Informing Morals to the Shepherd Maid,   10
Or taught the Swains that surest Bliss to find,
What Groves nor Streams bestow, a virtuous Mind.

When sweet and blushing, like a virgin Bride,
The radiant Morn resum'd her orient Pride,
When wanton Gales, along the Valleys play,   15
Breathe on each Flow'r, and bear their Sweets away:
By *Tigris'* wand'ring Waves he sate, and sung
This useful Lesson for the Fair and Young.

Ye *Persian* Dames, he said, to you belong,
Well may they please, the Morals of my Song;   20
No fairer Maids, I trust, than you are found,
Grac'd with soft Arts, the peopled World around!
The Morn that lights you, to your Loves supplies
Each gentler Ray delicious to your Eyes:
For you those Flow'rs her fragrant Hands bestow,   25
And yours the Love that Kings delight to know.
Yet think not these, all beauteous as they are,
The best kind Blessings Heav'n can grant the Fair!
Who trust alone in Beauty's feeble Ray,
Boast but the Worth ★ *Balsora's* Pearls display;   30

★ The Gulph of that Name, famous for the Pearl-fishery.

---

7 sung;] sung, *1757*
8   No Praise the Youth, but her's alone desir'd: *1742*
                    Nor praise, but such as Truth bestow'd, desir'd: *1757*
10 Maid,] maid; *1757*   13 blushing *1757*] od'rous *1742*   a virgin *1757*] an
Eastern *1742*   15 Gales,] gales *1757*   16 away:] away; *1757*   17 wand'ring
1757, *Dyce 1742 (where the initial 'w' has been cut off by the binder)*] Wand'rer *1742*
19, 21, 25 you *1757*, *Dyce 1742*] ye *1742*   20 Song;] song: *1757*
30–2   ★ *Balsora's* Pearls have more of Worth, than they;
                    Drawn from the Deep, they sparkle to the Sight,
                    And all-unconscious shoot a lust'rous Light: *1742*

                    Boast but the worth ★ Balsora's pearls display;
                    Drawn from the deep we own their surface bright,
                    But, dark within, they drink no lust'rous light: *1757*
30 *Balsora's*] Bassora's *Langhorne*

Drawn from the Deep we own their Surface bright,
But, dark within, they drink no lust'rous Light:
Such are the Maids, and such the Charms they boast,
By Sense unaided, or to Virtue lost.
Self-flattering Sex! your Hearts believe in vain   35
That Love shall blind, when once he fires the Swain;
Or hope a Lover by your Faults to win,
As Spots on Ermin beautify the Skin:
Who seeks secure to rule, be first her Care
Each softer Virtue that adorns the Fair,   40
Each tender Passion Man delights to find,
The lov'd Perfections of a female Mind.

Blest were the Days, when Wisdom held her Reign,
And Shepherds sought her on the silent Plain,
With Truth she wedded in the secret Grove,   45
Immortal Truth, and Daughters bless'd their Love.

O haste, fair Maids, ye Virtues come away,
Sweet Peace and Plenty lead you on your way!
The balmy Shrub, for you shall love our Shore,
By *Ind'* excell'd or *Araby* no more.   50

Lost to our Fields, for so the Fates ordain,
The dear Deserters shall return again.
Come thou whose Thoughts as limpid Springs are clear,
To lead the Train, sweet Modesty appear:
Here make thy Court amidst our rural Scene,   55
And Shepherd-Girls shall own Thee for their Queen.
With Thee be Chastity, of all afraid,
Distrusting all, a wise suspicious Maid;

40 Fair,] fair; *1757*   42 Mind.] mind! *1757*   44 Plain,] plain; *1757*
46 Immortal *1757*] The fair-eyed *1742*   47 Maids,] maids! *1757*   49 you
1757] ye *1742*   50 *Ind'*] Ind *1757*
53-4   O come, thou Modesty, as they decree,
             The Rose may then improve her Blush by Thee. *1742*

             Come thou whose thoughts as limpid springs are clear,
             To lead the train, sweet MODESTY appear: *1757*

But Man the most; not more the Mountain Doe
Holds the swift Falcon for her deadly Foe.   60
Cold is her Breast, like Flow'rs that drink the Dew,
A silken Veil conceals her from the View.
No wild Desires amidst thy Train be known,
But Faith, whose Heart is fix'd on one alone:
Desponding Meekness with her down-cast Eyes,   65
And friendly Pity full of tender Sighs;
And Love the last: By these your Hearts approve,
These are the Virtues that must lead to Love.

Thus sung the Swain, and ancient Legends say,
The Maids of *Bagdat* verify'd the Lay: 70
Dear to the Plains, the Virtues came along,
The Shepherds lov'd, and *Selim* bless'd his Song.

The END of the First ECLOGUE.

ECLOGUE the SECOND.

HASSAN; *or, the Camel-driver.*

SCENE, *the Desart.*

TIME, MID-DAY.

In silent Horror o'er the boundless Waste
The Driver *Hassan* with his Camels past.
One Cruise of Water on his Back he bore,
And his light Scrip contain'd a scanty Store:
A Fan of painted Feathers in his Hand,   5
To guard his shaded Face from scorching Sand.
The sultry Sun had gain'd the middle Sky,
And not a Tree, and not an Herb was nigh.
The Beasts, with Pain, their dusty Way pursue,
Shrill roar'd the Winds, and dreary was the View!   10

59 most; not] most—not *1757*   61 Dew,] dew; *1757*   69 Swain,] swain; *1757*
ancient *1757*] Eastern *1742*

1 boundless *1757*] Desart- *1742*   4 Store:] store; *1757*   8 nigh.] nigh; *1757*

With desp'rate Sorrow wild th' affrighted Man
Thrice sigh'd, thrice strook his Breast, and thus began:
Sad was the Hour, and luckless was the Day,
When first from Schiraz' *Walls I bent my Way.*

Ah! little thought I of the blasting Wind,   15
The Thirst or pinching Hunger that I find!
Bethink thee, *Hassan*, where shall Thirst assuage,
When fails this Cruise, his unrelenting Rage?
Soon shall this Scrip its precious Load resign,
Then what but Tears and Hunger shall be thine?   20

Ye mute Companions of my Toils, that bear
In all my Griefs a more than equal Share!
Here, where no Springs, in Murmurs break away,
Or Moss-crown'd Fountains mitigate the Day:
In vain ye hope the green Delights to know,   25
Which Plains more blest, or verdant Vales bestow.
Here Rocks alone, and tasteless Sands are found,
And faint and sickly Winds for ever howl around.
Sad was the Hour, &c.

                                                              (30)

Curst be the Gold and Silver which persuade
Weak Men to follow far-fatiguing Trade.
The Lilly-Peace outshines the silver Store,
And Life is dearer than the golden Ore.
Yet Money tempts us o'er the Desart brown,   35
To ev'ry distant Mart, and wealthy Town:
Full oft we tempt the Land, and oft the Sea,
And are we only yet repay'd by Thee?
Ah! why was Ruin so attractive made,
Or why fond Man so easily betray'd?   40

11 wild] wild, *1757*   13–14 *In 1757 the refrain is enclosed within quotation*
marks   14 *Way.*] way! *1757*   17 assuage] asswage *1757*   19 resign,]
resign; *1757*   23 Springs,] springs *1757*   24 Fountains] fountain *Pearch*
Day:] day, *1757*   26 bestow.] bestow: *1757*   29–30 *1757 prints the entire*
refrain here and in 47–8, 59–60, 69–70   32 Trade.] trade! *1757*   34 Ore.]
ore: *1757*   36 Mart,] mart *1757*   Town:] town. *1757*   37 Sea,] sea; *1757*
39 was] this *Pearch*

Why heed we not, whilst mad we haste along,
The gentle Voice of Peace, or Pleasure's Song?
Or wherefore think the flow'ry Mountain's Side,
The Fountain's Murmurs, and the Valley's Pride,
Why think we these less pleasing to behold,   45
Than dreary Desarts, if they lead to Gold?
    Sad was the Hour, &c.

    O cease, my Fears! all frantic as I go,
When Thought creates unnumber'd Scenes of Woe,   50
What if the Lion in his Rage I meet!
Oft in the Dust I view his printed Feet:
And fearful! oft, when Day's declining Light
Yields her pale Empire to the Mourner Night,
By Hunger rous'd, he scours the groaning Plain,   55
Gaunt Wolves and sullen Tygers in his Train:
Before them Death with Shrieks directs their Way,
Fills the wild Yell, and leads them to their Prey.
    Sad was the Hour, &c.

                                                            (60)

    At that dead Hour the silent Asp shall creep,
If ought of rest I find, upon my Sleep:
Or some swoln Serpent twist his Scales around,
And wake to Anguish with a burning Wound.
Thrice happy they, the wise contented Poor,   65
From Lust of Wealth, and Dread of Death secure;
They tempt no Desarts, and no Griefs they find;
Peace rules the Day, where Reason rules the Mind.
    Sad was the Hour, &c.

                                                            (70)

    O hapless Youth! for she thy Love hath won,
The tender *Zara*, will be most undone!
Big swell'd my Heart, and own'd the pow'rful Maid,
When fast she dropt her Tears, as thus she said;

45 these] then *Pearch*   49 Fears! all] fears!—All *1757*   51 meet!]
meet!— *1757*   66 secure;] secure! *1757*   74 said;] said: *1757*

"Farewel the Youth whom Sighs could not detain, 75
"Whom *Zara*'s breaking Heart implor'd in vain;
"Yet as thou go'st, may ev'ry Blast arise,
"Weak and unfelt as these rejected Sighs!
"Safe o'er the Wild, no Perils mayst thou see,
"No Griefs endure, nor weep, false Youth, like me." 80
O let me safely to the Fair return,
Say with a Kiss, she must not, shall not mourn.
O! let me teach my Heart to lose its Fears,
Recall'd by Wisdom's Voice, and *Zara*'s Tears.

He said, and call'd on Heav'n to bless the Day, 85
When back to *Schiraz*' Walls he bent his Way.

The END of the Second ECLOGUE.

ECLOGUE the THIRD.

ABRA; *or, the* Georgian *Sultana.*

SCENE, *a Forest.*

TIME, *the* EVENING.

In *Georgia*'s Land, where *Teflis*' Tow'rs are seen,
In distant View along the level Green,
While Ev'ning Dews enrich the glitt'ring Glade,
And the tall Forests cast a longer Shade,
What Time 'tis sweet o'er Fields of Rice to stray, 5
Or scent the breathing Maze at setting Day;
Amidst the Maids of *Zagen*'s peaceful Grove,
Emyra sung the pleasing Cares of Love.

Of *Abra* first began the tender Strain,
Who led her Youth, with Flocks upon the Plain: 10

75 Farewel] Farewell *1757*   76 vain;] vain! *1757*   82 mourn.] mourn; *1757*
83   Go teach my Heart, to lose its painful Fears, *1742*
           O! let me teach my heart to lose its fears, *1757*

5–6 *Added in 1757:*
           What time 'tis sweet o'er fields of rice to stray,
           Or scent the breathing maze at setting day;
10 Youth,] youth *1757*

At Morn she came those willing Flocks to lead,
Where Lillies rear them in the wat'ry Mead;
From early Dawn the live-long Hours she told,
'Till late at silent Eve she penn'd the Fold.
Deep in the Grove beneath the secret Shade,   15
A various Wreath of od'rous Flow'rs she made:
* Gay-motley'd Pinks and sweet Junquils she chose,
The Violet-blue, that on the Moss-bank grows;
All-sweet to Sense, the flaunting Rose was there;
The finish'd Chaplet well-adorn'd her Hair.   20

    Great *Abbas* chanc'd that fated Morn to stray,
By Love conducted from the Chace away;
Among the vocal Vales he heard her Song,
And sought the Vales and echoing Groves among:
At length he found, and woo'd the rural Maid,   25
She knew the Monarch, and with Fear obey'd.
    Be ev'ry Youth like Royal Abbas *mov'd,*
    And ev'ry Georgian *Maid like* Abra *lov'd.*

    The Royal Lover bore her from the Plain,
Yet still her Crook and bleating Flock remain: 30
Oft as she went, she backward turn'd her View,
And bad that Crook, and bleating Flock Adieu.
Fair happy Maid! to other Scenes remove,
To richer Scenes of golden Pow'r and Love!
Go leave the simple Pipe, and Shepherd's Strain,   35
With Love delight thee, and with *Abbas* reign.
    Be ev'ry Youth, &c.

    * That these Flowers are found in very great Abundance in some of the Provinces of *Persia*; see the *Modern History* of the ingenious Mr. *Salmon*.

---

17 Junquils] jonquils *1757*   17 n. *This note (to l. 15 in 1742) is crossed out in Dyce 1742 and bears a deletion mark in the margin. It was not, however, deleted in 1757*
18 Violet-blue,] violet-blue *1757*   19 there;] there: *1757*   25 Maid,]
maid; *1757*   27–8 *In 1757 the refrain is enclosed within quotation marks*   28 lov'd.]
lov'd! *1757*   29 Plain,] plain; *1757*   32 Crook,] crook *1757*   35 Strain,]
strain; *1757*   37–8 *1757 prints the entire refrain here and in 51–2, 59–60*

Yet midst the Blaze of Courts she fix'd her Love,
On the cool Fountain, or the shady Grove;   40
Still with the Shepherd's Innocence her Mind
To the sweet Vale, and flow'ry Mead inclin'd,
And oft as Spring renew'd the Plains with Flow'rs,
Breath'd his soft Gales, and led the fragrant Hours,
With sure Return she sought the sylvan Scene,   45
The breezy Mountains, and the Forests green.
Her Maids around her mov'd, a duteous Band!
Each bore a Crook all-rural in her Hand:
Some simple Lay, of Flocks and Herds they sung,
With Joy the Mountain, and the Forest rung.   50
    Be ev'ry Youth, &c.

And oft the Royal Lover left the Care,
And Thorns of State, attendant on the Fair:
Oft to the Shades and low-roof'd Cots retir'd,   55
Or sought the Vale where first his Heart was fir'd;
A Russet Mantle, like a Swain, he wore,
And thought of Crowns and busy Courts no more.
    Be ev'ry Youth, &c.

(60)

Blest was the Life, that Royal *Abbas* led:
Sweet was his Love, and innocent his Bed.
What if in Wealth the noble Maid excel;
The simple Shepherd Girl can love as well.
Let those who rule on *Persia*'s jewell'd Throne,   65
Be fam'd for Love, and gentlest Love alone:
Or wreath, like *Abbas*, full of fair Renown,
The Lover's Myrtle, with the Warrior's Crown.

Oh happy Days! the Maids around her say,
Oh haste, profuse of Blessings, haste away!   70
    Be ev'ry Youth, like Royal Abbas, *mov'd;*
    And ev'ry Georgian *Maid, like* Abra, *lov'd.*
     The END of the Third ECLOGUE.

39 Love,] love *1757*   42 inclin'd,] inclin'd; *1757*   49 sung,] sung; *1757*
53 Care,] care *1757*   54 Fair:] fair; *1757*   56 fir'd;] fir'd: *1757*   66 alone:]
alone; *1757*   69 say,] say; *1757*

ECLOGUE the FOURTH.
AGIB *and* SECANDER; *or, the Fugitives.*

SCENE, *a Mountain in* Circassia.

TIME, MIDNIGHT.

In fair *Circassia*, where to Love inclin'd,
Each Swain was blest, for ev'ry Maid was kind!
At that still Hour, when awful Midnight reigns,
And none, but Wretches, haunt the twilight Plains;
What Time the Moon had hung her Lamp on high,   5
And past in Radiance, thro' the cloudless Sky:
Sad o'er the Dews, two Brother Shepherds fled,
Where wild'ring Fear and desp'rate Sorrow led.
Fast as they prest their Flight, behind them lay
Wide ravag'd Plains, and Valleys stole away.   10
Along the Mountain's bending Sides they ran,
Till faint and weak *Secander* thus began.

SECANDER.

O stay thee, *Agib*, for my Feet deny,
No longer friendly to my Life, to fly.
Friend of my Heart, O turn thee and survey,   15
Trace our sad Flight thro' all its length of Way!
And first review that long-extended Plain,
And yon wide Groves, already past with Pain!
Yon ragged Cliff, whose dang'rous Path we try'd,
And last this lofty Mountain's weary Side!   20

AGIB.

Weak as thou art, yet hapless must thou know
The Toils of Flight, or some severer Woe!

---

1 where] where, *1757*   2 kind!] kind; *1757*   6 Radiance,] radiance *1757*
Sky:] sky; *1757*   8 led.] led: *1757*   10 Valleys] vallies *1757*   19 try'd,]
try'd! *1757*

Still as I haste, the *Tartar* shouts behind,
And Shrieks and Sorrows load the sad'ning Wind:
In rage of Heart, with Ruin in his Hand,   25
He blasts our Harvests, and deforms our Land.
Yon Citron Grove, whence first in Fear we came,
Droops its fair Honours to the conqu'ring Flame:
Far fly the Swains, like us, in deep Despair,
And leave to ruffian Bands their fleecy Care.   30

SECANDER.

Unhappy Land, whose Blessings tempt the Sword,
In vain, unheard, thou call'st thy *Persian* Lord!
In vain, thou court'st him, helpless to thine Aid,
To shield the Shepherd, and protect the Maid,
Far off in thoughtless Indolence resign'd,   35
Soft Dreams of Love and Pleasure sooth his Mind:
'Midst fair *Sultanas* lost in idle Joy,
No Wars alarm him, and no Fears annoy.

AGIB.

Yet these green Hills, in Summer's sultry Heat,
Have lent the Monarch oft a cool Retreat,   40
Sweet to the Sight is *Zabran*'s flow'ry Plain,
And once by Maids and Shepherds lov'd in vain!
No more the Virgins shall delight to rove,
By *Sargis*' Banks or *Irwan*'s shady Grove:
On *Tarkie*'s Mountain catch the cooling Gale,   45
Or breathe the Sweets of *Aly*'s flow'ry Vale:
Fair Scenes! but ah no more with Peace possest,
With Ease alluring, and with Plenty blest.
No more the Shepherds' whit'ning Tents appear,
Nor the kind Products of a bounteous Year;   50
No more the Date with snowy Blossoms crown'd,
But Ruin spreads her baleful Fires around.

24 sad'ning] sadd'ning *1757*   33 vain,] vain *1757*   34 Maid,] maid! *1757*
40 Retreat,] retreat. *1757*   44 Banks] banks, *1757*   Grove:] grove; *1757*
47 but ah] but, ah! *1757*   49 Shepherds'] Shepherds *1742*, shepherds' *1757*
Tents] Seats *1742*, tents *1757*, *Dyce 1742*   51 Date] Dale *1742*, date *1757*, Date
Dyce 1742   crown'd,] crown'd! *1757*

SECANDER.

In vain *Circassia* boasts her spicy Groves,
For ever fam'd for pure and happy Loves:
In vain she boasts her fairest of the Fair,   55
Their Eyes' blue languish, and their golden Hair!
Those Eyes in Tears, their fruitless Grief must send,
Those Hairs the *Tartar*'s cruel Hand shall rend.

AGIB.

Ye *Georgian* Swains that piteous learn from far
Circassia's Ruin, and the Waste of War: 60
Some weightier Arms than Crooks and Staves prepare,
To shield your Harvests, and defend your Fair:
The *Turk* and *Tartar* like Designs pursue,
Fix'd to destroy, and stedfast to undo.
Wild as his Land, in native Deserts bred,   65
By Lust incited, or by Malice led,
The Villain-*Arab*, as he prowls for Prey,
Oft marks with Blood and wasting Flames the Way;
Yet none so cruel as the *Tartar* Foe,
To Death inur'd, and nurst in Scenes of Woe.   70

He said, when loud along the Vale was heard
A shriller Shriek, and nearer Fires appear'd:
Th' affrighted Shepherds thro' the Dews of Night
Wide o'er the Moon-light Hills, renew'd their Flight.

The END of the Fourth and last ECLOGUE.

57 Tears,] tears *1757*   send,] send; *1757*   60 War:] war; *1757*   65 Deserts]
desarts *1757*   67 Villain-*Arab*] villain Arab *1757*   71 said,] said; *1757*
73 Night] night, *1757*   74 Hills,] hills *1757*

AN
EPISTLE:
ADDREST TO
Sir *THOMAS HANMER*,
On his EDITION of
Shakespear's WORKS.

TO
Sir *Thomas Hanmer*.

SIR,
While born to bring the Muse's happier Days,
A Patriot's Hand protects a Poet's Lays:
While nurst by you she sees her Myrtles bloom,
Green and unwither'd o'er his honour'd Tomb:
Excuse her Doubts, if yet she fears to tell   5
What secret Transports in her Bosom swell:
With conscious Awe she hears the Critic's Fame,
And blushing hides her Wreath at *Shakespear*'s Name.
Hard was the Lot those injur'd Strains endur'd,

Title. VERSES / HUMBLY ADDRESS'D / TO / Sir *THOMAS HANMER.* /
On his EDITION of / *Shakespear*'s WORKS. *1743*   *Salutation.* SIR,] *SIR 1744*
1–6   While, own'd by You, with Smiles the Muse surveys,
             Th' expected Triumph of her sweetest Lays:
             While, stretch'd at Ease, she boasts your Guardian Aid,
             Secure, and happy in her sylvan Shade:
             Excuse her Fears, who scarce a Verse bestows,
             In just Remembrance of the Debt she owes; *1743*
9–16 *These lines replace a much longer passage in 1743*:
             Long slighted *Fancy*, with a Mother's Care,
             Wept o'er his Works, and felt the last Despair.
             Torn from her Head, she saw the Roses fall,
             By all deserted, tho' admir'd by all.
             "And oh! she cry'd, shall Science still resign
             "Whate'er is Nature's, and whate'er is mine?
             "Shall *Taste* and *Art*, but shew a cold Regard,
             "And scornful Pride reject th' unletter'd Bard?
             "Ye myrtled Nymphs, who own my gentle Reign,
             "Tune the sweet Lyre, and grace my airy Train!
             "If, where ye rove, your searching Eyes have known
             "One perfect Mind, which Judgment calls its own:

Unown'd by Science, and by Years obscur'd: 10
Fair Fancy wept; and echoing Sighs confest
A fixt Despair in ev'ry tuneful Breast.
Not with more Grief th' afflicted Swains appear
When wintry Winds deform the plenteous Year:
When ling'ring Frosts the ruin'd Seats invade   15
Where Peace resorted, and the Graces play'd.

    Each rising Art by just Gradation moves,
Toil builds on Toil, and Age on Age improves.
The Muse alone unequal dealt her Rage,
And grac'd with noblest Pomp her earliest Stage.   20
Preserv'd thro' Time, the speaking Scenes impart
Each changeful Wish of *Phædra*'s tortur'd Heart:
Or paint the Curse, that mark'd the ★ *Theban*'s Reign,
A Bed incestuous, and a Father slain.
With kind Concern our pitying Eyes o'erflow,   25
Trace the sad Tale, and own another's Woe.

    To *Rome* remov'd, with Wit secure to please,
The *Comic* Sisters kept their native Ease.
With jealous Fear declining *Greece* beheld
Her own *Menander*'s Art almost excell'd!   30
But ev'ry Muse essay'd to raise in vain
Some labour'd Rival of her *Tragic* Strain;
Ilissus' Laurels, tho' transferr'd with Toil,
Droop'd their fair Leaves, nor knew th' unfriendly Soil.

★ The *Oedipus* of *Sophocles*.

"There ev'ry Breast its fondest Hopes must bend,
"And ev'ry Muse with Tears await her Friend.

   'Twas then fair *Isis* from her Stream arose,
In kind Compassion of her Sister's Woes.
'Twas then she promis'd to the mourning Maid
Th' immortal Honours, which thy Hands have paid:
"My best-lov'd Son (she said) shall yet restore
"Thy ruin'd Sweets, and Fancy weep no more.

17 just *1744*] slow *1743*   25 With kind Concern *1744*] Line after Line, *1743*
27 Wit secure *1744*] equal Pow'r *1743*

As Arts expir'd, resistless Dulness rose;   35
Goths, *Priests*, or *Vandals*,----all were Learning's Foes.
Till * *Julius* first recall'd each exil'd Maid,
And *Cosmo* own'd them in th' *Etrurian* Shade:
Then deeply skill'd in Love's engaging Theme,
The soft *Provencial* past to *Arno*'s Stream: 40
With graceful Ease the wanton Lyre he strung,
Sweet flow'd the Lays, but Love was all he sung.
The gay Description could not fail to move,
For, led by Nature, all are Friends to Love.

But Heav'n, still various in its Works, decreed   45
The perfect Boast of Time should last succeed.
The beauteous Union must appear at length,
Of *Tuscan* Fancy, and *Athenian* Strength:
One greater Muse *Eliza*'s Reign adorn,
And ev'n a *Shakespear* to her Fame be born!   50

Yet ah! so bright her Morning's op'ning Ray,
In vain our *Britain* hop'd an equal Day!
No second Growth the Western Isle could bear,
At once exhausted with too rich a Year.
Too nicely *Johnson* knew the Critic's Part;   55
Nature in him was almost lost in Art.
Of softer Mold the gentle *Fletcher* came,
The next in Order, as the next in Name.
With pleas'd Attention 'midst his Scenes we find
Each glowing Thought, that warms the Female Mind;   60

* *Julius* the Second, the immediate Predecessor of *Leo* the Tenth.

35-41   When *Rome* herself, her envy'd Glories dead,
               No more Imperial, stoop'd her conquer'd Head:
               Luxuriant *Florence* chose a softer Theme,
               While all was Peace, by *Arno*'s silver Stream.
               With sweeter Notes th' *Etrurian* Vales complain'd,
               And Arts reviving told------ a *Cosmo* reign'd.
               Their wanton Lyres the Bards of *Provence* strung, *1743*
37 n. *Added in 1744*   42 Lays, but] Lays---- but *1744*   he *1744*] they *1743*
43 move,] move; *1744*   45 various *1744*] rising *1743*

Each melting Sigh, and ev'ry tender Tear,
The Lover's Wishes and the Virgin's Fear.
His ‡ ev'ry Strain the Smiles and Graces own;
But stronger *Shakespear* felt for *Man* alone:
Drawn by his Pen, our ruder Passions stand   65
Th' unrivall'd Picture of his early Hand.

† With gradual Steps, and slow, exacter *France*
Saw Art's fair Empire o'er her Shores advance:
By length of Toil, a bright Perfection knew,
Correctly bold, and just in all she drew.   70
Till late *Corneille*, with ★ *Lucan*'s spirit fir'd,
Breath'd the free Strain, as *Rome* and He inspir'd:
And classic Judgment gain'd to sweet *Racine*
The temp'rate Strength of *Maro*'s chaster Line.

But wilder far the *British* Laurel spread,   75
And Wreaths less artful crown our Poet's Head.
Yet He alone to ev'ry Scene could give
Th' Historian's Truth, and bid the Manners live.
Wak'd at his Call I view, with glad Surprize,
Majestic Forms of mighty Monarchs rise.   80
There *Henry*'s Trumpets spread their loud Alarms,
And laurel'd Conquest waits her Hero's Arms.
Here gentler *Edward* claims a pitying Sigh,
Scarce born to Honours, and so soon to die!
Yet shall thy Throne, unhappy Infant, bring   85

---

‡ Their Characters are thus distinguish'd by Mr. *Dryden*.
† About the Time of *Shakespear*, the Poet *Hardy* was in great Repute in *France*. He wrote, according to *Fontenelle*, six hundred Plays. The *French* Poets after him applied themselves in general to the correct Improvement of the Stage, which was almost totally disregarded by those of our own Country, *Johnson* excepted.
★ The favourite Author of the Elder *Corneille*.

---

63 Smiles and Graces] Loves and Graces *1743*, Smiles and *Graces 1744*   66 un-
rivall'd] unrival'd *1744*   67 n. *Added in 1744*
71–2   Till late *Corneille* from Epick † *Lucan* brought
               The full Expression, and the *Roman* Thought; *1743*

No Beam of Comfort to the guilty King?
The ‡ Time shall come, when *Glo'ster*'s Heart shall bleed
In Life's last Hours, with Horror of the Deed:
When dreary Visions shall at last present
Thy vengeful Image, in the midnight Tent: 90
Thy Hand unseen the secret Death shall bear,
Blunt the weak Sword, and break th' oppressive Spear.

  Where'er we turn, by Fancy charm'd, we find
Some sweet Illusion of the cheated Mind.
Oft, wild of Wing, she calls the Soul to rove   95
With humbler Nature, in the rural Grove;
Where Swains contented own the quiet Scene,
And twilight Fairies tread the circled Green:
Drest by her Hand, the Woods and Vallies smile,
And Spring diffusive decks th' *enchanted Isle*.   100

  O more than all in pow'rful Genius blest,
Come, take thine Empire o'er the willing Breast!
Whate'er the Wounds this youthful Heart shall feel,
Thy Songs support me, and thy Morals heal!
There ev'ry Thought the Poet's Warmth may raise,   105
There native Music dwells in all the Lays.
O might some Verse with happiest Skill persuade
Expressive Picture to adopt thine Aid!
What wond'rous Draughts might rise from ev'ry Page!
What other *Raphaels* Charm a distant Age!   110

         ‡ Tempus erit Turno, magno cum optaverit emptum
           Intactum Pallanta, *&c.*

87 bleed] d *missing in at least one copy of 1744*   94 cheated] created *Poetical
Dictionary*
101-10   O blest in all that Genius gives to charm,
                    Whose Morals mend us, and whose Passions warm!
                    Oft let my Youth attend thy various Page,
                    Where rich Invention rules th' unbounded Stage.
                    There ev'ry Scene the Poet's Warmth may raise,
                    And melting Music find the softest Lays.
                    O might the Muse with equal Ease persuade,
                    Expressive Picture, to adopt thine Aid!
                    Some pow'rful *Raphael* shou'd again appear,
                    And Arts consenting fix their Empire here. *1743*

Methinks ev'n now I view some free Design,
Where breathing Nature lives in ev'ry Line:
Chaste, and subdu'd, the modest Lights decay,
Steal into Shade, and mildly melt away.
----And see, where † *Antony* in Tears approv'd,   115
Guards the pale Relicks of the Chief he lov'd:
O'er the cold Corse the Warrior seems to bend,
Deep sunk in Grief, and mourns his murther'd Friend!
Still as they press, he calls on all around,
Lifts the torn Robe, and points the bleeding Wound.   120

But ‡ who is he, whose Brows exalted bear
A Wrath impatient, and a fiercer Air?
Awake to all that injur'd Worth can feel,
On his own *Rome* he turns th' avenging Steel.
Yet shall not War's insatiate Fury fall,   125
(So Heav'n ordains it) on the destin'd Wall.
See the fond Mother 'midst the plaintive Train
Hung on his Knees, and prostrate on the Plain!
Touch'd to the Soul, in vain he strives to hide
The Son's Affection, in the *Roman*'s Pride: 130
O'er all the Man conflicting Passions rise,
Rage grasps the Sword, while *Pity* melts the Eyes.

† See the Tragedy of *Julius Cæsar*.
‡ *Coriolanus*. See Mr. *Spence*'s Dialogues on the *Odyssey*.

111 free *1744*] fair *1743* (*MH* and *DFo*) fair *is deleted and* just,
apparently in Collins's hand, is written above   113 Chaste, and subdu'd,] Chast
and subdu'd *1744*   Lights decay *1744*] Colours lie *1743*
114–16   In fair Proportion to th' approving Eye.----
             And see, where † *Antony* lamenting stands
             In fixt Distress, and spreads his pleading Hands! *1743*
114 Shade] shades *Collection, Poetical Calendar, Langhorne*   115 Antony] *Anthony*
1744   117 cold *1744*] pale *1743*   122 Wrath *1744*] Rage *1743*
123–30   Ev'n now, his Thoughts with eager Vengeance doom
             The last sad Ruin of ungrateful *Rome*.
             Till, slow-advancing o'er the tented Plain,
             In sable Weeds, appear the Kindred-train:
             The frantic Mother leads their wild Despair,
             Beats her swoln Breast, and rends her silver Hair.
             And see he yields! ----the Tears unbidden start,
             And conscious Nature claims th' unwilling Heart! *1743*

Thus, gen'rous Critic, as thy Bard inspires,
The Sister Arts shall nurse their drooping Fires;
Each from his Scenes her Stores alternate bring,   135
Blend the fair Tints, or wake the vocal String:
Those *Sibyl*-Leaves, the Sport of ev'ry Wind,
(For Poets ever were a careless Kind)
By thee dispos'd, no farther Toil demand,
But, just to Nature, own thy forming Hand.   140

So spread o'er *Greece*, th' harmonious Whole unknown,
Ev'n *Homer*'s Numbers charm'd by Parts alone.
Their own *Ulysses* scarce had wander'd more,
By Winds and Water cast on ev'ry Shore:
When, rais'd by Fate, some former *Hanmer* join'd   145
Each beauteous Image of the boundless Mind:
And bad, like Thee, his *Athens* ever claim,
A fond Alliance, with the Poet's Name.

A SONG FROM
Shakespear's CYMBELYNE.
Sung by GUIDERUS *and* ARVIRAGUS *over* FIDELE,
suppos'd to be Dead.

See page 278 *of the* 7*th Vol. of* THEOBALD'*s Edition of*
SHAKESPEAR.

I.

To fair FIDELE's grassy Tomb
    Soft Maids, and Village Hinds shall bring
Each op'ning Sweet, of earliest Bloom,
    And rifle all the breathing Spring.

136 Blend *1744*] Spread *1743*   144 Water *1744*] Waters *1743*   146 boundless
1744] tuneful *1743*   148 Alliance,] Alliance *1744*

Title. ELEGIAC SONG. GM   CYMBELYNE] CYMBELINE *Collection 1758b*
1 FIDELE's] *Pastora's* GM

II.

No wailing Ghost shall dare appear 5
 To vex with Shrieks this quiet Grove:
But Shepherd Lads assemble here,
 And melting Virgins own their Love.

III.

No wither'd Witch shall here be seen,
 No Goblins lead their nightly Crew: 10
The Female Fays shall haunt the Green,
 And dress thy Grave with pearly Dew!

IV.

The Redbreast oft at Ev'ning Hours
 Shall kindly lend his little Aid:
With hoary Moss, and gather'd Flow'rs, 15
 To deck the Ground where thou art laid.

V.

When howling Winds, and beating Rain,
 In Tempests shake the sylvan Cell:
Or midst the Chace on ev'ry Plain,
 The tender Thought on thee shall dwell. 20

VI.

Each lonely Scene shall thee restore,
 For thee the Tear be duly shed:
Belov'd, till Life could charm no more;
 And mourn'd, till Pity's self be dead.

---

5 Ghost] ghosts *Lyric Harmony*   7 Shepherd] Shepherd's *Lyric Harmony*   Lads] swains *GM*   11 The] But *GM*   12 Grave] bed *GM*   pearly] early *Lyric Harmony*   14 lend] bend *Johnson's Shakespeare*   17 howling] chiding *GM* 18 Tempests] tempest *GM*, Tempest *Lyric Harmony*   19 Chace] flocks *GM* 21 lonely] lovely *GM*   23 could] can *GM, Langhorne, Dyce*

SONG. *The Sentiments borrowed from* SHAKSPEARE.

Young Damon of the vale is dead,
  Ye lowland hamlets moan:
A dewy turf lies o'er his head,
  And at his feet a stone.

His shroud, which death's cold damps destroy,   5
  Of snow-white threads was made:
All mourn'd to see so sweet a boy
  In earth for ever laid.

Pale pansies o'er his corpse were plac'd,
  Which, pluck'd before their time,   10
Bestrew'd the boy like him to waste,
  And wither in their prime.

But will he ne'er return, whose tongue
  Could tune the rural lay?
Ah, no! his bell of peace is rung,   15
  His lips are cold as clay.

They bore him out at twilight hour,
  The youth who lov'd so well:
Ah me! how many a true-love shower
  Of kind remembrance fell!   20

Each maid was woe—but Lucy chief,
  Her grief o'er all was tried,
Within his grave she dropp'd in grief,
  And o'er her lov'd-one died.

2 lowland] lowly *Dyce*   moan] mourn *Beloe*   5 death's] death *Beloe*
12 wither] whither *General Evening Post* (*misprint?*)   13 will he] he will *Public
Advertiser* (*misprint?*)   18 who lov'd] belov'd *Public Advertiser, General Evening
Post*

Written on a paper, which contained a piece of Bride Cake given to the author by a Lady.

Ye curious hands, that, hid from vulgar eyes,
  By search profane shall find this hallow'd cake,
With virtue's awe forbear the sacred prize,
  Nor dare a theft for love and pity's sake!

This precious relick, form'd by magick pow'r,   5
  Beneath her shepherd's haunted pillow laid,
Was meant by love to charm the silent hour,
  The secret present of a matchless maid.

The *Cypryan* queen, at hymen's fond request,
  Each nice ingredient chose with happiest art;   10
Fears, sighs, and wishes of th' enamoured breast,
  And pains that please, are mixt in every part.

With rosy hand the spicy fruit she brought
  From *Paphian* hills, and fair *Cythera's* isle;
And tempered sweet with these the melting thought,   15
  The kiss ambrosial and the yielding smile.

Ambiguous looks, that scorn and yet relent,
  Denials mild, and firm unalter'd truth,
Reluctant pride, and amorous faint consent,
  And meeting ardors and exulting youth.   20

Sleep, wayward God! hath sworn while these remain,
  With flattering dreams to dry his nightly tear,
And chearful *Hope*, so oft invok'd in vain,
  With fairy songs shall soothe his pensive ear.

If bound by vows to friendship's gentle side,   25
  And fond of soul, thou hop'st an equal grace,

6 her] the *Pearch*

If youth or maid thy joys and griefs divide,
  O much intreated leave this fatal place.

Sweet *Peace*, who long hath shunn'd my plaintive day,
  Consents at length to bring me short delight,   30
Thy careless steps may scare her doves away,
  And grief with raven note usurp the night.

ODES
ON SEVERAL
Descriptive and *Allegoric*
SUBJECTS.

——Ειην
Ευρησιεπης αναγεισθαι
Προσφορος εν Μοισᾶν Διφρω·
Τολμα δε και αμφιλαφης Δυναμις
Εσποιτο.——
          Πινδαρ. Ολυμπ. Θ.

ODE *to* PITY.

O Thou, the Friend of Man assign'd,
With balmy Hands his Wounds to bind,
  And charm his frantic Woe:
When first *Distress* with Dagger keen
Broke forth to waste his destin'd Scene,   5
  His wild unsated Foe!

2.

By *Pella*'s * Bard, a magic Name,
By all the Griefs his Thought could frame,
  Receive my humble Rite:

---

* *Euripides*, of whom *Aristotle* pronounces, on a Comparison of him with *Sophocles*, That he was the greater Master of the tender Passions, ἦν τραγικώτερος.

Long, *Pity*, let the Nations view
Thy sky-worn Robes of tend'rest Blue,
    And Eyes of dewy Light!

3.

But wherefore need I wander wide
To old *Ilissus'* distant Side,
    Deserted Stream, and mute?   15
Wild *Arun* † too has heard thy Strains,
And Echo, 'midst my native Plains,
    Been sooth'd by *Pity's* Lute.

4.

There first the Wren thy Myrtles shed
On gentlest *Otway's* infant Head,   20
    To Him thy Cell was shown;
And while He sung the Female Heart,
With Youth's soft Notes unspoil'd by Art,
    Thy Turtles mix'd their own.

5.

Come, *Pity*, come, by Fancy's Aid,   25
Ev'n now my Thoughts, relenting Maid,
    Thy Temple's Pride design:
Its Southern Site, its Truth compleat
Shall raise a wild Enthusiast Heat,
    In all who view the Shrine.   30

6.

There Picture's Toils shall well relate,
How Chance, or hard involving Fate,
    O'er mortal Bliss prevail:
The Buskin'd Muse shall near her stand,
And sighing prompt her tender Hand,   35
    With each disastrous Tale.

† The River *Arun* runs by the Village in *Sussex*, where *Otway* had his Birth.

31 Toils] toil *Langhorne*

7.

There let me oft, retir'd by Day,
In Dreams of Passion melt away,
  Allow'd with Thee to dwell:
There waste the mournful Lamp of Night,   40
Till, Virgin, Thou again delight
  To hear a *British* Shell!

ODE *to* FEAR.

Thou, to whom the World unknown
With all its shadowy Shapes is shown;
Who see'st appall'd th' unreal Scene,
While Fancy lifts the Veil between:
    Ah *Fear!* Ah frantic *Fear!*   5
    I see, I see Thee near.
I know thy hurried Step, thy haggard Eye!
Like Thee I start, like Thee disorder'd fly,
For lo what *Monsters* in thy Train appear!
Danger, whose Limbs of Giant Mold   10
What mortal Eye can fix'd behold?
Who stalks his Round, an hideous Form,
Howling amidst the Midnight Storm,
Or throws him on the ridgy Steep
Of some loose hanging Rock to sleep: 15
And with him thousand Phantoms join'd,
Who prompt to Deeds accurs'd the Mind:
And those, the Fiends, who near allied,
O'er Nature's Wounds, and Wrecks preside;
Whilst *Vengeance*, in the lurid Air,   20
Lifts her red Arm, expos'd and bare:
On whom that rav'ning * Brood of Fate,
Who lap the Blood of Sorrow, wait;

---

* Alluding to the Κυνας αφυκτους of *Sophocles*. See the ELECTRA.

---

2 shadowy] shadow *Pearch* (*misprint?*)

Who, *Fear*, this ghastly Train can see,
And look not madly wild, like Thee?   25

EPODE.

In earliest *Grece* to Thee with partial Choice,
   The Grief-full Muse addrest her infant Tongue;
The Maids and Matrons, on her awful Voice,
   Silent and pale in wild Amazement hung.

Yet He the Bard ★ who first invok'd thy Name,   30
   Disdain'd in *Marathon* its Pow'r to feel:
For not alone he nurs'd the Poet's flame,
   But reach'd from Virtue's Hand the Patriot's Steel.

But who is He whom later Garlands grace,
   Who left a-while o'er *Hybla*'s Dews to rove,   35
With trembling Eyes thy dreary Steps to trace,
   Where Thou and *Furies* shar'd the baleful Grove?

Wrapt in thy cloudy Veil th' *Incestuous Queen* †
   Sigh'd the sad Call ‖ her Son and Husband hear'd,
When once alone it broke the silent Scene,   40
   And He the Wretch of *Thebes* no more appear'd.

O *Fear*, I know Thee by my throbbing Heart,
   Thy with'ring Pow'r inspir'd each mournful Line,
Tho' gentle *Pity* claim her mingled Part,
   Yet all the Thunders of the Scene are thine!   45

ANTISTROPHE.

Thou who such weary Lengths hast past,
Where wilt thou rest, mad Nymph, at last?

★ *Æschylus.*   † *Jocasta.*

‖ ——ουδ ετ' ὀρωρει βοη
Ην μεν Σιωπη; φθεγμα δ'εξαιφνης τινος
Θωυξεν αυτον, ωστε παντας ορθιας
Στησαι φοβω δεισαντας εξαιφνης Τριχας.
See the Œdip. Colon. of *Sophocles.*

Say, wilt thou shroud in haunted Cell,
Where gloomy *Rape* and *Murder* dwell?
Or in some hollow'd Seat,   50
'Gainst which the big Waves beat,
Hear drowning Sea-men's Cries in Tempests brought!
Dark Pow'r, with shudd'ring meek submitted Thought
Be mine, to read the Visions old,
Which thy awak'ning Bards have told: 55
And lest thou meet my blasted View,
Hold each strange Tale devoutly true;
Ne'er be I found, by Thee o'eraw'd,
In that thrice-hallow'd Eve abroad,
When Ghosts, as Cottage-Maids believe,   60
Their pebbled Beds permitted leave,
And *Gobblins* haunt from Fire, or Fen,
Or Mine, or Flood, the Walks of Men!
  O Thou whose Spirit most possest
The sacred Seat of *Shakespear*'s Breast!   65
By all that from thy Prophet broke,
In thy Divine Emotions spoke:
Hither again thy Fury deal,
Teach me but once like Him to feel:
His *Cypress Wreath* my Meed decree,   70
And I, O *Fear*, will dwell with *Thee!*

ODE *to* SIMPLICITY.

I.

O Thou by *Nature* taught,
  To breathe her genuine Thought,
In Numbers warmly pure, and sweetly strong:
  Who first on Mountains wild,
  In *Fancy* loveliest Child,   5
Thy Babe, or *Pleasure's*, nurs'd the Pow'rs of Song!

6 or] and *Langhorne*

2.

Thou, who with Hermit Heart
Disdain'st the Wealth of Art,
And Gauds, and pageant Weeds, and trailing Pall:
But com'st a decent Maid   10
In *Attic* Robe array'd,
O chaste unboastful Nymph, to Thee I call!

3.

By all the honey'd Store
On *Hybla*'s Thymy Shore,
By all her Blooms, and mingled Murmurs dear,   15
By Her ★, whose Love-lorn Woe
In Ev'ning Musings slow
Sooth'd sweetly sad *Electra*'s Poet's Ear:

4.

By old *Cephisus* deep,
Who spread his wavy Sweep   20
In warbled Wand'rings round thy green Retreat,
On whose enamel'd Side
When holy *Freedom* died
No equal Haunt allur'd thy future Feet.

5.

O Sister meek of Truth,   25
To my admiring Youth,
Thy sober Aid and native Charms infuse!
The Flow'rs that sweetest breathe,
Tho' Beauty cull'd the Wreath,
Still ask thy Hand to range their order'd Hues.   30

★ The αηδων, or Nightingale, for which *Sophocles* seems to have entertain'd a
peculiar Fondness.

---

16 Love-lorn] Love-born *Odes (corrected in Errata)*   16 n. Sophocles] s *missing or
blurred in several copies of Odes*   21 thy] the *Pearch*

6.

While *Rome* could none esteem
  But Virtue's Patriot Theme,
You lov'd her Hills, and led her Laureate Band:
  But staid to sing alone
  To one distinguish'd Throne,   35
And turn'd thy Face, and fled her alter'd Land.

7.

No more, in Hall or Bow'r,
  The Passions own thy Pow'r,
Love, only Love her forceless Numbers mean:
  For Thou hast left her Shrine,   40
  Nor Olive more, nor Vine,
Shall gain thy Feet to bless the servile Scene.

8.

Tho' Taste, tho' Genius bless,
  To some divine Excess,
Faints the cold Work till Thou inspire the whole;   45
  What each, what all supply,
  May court, may charm our Eye,
Thou, only Thou can'st raise the meeting Soul!

9.

Of These let others ask,
  To aid some mighty Task,   50
I only seek to find thy temp'rate Vale:
  Where oft my Reed might sound
  To Maids and Shepherds round,
And all thy Sons, O *Nature*, learn my Tale.

33 her Laureate] the laureat *Pearch*   45 Faints] Faint's *Poetical Calendar,*
Langhorne, Pearch   47 our] your *Pearch*

ODE *on the* POETICAL CHARACTER.

As once, if not with light Regard,
I read aright that gifted Bard,
(Him whose School above the rest
His Loveliest *Elfin* Queen has blest.)
One, only One, unrival'd Fair *,   5
Might hope the magic Girdle wear,
At solemn Turney hung on high,
The Wish of each love-darting Eye;
Lo! to each other Nymph in turn applied,
    As if, in Air unseen, some hov'ring Hand,   10
Some chaste and Angel-Friend to Virgin-Fame,
    With whisper'd Spell had burst the starting Band,
It left unblest her loath'd dishonour'd Side;
        Happier hopeless Fair, if never
        Her baffled Hand with vain Endeavour   15
Had touch'd that fatal Zone to her denied!
Young *Fancy* thus, to me Divinest Name,
        To whom, prepar'd and bath'd in Heav'n,
        The Cest of amplest Pow'r is giv'n:
        To few the God-like Gift assigns,   20
        To gird their blest prophetic Loins,
And gaze her Visions wild, and feel unmix'd her Flame!

                                2.

The Band, as Fairy Legends say,
Was wove on that creating Day,
When He, who call'd with Thought to Birth   25
Yon tented Sky, this laughing Earth,
And drest with Springs, and Forests tall,
And pour'd the Main engirting all,
Long by the lov'd *Enthusiast* woo'd,
Himself in some Diviner Mood,   30

★ *Florimel.* See *Spenser* Leg. 4th.

Retiring, sate with her alone,
And plac'd her on his Saphire Throne,
The whiles, the vaulted Shrine around,
Seraphic Wires were heard to sound,
Now sublimest Triumph swelling,   35
Now on Love and Mercy dwelling;
And she, from out the veiling Cloud,
Breath'd her magic Notes aloud:
And Thou, Thou rich-hair'd Youth of Morn,
And all thy subject Life was born!   40
The dang'rous Passions kept aloof,
Far from the sainted growing Woof:
But near it sate Ecstatic *Wonder*,
List'ning the deep applauding Thunder:
And *Truth*, in sunny Vest array'd,   45
By whose the Tarsel's Eyes were made;
All the shad'wy Tribes of *Mind*,
In braided Dance their Murmurs join'd,
And all the bright uncounted *Pow'rs*,
Who feed on Heav'n's ambrosial Flow'rs.   50
Where is the Bard, whose Soul can now
Its high presuming Hopes avow?
Where He who thinks, with Rapture blind,
This hallow'd Work for Him design'd?

3.

High on some Cliff, to Heav'n up-pil'd,   55
Of rude Access, of Prospect wild,
Where, tangled round the jealous Steep,
Strange Shades o'erbrow the Valleys deep,
And holy *Genii* guard the Rock,
Its Gloomes embrown, its Springs unlock,   60
While on its rich ambitious Head,
An *Eden*, like his own, lies spread.
I view that Oak, the fancied Glades among,

58 o'erbrow] o'erbow *Pearch*

By which as *Milton* lay, His Ev'ning Ear,
From many a Cloud that drop'd Ethereal Dew,   65
Nigh spher'd in Heav'n its native Strains could hear:
On which that ancient Trump he reach'd was hung;
    Thither oft his Glory greeting,
    From *Waller*'s Myrtle Shades retreating,
With many a Vow from Hope's aspiring Tongue,   70
My trembling Feet his guiding Steps pursue;
    In vain— Such Bliss to One alone,
    Of all the Sons of Soul was known,
    And Heav'n, and *Fancy*, kindred Pow'rs,
    Have now o'erturn'd th' inspiring Bow'rs,   75
Or curtain'd close such Scene from ev'ry future View.

ODE, *Written in the beginning of the Year* 1746.

How sleep the Brave, who sink to Rest,
By all their Country's Wishes blest!
When *Spring*, with dewy Fingers cold,
Returns to deck their hallow'd Mold,
She there shall dress a sweeter Sod,   5
Than *Fancy*'s Feet have ever trod.

2.

By Fairy Hands their Knell is rung,
By Forms unseen their Dirge is sung;
There *Honour* comes, a Pilgrim grey,
To bless the Turf that wraps their Clay,   10
And *Freedom* shall a-while repair,
To dwell a weeping Hermit there!

Title. ODE, *Written in the same Year* [1745]. *Collection*   2 their] the *Collection*
1758a   5 there] *then Alfred*
7-8   *By Hands unseen the Knell is rung;*
                   By FAIRY *Forms their Dirge is sung. Alfred*

ODE *to* MERCY.

STROPHE.

O Thou, who sit'st a smiling Bride
  By *Valour's* arm'd and awful Side,
Gentlest of Sky-born Forms, and best ador'd:
  Who oft with Songs, divine to hear,
  Win'st from his fatal Grasp the Spear,   5
And hid'st in Wreaths of Flow'rs his bloodless Sword!
  Thou who, amidst the deathful Field,
  By Godlike Chiefs alone beheld,
Oft with thy Bosom bare art found,
Pleading for him the Youth who sinks to Ground: 10
  See, *Mercy*, see, with pure and loaded Hands,
  Before thy Shrine my Country's Genius stands,
And decks thy Altar still, tho' pierc'd with many a Wound!

ANTISTROPHE.

When he whom ev'n our Joys provoke,
  The *Fiend of Nature* join'd his Yoke,   15
And rush'd in Wrath to make our Isle his Prey;
  Thy Form, from out thy sweet Abode,
  O'ertook Him on his blasted Road,
And stop'd his Wheels, and look'd his Rage away.
  I see recoil his sable Steeds,   20
  That bore Him swift to Salvage Deeds,
Thy tender melting Eyes they own;
O Maid, for all thy Love to *Britain* shown,
  Where *Justice* bars her Iron Tow'r,
  To Thee we build a roseate Bow'r,   25
Thou, Thou shalt rule our Queen, and share our
    Monarch's Throne!

ODE *to* LIBERTY.

STROPHE.

Who shall awake the *Spartan* Fife,
And call in solemn Sounds to Life,
The Youths, whose Locks divinely spreading,
  Like vernal Hyacinths in sullen Hue,
At once the Breath of Fear and Virtue shedding,   5
  Applauding *Freedom* lov'd of old to view?
What New *Alcæus* ★, Fancy-blest,
Shall sing the Sword, in Myrtles drest,
  At *Wisdom's* Shrine a-while its Flame concealing,
(What Place so fit to seal a Deed renown'd?)   10
  Till she her brightest Lightnings round revealing,
It leap'd in Glory forth, and dealt her prompted Wound!
    O Goddess, in that feeling Hour,
    When most its Sounds would court thy Ears,
    Let not my Shell's misguided Pow'r ★,   15
    E'er draw thy sad, thy mindful Tears.
No, *Freedom*, no, I will not tell,
How *Rome*, before thy weeping Face,
With heaviest Sound, a Giant-statue, fell,
Push'd by a wild and artless Race,   20
From off its wide ambitious Base,

★ Alluding to that beautiful Fragment of *Alcæus*.

      Εν Μυρτου κλαδι το ξιφος φορησω,
      Ωσπερ Αρμοδιος και Αριστογειτων,
      Φιλταθ' Αρμοδι ουπω Τεθνηκας,
      Νησοις δ' εν Μακαρων Σε φασιν ειναι·
      Εν μυρτου κλαδι το ξιφος φορησω,
      Ωσπερ Αρμοδιος και Αριστογειτων,
      Οτ' Αθηναιης εν θυσιαις,
      Ανδρα Τυραννον ιππαρχον εκαινετην.
      Αει Σφων κλεος εσσεται κατ' αιαν,
      Φιλταθ' Αρμοδι', και Αριστογειτων.

   ★ Μη μη ταυτα λεγωμες, ὰ Δακρυον ἥγαγε Δηοι.
               Callimach. Υμνος εις Δημητρα

---

7 n. that] a *Poetical Calendar*

When Time his Northern Sons of Spoil awoke,
  And all the blended Work of Strength and Grace,
  With many a rude repeated Stroke,
And many a barb'rous Yell, to thousand Fragments broke.   25

EPODE.

2.

Yet ev'n, where'er the least appear'd,
Th' admiring World thy Hand rever'd;
Still 'midst the scatter'd States around,
Some Remnants of Her Strength were found;
They saw by what escap'd the Storm,   30
How wond'rous rose her perfect Form;
How in the great the labour'd Whole,
Each mighty Master pour'd his Soul!
For sunny *Florence*, Seat of Art,
Beneath her Vines preserv'd a part,   35
Till They ★, whom Science lov'd to name,
(O who could fear it?) quench'd her Flame.
And lo, an humbler Relick laid
In jealous *Pisa*'s Olive Shade!
See small *Marino* † joins the Theme,   40
Tho' least, not last in thy Esteem:
Strike, louder strike th' ennobling Strings
To those ★, whose Merchant Sons were Kings;
To Him †, who deck'd with pearly Pride,
In *Adria* weds his green-hair'd Bride;   45
Hail Port of Glory, Wealth, and Pleasure,
Ne'er let me change this *Lydian* Measure:
Nor e'er her former Pride relate,
To sad *Liguria*'s ‖ bleeding State.
Ah no! more pleas'd thy Haunts I seek,   50
On wild *Helvetia*'s ★★ Mountains bleak:

★ The Family of the *Medici*.   † The little Republic of *San Marino*.
★ The *Venetians*.   † The Doge of *Venice*.
‖ *Genoa*.   ★★ *Switzerland*.

(Where, when the favor'd of thy Choice,
The daring Archer heard thy Voice;
Forth from his Eyrie rous'd in Dread,
The rav'ning *Eagle* northward fled.)   55
Or dwell in willow'd Meads more near,
With Those †† to whom thy Stork is dear:
Those whom the Rod of *Alva* bruis'd,
Whose Crown a *British* Queen * refus'd!
The Magic works, Thou feel'st the Strains,   60
One holier Name alone remains;
The perfect Spell shall then avail,
Hail Nymph, ador'd by *Britain*, Hail!

ANTISTROPHE.

Beyond the Measure vast of Thought,
The Works, the Wizzard *Time* has wrought!   65
    The *Gaul*, 'tis held of antique Story,
Saw *Britain* link'd to his now adverse Strand ||,
    No Sea between, nor Cliff sublime and hoary,
He pass'd with unwet Feet thro' all our Land.
    To the blown *Baltic* then, they say,   70
    The wild Waves found another way,
Where *Orcas* howls, his wolfish Mountains rounding;
    Till all the banded West at once 'gan rise,
A wide wild Storm ev'n Nature's self confounding,
    With'ring her Giant Sons with strange uncouth Surprise.   75
    This pillar'd Earth so firm and wide,
    By Winds and inward Labors torn,
    In Thunders dread was push'd aside,
    And down the should'ring Billows born.

†† The *Dutch*, amongst whom there are very severe Penalties for those who are convicted of killing this Bird. They are kept tame in almost all their Towns, and particularly at the *Hague*, of the Arms of which they make a Part. The common People of *Holland* are said to entertain a superstitious Sentiment, That if the whole Species of them should become extinct, they should lose their Liberties.

* Queen *Elizabeth*.

|| This Tradition is mention'd by several of our old Historians. Some Naturalists too have endeavour'd to support the Probability of the Fact, by Arguments drawn from the correspondent Disposition of the two opposite Coasts. I don't remember that any Poetical Use has been hitherto made of it.

And see, like Gems, her laughing Train,   80
    The little Isles on ev'ry side,
Mona *, once hid from those who search the Main,
    Where thousand Elfin Shapes abide,
And *Wight* who checks the west'ring Tide,
    For Thee consenting Heav'n has each bestow'd,   85
A fair Attendant on her sov'reign Pride:
    To Thee this blest Divorce she ow'd,
For thou hast made her Vales thy lov'd, thy last Abode!

SECOND EPODE.

Then too, 'tis said, an hoary Pile,
'Midst the green Navel of our Isle,   90
Thy Shrine in some religious Wood,
O Soul-enforcing Goddess stood!
There oft the painted Native's Feet,
Were wont thy Form celestial meet:
Tho' now with hopeless Toil we trace   95
Time's backward Rolls, to find its place;
Whether the fiery-tressed *Dane*,
Or *Roman*'s self o'erturn'd the Fane,
Or in what Heav'n-left Age it fell,
'Twere hard for modern Song to tell.   100
Yet still, if Truth those Beams infuse,
Which guide at once, and charm the Muse,
Beyond yon braided Clouds that lie,
Paving the light-embroider'd Sky:
Amidst the bright pavilion'd Plains,   105
The beauteous *Model* still remains.
There happier than in Islands blest,
Or Bow'rs by Spring or *Hebe* drest,

* There is a Tradition in the Isle of *Man*, that a Mermaid becoming enamour'd of a young Man of extraordinary Beauty, took an Opportunity of meeting him one day as he walked on the Shore, and open'd her Passion to him, but was receiv'd with a Coldness, occasion'd by his Horror and Surprize at her Appearance. This however was so misconstrued by the Sea-Lady, that in revenge for his Treatment of her, she punish'd the whole Island, by covering it with a Mist, so that all who attempted to carry on any Commerce with it, either never arriv'd at it, but wander'd up and down the Sea, or were on a sudden wreck'd upon its Cliffs.

The Chiefs who fill our *Albion*'s Story,
In warlike Weeds, retir'd in Glory,   110
Hear their consorted *Druids* sing
Their Triumphs to th' immortal String.
  How may the Poet now unfold,
What never Tongue or Numbers told?
How learn delighted, and amaz'd,   115
What Hands unknown that Fabric rais'd?
Ev'n now before his favor'd Eyes,
In *Gothic* Pride it seems to rise!
Yet *Græcia*'s graceful Orders join,
Majestic thro' the mix'd Design;   120
The secret Builder knew to chuse,
Each sphere-found Gem of richest Hues:
Whate'er Heav'n's purer Mold contains,
When nearer Suns emblaze its Veins;
There on the Walls the *Patriot's* Sight,   125
May ever hang with fresh Delight,
And, grav'd with some Prophetic Rage,
Read *Albion*'s Fame thro' ev'ry Age.
  Ye Forms Divine, ye Laureate Band,
That near her inmost Altar stand!   130
Now sooth Her, to her blissful Train
Blithe *Concord's* social Form to gain:
Concord, whose Myrtle Wand can steep
Ev'n *Anger's* blood-shot Eyes in Sleep:
Before whose breathing Bosom's Balm,   135
Rage drops his Steel, and Storms grow calm;
Her let our Sires and Matrons hoar
Welcome to *Britain*'s ravag'd Shore,
Our Youths, enamour'd of the Fair,
Play with the Tangles of her Hair,   140
Till in one loud applauding Sound,
The Nations shout to Her around,
O how supremely art thou blest,
Thou, Lady, Thou shalt rule the West!

ODE, *to a Lady on the Death of Colonel* ROSS *in the Action of* Fontenoy.

1.

While, lost to all his former Mirth,
Britannia's Genius bends to Earth,
    And mourns the fatal Day:
While stain'd with Blood he strives to tear
Unseemly from his Sea-green Hair   5
    The Wreaths of chearful *May*:

2.

The Thoughts which musing Pity pays,
And fond Remembrance loves to raise,
    Your faithful Hours attend:
Still Fancy to Herself unkind,   10
Awakes to Grief the soften'd Mind,
    And points the bleeding Friend.

3.

By rapid *Scheld*'s descending Wave
His Country's Vows shall bless the Grave,
    Where'er the Youth is laid: 15
That sacred Spot the Village Hind
With ev'ry sweetest Turf shall bind,
    And Peace protect the Shade.

Title. ODE *to a LADY, On the Death of Col.* CHARLES ROSS, *in the Action at* Fontenoy. *Written* May, 1745. *Museum; An* ODE *to the Memory of Colonel* CHARLES ROSS *of* Balnagown, *who was killed in the Action at* Fontenoy. *British Magazine;* ODE, to a LADY, On the Death of Col. CHARLES ROSS, in the Action at *Fontenoy.* Written *May*, 1745. *Collection 1748*   4 stain'd with Blood] sunk in grief *Warton MS.*

4.

O'er him, whose Doom thy Virtues grieve,
Aërial Forms shall sit at Eve   20
    And bend the pensive Head!
And, fall'n to save his injur'd Land,
Imperial *Honor*'s awful Hand
    Shall point his lonely Bed!

5.

The warlike Dead of ev'ry Age,   25
Who fill the fair recording Page,
    Shall leave their sainted Rest:
And, half-reclining on his Spear,
Each wond'ring Chief by turns appear,
    To hail the blooming Guest.   30

6.

Old *Edward*'s Sons, unknown to yield,
Shall croud from *Cressy*'s laurell'd Field,
    And gaze with fix'd Delight:

19–24   Ev'n now, regardful of his Doom,
           Applauding *Honour* haunts his Tomb,
               With shadowy Trophies crown'd:
           Whilst *Freedom*'s Form beside her roves
           Majestic thro' the twilight Groves,
               And calls her Heroes round. *Museum*

           Blest Youth, regardful of thy Doom,
           Aërial Hands shall build thy Tomb,
               With shadowy Trophies crown'd:
           Whilst *Honor* bath'd in Tears shall rove
           To sigh thy Name thro' ev'ry Grove,
               And call his Heros round. *Odes*

           O'er him, whose doom thy virtues grieve,
           Aërial forms shall sit at eve
               And bend the pensive head!
           And, fall'n to save his injur'd land,
           Imperial Honor's awful hand
               Shall point his lonely bed! *Collection 1748*

The Warton MS. follows the substantives of the Museum text exactly except in l.19: regardless
for regardful (*Warton's mistake?*)   31 unknown] untaught *Warton MS.*

Again for *Britain*'s Wrongs they feel,
Again they snatch the gleamy Steel,   35
    And wish th' avenging Fight.

7.·

But lo where, sunk in deep Despair,
Her Garments torn, her Bosom bare,
    Impatient *Freedom* lies!
Her matted Tresses madly spread,   40
To ev'ry Sod, which wraps the Dead,
    She turns her joyless Eyes.

8.

Ne'er shall she leave that lowly Ground,
Till Notes of Triumph bursting round
    Proclaim her Reign restor'd: 45
Till *William* seek the sad Retreat,
And bleeding at her sacred Feet,
    Present the sated Sword.

9.

If, weak to sooth so soft an Heart,
These pictur'd Glories nought impart,   50
    To dry thy constant Tear:
If yet, in Sorrow's distant Eye,
Expos'd and pale thou see'st him lie,
    Wild War insulting near:

10.

Where'er from Time Thou court'st Relief,   55
The Muse shall still, with social Grief,
    Her gentlest Promise keep:

37–48 *Added in Odes (and British Magazine); removed in Collection 1748*   49 If
drawn by all a Lover's Art *Warton MS.*   an] a *Museum*   57 gentlest] gentle
Collection 1758 b

Ev'n humble *Harting*'s cottag'd Vale
Shall learn the sad repeated Tale,
And bid her Shepherds weep.   60

ODE *to* EVENING.

If ought of Oaten Stop, or Pastoral Song,
May hope, chaste *Eve*, to sooth thy modest Ear,
    Like thy own solemn Springs,
    Thy Springs, and dying Gales,
O *Nymph* reserv'd, while now the bright-hair'd Sun   5
Sits in yon western Tent, whose cloudy Skirts,
    With Brede ethereal wove,
    O'erhang his wavy Bed:
Now Air is hush'd, save where the weak-ey'd Bat,
With short shrill Shriek flits by on leathern Wing,   10
    Or where the Beetle winds
    His small but sullen Horn,
As oft he rises 'midst the twilight Path,
Against the Pilgrim born in heedless Hum:
    Now teach me, *Maid* compos'd,   15
    To breathe some soften'd Strain,
Whose Numbers stealing thro' thy darkning Vale,
May not unseemly with its Stillness suit,
    As musing slow, I hail
    Thy genial lov'd Return!   20
For when thy folding Star arising shews
His paly Circlet, at his warning Lamp
    The fragrant *Hours*, and *Elves*
    Who slept in Flow'rs the Day,
And many a *Nymph* who wreaths her Brows with Sedge,   25

58 *Harting*'s] *H------*'s *Museum*   cottag'd] cottage *Collection 1748–1758a*

2   May hope, O pensive *Eve*, to sooth thine Ear, *Odes*
        May hope, chaste EVE, to sooth thy modest ear, *Collection 1748*
3 solemn *Collection 1748*] brawling *Odes*   6 in] on *Collection 1758b*   9 Now]
Nor *Union 1753a*, While *Collection 1758b*   10 Shriek] shrieks *Collection 1751–8*,
Poetical Calendar   24 Flow'rs] Buds *Odes*, flow'rs *Collection 1748*

And sheds the fresh'ning Dew, and lovelier still,
    The *Pensive Pleasures* sweet
    Prepare thy shadowy Car.
Then lead, calm *Vot'ress*, where some sheety Lake
Cheers the lone Heath, or some time-hallow'd Pile,   30
    Or up-land Fallows grey
    Reflect it's last cool Gleam.
But when chill blustring Winds, or driving Rain,
Forbid my willing Feet, be mine the Hut,
    That from the Mountain's Side,   35
    Views Wilds, and swelling Floods,
And Hamlets brown, and dim-discover'd Spires,
And hears their simple Bell, and marks o'er all
    Thy Dewy Fingers draw
    The gradual dusky Veil.   40
While *Spring* shall pour his Show'rs, as oft he wont,
And bathe thy breathing Tresses, meekest *Eve!*
    While *Summer* loves to sport,
    Beneath thy ling'ring Light:
While sallow *Autumn* fills thy Lap with Leaves,   45
Or *Winter* yelling thro' the troublous Air,
    Affrights thy shrinking Train,
    And rudely rends thy Robes.
So long, sure-found beneath the Sylvan Shed,
Shall *Fancy, Friendship, Science*, rose-lip'd *Health*,   50
    Thy gentlest Influence own,
    And hymn thy fav'rite Name!

29–32   Then let me rove some wild and heathy Scene,
        Or find some Ruin 'midst its dreary Dells,
          Whose Walls more awful nod
          By thy religious Gleams. *Odes*

        Then lead, calm Vot'ress, where some sheety lake
        Cheers the lone heath, or some time-hallow'd pile,
          Or up-land fallows grey
          Reflect it's last cool gleam. *Collection 1748*

33 But when *Collection 1748*] Or if *Odes*   34 Forbid *Collection 1748*] Prevent *Odes*
45 sallow] fallow *Collection 1749 (corrected in subsequent editions)*
49   So long regardful of thy quiet Rule, *Odes*
        So long, sure-found beneath the Sylvan shed, *Collection 1748*
the] thy *Collection 1749, Union*   50 rose-lip'd *Health*] smiling *Peace Odes*,
rose-lip'd HEALTH *Collection 1748*   52 hymn *Collection 1748*] love *Odes*

ODE *to* PEACE.

O Thou, who bad'st thy Turtles bear
Swift from his Grasp thy golden Hair,
 And sought'st thy native Skies:
When *War*, by Vultures drawn from far,
To *Britain* bent his Iron Car,   5
 And bad his Storms arise!

2.

Tir'd of his rude tyrannic Sway,
Our Youth shall fix some festive Day,
 His sullen Shrines to burn:
But Thou who hear'st the turning Spheres,   10
What Sounds may charm thy partial Ears,
 And gain thy blest Return!

3.

O *Peace*, thy injur'd Robes up-bind,
O rise, and leave not one behind
 Of all thy beamy Train: 15
The *British* Lion, Goddess sweet,
Lies stretch'd on Earth to kiss thy Feet,
 And own thy holier Reign.

4.

Let others court thy transient Smile,
But come to grace thy western Isle,   20
 By warlike *Honour* led!
And, while around her Ports rejoice,
While all her Sons adore thy Choice,
 With Him for ever wed!

The MANNERS. *An* ODE.

Farewell, for clearer Ken design'd,
The dim-discover'd Tracts of Mind:

Truths which, from Action's Paths retir'd,
My silent Search in vain requir'd!
No more my Sail that Deep explores,   5
No more I search those magic Shores,
What Regions part the World of Soul,
Or whence thy Streams, *Opinion*, roll:
If e'er I round such Fairy Field,
Some Pow'r impart the Spear and Shield,   10
At which the Wizzard *Passions* fly,
By which the Giant *Follies* die!
  Farewell the Porch, whose Roof is seen,
Arch'd with th' enlivening Olive's Green:
Where *Science*, prank'd in tissued Vest,   15
By *Reason*, *Pride*, and *Fancy* drest,
Comes like a Bride so trim array'd,
To wed with *Doubt* in *Plato*'s Shade!
  Youth of the quick uncheated Sight,
Thy Walks, *Observance*, more invite!   20
O Thou, who lov'st that ampler Range,
Where Life's wide Prospects round thee change,
And with her mingling Sons ally'd,
Throw'st the prattling Page aside:
To me in Converse sweet impart,   25
To read in Man the native Heart,
To learn, where Science sure is found,
From Nature as she lives around:
And gazing oft her Mirror true,
By turns each shifting Image view!   30
Till meddling *Art*'s officious Lore,
Reverse the Lessons taught before,
Alluring from a safer Rule,
To dream in her enchanted School;
Thou Heav'n, whate'er of Great we boast,   35
Hast blest this social Science most.

23 mingling] mingled *Langhorne*   33 Alluring from] Alluring him from *Odes*
(*corrected in Errata*)

Retiring hence to thoughtful Cell,
As *Fancy* breathes her potent Spell,
Not vain she finds the charmful Task,
In Pageant quaint, in motley Mask,   40
Behold before her musing Eyes,
The countless *Manners* round her rise;
While ever varying as they pass,
To some *Contempt* applies her Glass:
With these the *white-rob'd Maids* combine,   45
And those the laughing *Satyrs* join!
But who is He whom now she views,
In Robe of wild contending Hues?
Thou by the Passions nurs'd, I greet
The comic Sock that binds thy Feet!   50
O *Humour*, Thou whose Name is known,
To *Britain*'s favor'd Isle alone:
Me too amidst thy Band admit,
There where the young-eyed healthful *Wit*,
(Whose Jewels in his crisped Hair   55
Are plac'd each other's Beams to share,
Whom no Delights from Thee divide)
In Laughter loos'd attends thy Side!
By old *Miletus* ★ who so long
Has ceas'd his Love-inwoven Song: 60
By all you taught the *Tuscan* Maids,
In chang'd *Italia*'s modern Shades:
By Him †, whose *Knight*'s distinguish'd Name
Refin'd a Nation's Lust of Fame;
Whose Tales ev'n now, with Echos sweet,   65
Castilia's *Moorish* Hills repeat:
Or Him ★, whom *Seine*'s blue Nymphs deplore,
In watchet Weeds on *Gallia*'s Shore,
Who drew the sad *Sicilian* Maid,

★ Alluding to the *Milesian* Tales, some of the earliest Romances.
† *Cervantes.*
★ Monsieur *Le Sage*, Author of the incomparable Adventures of *Gil Blas de Santillane*, who died in *Paris* in the Year 1745.

By Virtues in her Sire betray'd: 70
   O Nature boon, from whom proceed
Each forceful Thought, each prompted Deed;
If but from Thee I hope to feel,
On all my Heart imprint thy Seal!
Let some retreating Cynic find,   75
Those oft-turn'd Scrolls I leave behind,
The *Sports* and I this Hour agree,
To rove thy Scene-full World with Thee!

The PASSIONS.
An ODE *for Music.*

When Music, Heav'nly Maid, was young,
While yet in early *Greece* she sung,
The Passions oft to hear her Shell,
Throng'd around her magic Cell,
Exulting, trembling, raging, fainting,   5
Possest beyond the Muse's Painting;
By turns they felt the glowing Mind,
Disturb'd, delighted, rais'd, refin'd.
Till once, 'tis said, when all were fir'd,
Fill'd with Fury, rapt, inspir'd,   10
From the supporting Myrtles round,
They snatch'd her Instruments of Sound,
And as they oft had heard a-part
Sweet Lessons of her forceful Art,
Each, for Madness rul'd the Hour,   15
Would prove his own expressive Pow'r.

First *Fear* his Hand, its Skill to try,
   Amid the Chords bewilder'd laid,
And back recoil'd he knew not why,
   Ev'n at the Sound himself had made.   20

4 around] round *Hayes B*   16 expressive] excessive *Pearch*   17 its] his *Hayes E*

Next *Anger* rush'd, his Eyes on fire,
    In Lightnings own'd his secret Stings,
In one rude Clash he struck the Lyre,
    And swept with hurried Hand the Strings.

With woful Measures wan *Despair*   25
    Low sullen Sounds his Grief beguil'd,
A solemn, strange, and mingled Air,
    'Twas sad by Fits, by Starts 'twas wild.

But Thou, O *Hope*, with Eyes so fair,
    What was thy delightful Measure?   30
Still it whisper'd promis'd Pleasure,
    And bad the lovely Scenes at distance hail!
Still would Her Touch the Strain prolong,
    And from the Rocks, the Woods, the Vale,
She call'd on Echo still thro' all the Song;   35
    And where Her sweetest Theme She chose,
    A soft responsive Voice was heard at ev'ry Close,
And *Hope* enchanted smil'd, and wav'd Her golden Hair.

And longer had She sung,—but with a Frown,
    Revenge impatient rose,   40
He threw his blood-stain'd Sword in Thunder down,
    And with a with'ring Look,
    The War-denouncing Trumpet took,
And blew a Blast so loud and dread,
Were ne'er Prophetic Sounds so full of Woe.   45
    And ever and anon he beat
    The doubling Drum with furious Heat;
And tho' sometimes each dreary Pause between,
    Dejected *Pity* at his Side,
    Her Soul-subduing Voice applied,   50
    Yet still He kept his wild unalter'd Mien,

22 Stings] Strings *Hayes* E (*misprint?*)   23 In] with *Hayes* D   30 delightful]
delighted *Poetical Calendar, Langhorne*

While each strain'd Ball of Sight seem'd bursting from
    his Head.

Thy Numbers, *Jealousy*, to nought were fix'd,
    Sad Proof of thy distressful State,
Of diff'ring Themes the veering Song was mix'd,   55
    And now it courted *Love*, now raving call'd on *Hate*.

With Eyes up-rais'd, as one inspir'd,
Pale *Melancholy* sate retir'd,
And from her wild sequester'd Seat,
In Notes by Distance made more sweet,   60
Pour'd thro' the mellow *Horn* her pensive Soul:
    And dashing soft from Rocks around,
    Bubbling Runnels join'd the Sound;
Thro' Glades and Glooms the mingled Measure stole,
    Or o'er some haunted Stream with fond Delay,   65
      Round an holy Calm diffusing,
      Love of Peace, and lonely Musing,
    In hollow Murmurs died away.

But O how alter'd was its sprightlier Tone!
When *Chearfulness*, a Nymph of healthiest Hue,   70
    Her Bow a-cross her Shoulder flung,
    Her Buskins gem'd with Morning Dew,
Blew an inspiring Air, that Dale and Thicket rung,
    The Hunter's Call to *Faun* and *Dryad* known!
    The Oak-crown'd *Sisters*, and their chast-eye'd *Queen*,   75
    Satyrs and sylvan Boys were seen,
    Peeping from forth their Alleys green;
Brown *Exercise* rejoic'd to hear,
    And *Sport* leapt up, and seiz'd his Beechen Spear.

Last came *Joy's* Ecstatic Trial,   80
He with viny Crown advancing,

---

52 seem'd] seems *Hayes D*   55 diff'ring] different *Hayes A, C, E*   63 Bubbling
Runnels] Bublings, runnels *Hayes B*   65 Stream] streams *Langhorne*
69 sprightlier] sprightliest *Hayes C*   76 *Satyrs* and] Satyrs *Hayes C*

First to the lively Pipe his Hand addrest,
But soon he saw the brisk awak'ning Viol,
   Whose sweet entrancing Voice he lov'd the best.
      They would have thought who heard the Strain,   85
      They saw in *Tempe*'s Vale her native Maids,
      Amidst the festal sounding Shades,
To some unwearied Minstrel dancing,
   While as his flying Fingers kiss'd the Strings,
   LOVE fram'd with *Mirth*, a gay fantastic Round,   90
   Loose were Her Tresses seen, her Zone unbound,
   And HE amidst his frolic Play,
As if he would the charming Air repay,
Shook thousand Odours from his dewy Wings.

O *Music*, Sphere-descended Maid,   95
Friend of Pleasure, *Wisdom*'s Aid,
Why, Goddess, why to us deny'd?
Lay'st Thou thy antient Lyre aside?
As in that lov'd *Athenian* Bow'r,
You learn'd an all-commanding Pow'r,   100
Thy mimic Soul, O Nymph endear'd,
Can well recall what then it heard.
Where is thy native simple Heart,
Devote to Virtue, Fancy, Art?
Arise as in that elder Time,   105
Warm, Energic, Chaste, Sublime!
Thy Wonders in that God-like Age,
Fill thy recording *Sister*'s Page——
'Tis said, and I believe the Tale,
Thy humblest *Reed* could more prevail,   110
Had more of Strength, diviner Rage,
Than all which charms this laggard Age,
Ev'n all at once together found,
Cæcilia's mingled World of Sound——

84 lov'd] lik'd *Hayes B, D*   85 Strain] strains *Hayes D*   87 Shades] shade
Hayes C   93–118 *Hayes A–E follow an entirely different text by the Earl of Litch-
field (see head-note)*

O bid our vain Endeavors cease,
Revive the just Designs of *Greece*,
Return in all thy simple State!
Confirm the Tales Her Sons relate!

ODE
Occasion'd by the DEATH of
Mr. *THOMSON*.

*Hæc tibi semper erunt, & cum solennia Vota
Reddemus Nymphis, & cum lustrabimus Agros.*
— —*Amavit nos quoque Daphnis.*
                    VIRG. Bucol. Eclog. v.

TO

GEORGE LYTTLETON, Esq;
THIS
ODE
IS INSCRIB'D BY
The AUTHOR.

ADVERTISEMENT.

The Scene of the following STANZAS is suppos'd to lie
on the *Thames* near *Richmond*.

ODE
ON THE
DEATH of Mr. *THOMSON*.

I.

In yonder Grave a DRUID lies
Where slowly winds the stealing Wave!

1 Grave] grove *Poetical Calendar*

The *Year*'s best Sweets shall duteous rise
  To deck *it's* POET'*s* sylvan Grave!

II.

In yon deep Bed of whisp'ring Reeds   5
  His airy Harp ★ shall now be laid,
That He, whose Heart in Sorrow bleeds
  May love thro' Life the soothing Shade.

III.

Then Maids and Youths shall linger here,
  And while it's Sounds at distance swell,   10
Shall sadly seem in Pity's Ear
  To hear the WOODLAND PILGRIM'S Knell.

IV.

REMEMBRANCE oft shall haunt the Shore
  When THAMES in Summer-wreaths is drest,
And oft suspend the dashing Oar   15
  To bid his gentle Spirit rest!

V.

And oft as EASE and HEALTH retire
  To breezy Lawn, or Forest deep,
The Friend shall view yon whit'ning Spire ★,
  And 'mid the varied Landschape weep.   20

VI.

But Thou, who own'st that Earthy Bed,
  Ah! what will ev'ry Dirge avail?
Or Tears, which LOVE and PITY shed
  That mourn beneath the gliding Sail!

★ The Harp of *Æolus*, of which see a Description in the *Castle of Indolence*.
★ *Richmond*-Church.

---

21 Earthy] earthly *Langhorne*

VII.

Yet lives there one, whose heedless Eye   25
    Shall scorn thy pale Shrine glimm'ring near?
With Him, Sweet Bard, may FANCY die,
    And JOY desert the blooming Year.

VIII.

But thou, lorn STREAM, whose sullen Tide
    No sedge-crown'd SISTERS now attend,   30
Now waft me from the green Hill's Side
    Whose cold Turf hides the buried FRIEND!

IX.

And see, the Fairy Valleys fade,
    Dun *Night* has veil'd the solemn View!
—Yet once again, Dear parted SHADE   35
    Meek NATURE'S CHILD again adieu!

X.

The genial Meads assign'd to bless
    Thy Life, shall mourn thy early Doom,
Their Hinds, and Shepherd-Girls shall dress
    With simple Hands thy rural Tomb.   40

XI.

Long, long, thy Stone and pointed Clay
    Shall melt the musing BRITON'S Eyes,
O! VALES, and WILD WOODS, shall HE say
    In yonder Grave YOUR DRUID lies!

38 Thy Life] The life *Union 1759*

Ode to a Friend on his Return &c

[*An* Ode *on the* Popular Superstitions *of the* Highlands *of*
Scotland, *considered as the Subject of Poetry.*]

I

H—— Thou return'st from Thames, whose Naiads long
  Have seen Thee ling'ring with a fond delay
  Mid' those soft Friends, whose hearts some future day
Shall melt perhaps to hear thy Tragic Song
Go not unmindfull of that cordial Youth   5
  Whose
Together let us wish Him lasting truth
  And Joy untainted with his destin'd Bride
Go! nor regardless, while these Numbers boast
  My short-liv'd bliss, forget my social Name   10
But think far-off how on the Southern coast
  I met thy Friendship with an equal Flame!
Fresh to that soil thou turn'st, whose ev'ry Vale
  Shall prompt the Poet, and his Song demand;
    To Thee thy copious Subjects ne'er shall fail   15
  Thou need'st but take the Pencil to thy Hand
And paint what all believe who own thy Genial Land.

2.

There must Thou wake perforce thy *Doric* Quill
  'Tis Fancy's Land to which thou set'st thy Feet
  Where still, tis said, the Fairy People meet   20
Beneath Each birken Shade, on mead or Hill
  There Each Trim Lass that Skims the milky store
  To the Swart Tribes their creamy Bowl allots,
By Night They sip it round the cottage Door

---

1 H——] Home *Bell*   from *cancels* to   3 Mid' *above* 'Mid *deleted (apparently to*
indicate indentation as in l. 2)   4 Shall *precedes* Shall *deleted (apparently to indicate*
that this line is not indented)   6 Whose *above* Whom long endear'd thou leav'st
by Lavant's side *deleted*   13 whose] where *Bell*   16 the] thy *Bell*
23 Bowl] bowls *Bell*

1

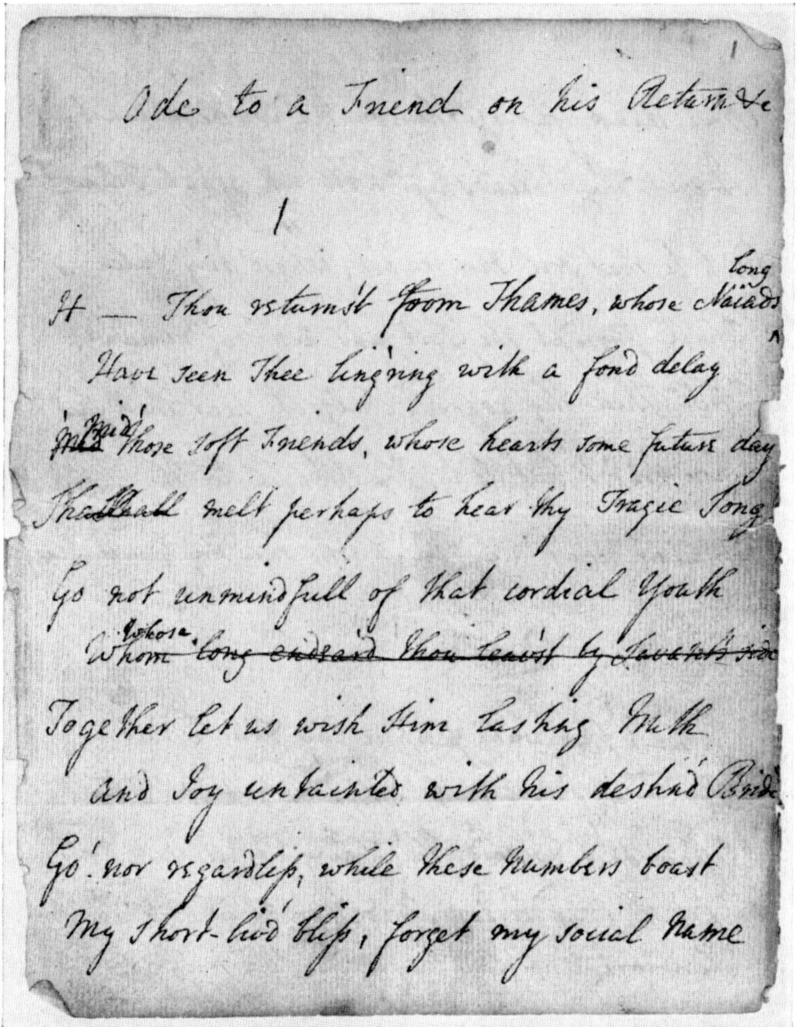

Ode to a Friend on his Return &c

1

If — Thou return'st from Thames, whose Naiads long
Have seen Thee lingring with a fond delay
Mid those soft Friends, whose hearts some future day
Shall melt perhaps to hear thy Tragic Song
Go not unmindfull of that cordial Youth
Whose ~~long endear'd thou leav'st by Lavant's side~~
Together let us wish Him lasting Truth
And Joy untainted with his destin'd Bride
Go! nor regardless, while these Numbers boast
My short-liv'd bliss, forget my social Name

PLATE I

The first page of Collins's unfinished manuscript of the 'Ode to a Friend on his Return &c', which was rediscovered in 1967 (Bodleian MS. Dep. e. 87, f. 1r). Reproduced by permission of Colonel A. E. Cameron of Aldouri Castle, Inverness-shire, and the Bodleian Library

While Airy Minstrels warble jocund notes   25
  There ev'ry Herd by sad experience knows
    How wing'd with fate their Elph-shot arrows fly
When the Sick Ewe her summer food foregoes
  Or stretch'd on Earth the Heart-smit Heifers lie!
Such Airy Beings awe th' untutor'd Swain;   30
  Nor Thou, tho learn'd, his homelier thoughts neglect
Let thy sweet Muse the rural faith sustain;
  These are the Themes of simple sure Effect
That add New conquests to her boundless reign
And fill with double force her heart commanding Strain.   35

                        3

Ev'n yet preserv'd how often may'st thou hear
  Where to the Pole the Boreal Mountains run
    Taught by the Father to his list'ning Son
Strange lays whose pow'r had charm'd a Spenser's Ear
  At Ev'ry Pause, before thy Mind possest,   40
Old Runic Bards shall seem to rise around
  With uncouth Lyres, in many-colour'd Vest,
    Their Matted Hair with boughs fantastic crown'd
Whether Thou bidst the well-taught Hind repeat
  The Choral Dirge that mourns some Chieftain brave   45
When Ev'ry Shrieking Maid her bosom beat
  And strew'd with choicest herbs his scented Grave
Or whether sitting in the Shepherd's ˣ Shiel
  Thou hear'st some Sounding Tale of War's alarms
When at the Bugle's call with fire and steel   50
  The Sturdy Clans pour'd forth their bonny Swarms
And hostile Brothers met to prove each Other's Arms.

ˣ a Kind of Hut built ev'ry summer for the convenience of milking the Cattle

---

25 Airy *above* viewless *deleted* (*above* Airy, *deleted in original line*)   44 repeat] peat
above late *of* relate *deleted*   51 The] e *above* ey *of* They *deleted*   bonny] bony
Transactions, brawny *Bell*

4

'Tis thine to Sing how framing hideous Spells
  In Skys lone Isle the Gifted Wizzard Seer
Lodg'd in the Wintry cave with   55
Or in the depth of Ust's dark forrests dwells
    How They whose Sight such dreary dreams engross
      With their own Visions oft astonish'd droop
When o'er the watry strath or quaggy Moss
    They see the gliding Ghosts unbodied troop   60
Or if in Sports or on the festive Green
    Their   glance some fated Youth descry
Who now perhaps in lusty Vigour seen
  And rosy health shall soon lamented die
For them the viewless Forms of Air obey   65
    Their bidding heed, and at their beck repair
They know what Spirit brews the storm full day
    And heartless oft like moody Madness stare
To see the Phantom train their secret work prepare!

5.

[stanza missing]

[6]

[8 lines missing]

What tho far off from some dark dell espied   95
  His glimm'ring Mazes cheer th' excursive sight
Yet turn ye Wandrers turn your steps aside
  Nor chuse the Guidance of that faithless light!
For watchfull lurking mid th' unrustling Reed
  At those sad hours the wily Monster lies   100
And listens oft to hear the passing Steed

54 Ione] long *Dobson*   56 depth *above* gloom *deleted*   58 Visions]
vision *Bell*   astonish'd *above* afflicted *deleted*   66 heed *above* mark *deleted*
67 Spirit *cancels* Fiend   70–94 *One leaf of the MS. is missing here, comprising stanza*
5 and the first eight lines of stanza 6 (see head-note)   98 chuse] trust *Transactions,*
Bell   99 th'] e *of original* the *deleted*   100 mirk *suggested above* sad

And frequent round him rolls his sullen Eyes
If Chance his Savage wrath may some weak wretch surprise.

7

Ah luckless Swain, oer All Unblest indeed!
    Whom late bewilder'd in the dank dark Fen   105
Far from his Flocks and smoaking Hamlet then!
    To that sad spot his
On Him enrag'd the Fiend in Angry mood
    Shall never look with Pity's kind concern
But Instant Furious rouse the whelming Flood   110
O'er it's drown'd Banks forbidding All return
Or If He meditate his wish'd Escape
    To some dim Hill that seems uprising near
To his faint Eye the Grim and Griesly Shape
    In all its Terrors clad shall wild appear.   115
Mean time the Watry Surge shall round him rise
    Pour'd sudden forth from evry swelling source
What now remains but Tears and hopeless sighs?
    His Fear-shook limbs have lost their Youthly force
And down the waves He floats a Pale and breathless
        Corse.   120

8.

For Him in vain his anxious Wife shall wait
    Or wander forth to meet him on his way
    For Him in vain at To fall of the Day
His Bairns shall linger at the unclosing Gate
Ah neer shall He return—Alone if Night   125
    Her travell'd limbs in broken slumbers steep
With Dropping Willows drest his mournfull Sprite
    Shall visit sad perhaps her silent Sleep

110 rouse] raise *Transactions, Bell*   111 Banks] bank *Transactions,* banks *Bell*
119 Youthly] *the first letters are written over one or two illegible letters of another word*
124 Bairns] babes *Transactions, Bell*   unclosing *above* Cottage *deleted* (*Collins would presumably have revised this to* th' unclosing)   127 Dropping (*cancels part of an illegible word*)] drooping *Bell*   Willows *above* Dropping drest *for insertion*   128 perhaps] perchance *Transactions, Bell*

Then He perhaps with moist and watry hand
  Shall fondly seem to press her shuddring cheek   130
And with his blue swoln face before her stand
  And Shivring cold these piteous accents speak
'Pursue Dear Wife, thy daily toils pursue
'At Dawn, or dusk Industrious as before
'Nor e'er of Me one hapless thought renew   135
'While I lie weltring on the Osier'd Shore
'Drown'd by the Kaelpie's wrath nor eer shall aid thee more

9.

Unbounded is thy range, with varied style
  Thy Muse may like those feath'ry tribes which spring
From their Rude Rocks extend her skirting wing   140
  Round the Moist Marge of each cold Hebrid Isle
To that hoar Pile which still its ruin shows
  In whose small vaults a Pigmie-Folk is found
Whose Bones the Delver with his Spade up-throws
  And culls them wondring from the hallow'd Ground! 145
Or thither, where beneath the show'ry west
  The Mighty Kings of three fair Realms are laid
Once Foes perhaps together now they rest
  No Slaves revere them, and no Wars invade:
Yet frequent now at Mid night's solemn hour   150
  The Rifted Mounds their yawning cells unfold
And forth the Monarchs stalk with sovreign Pow'r
In pageant Robes, and wreath'd with sheeny Gold
And on their twilight tombs Aerial council hold.

10.

But O o'er all forget not Kilda's race   155
  On Whose bleak rocks which brave the wasting tides

130 fondly *above* Shall seem (*for insertion*) shuddring *above* cold and shuddring *deleted* 133 Pursue] ursue *above* roceed *of* Proceed *deleted* daily] *omitted in* Dobson 133–7 *These lines are preceded by signs resembling question marks, apparently functioning here as quotation marks (see head-note)* 135 hapless] helpless *Bell* 150 Mid night's] midnight *Bell* 151 Rifted *above* Yawning *deleted* 152 Monarchs] monarch's *Transactions* (*misprint?*)

Fair Nature's Daughter Virtue yet Abides!
Go just, as They, their blameless Manners trace!
  Then to my Ear transmit some gentle Song
  Of Those whose Lives are yet sincere and plain   160
Their bounded walks the ragged Cliffs Along
  And all their Prospect but the wintry Main.
With sparing Temp'rance at the needfull Time
  They drain the Sainted Spring, or Hunger-prest
Along th' Atlantic Rock undreading climb   165
  And of its Eggs despoil the *Solan*'s nest
Thus blest in primal Innocence they live
  Suffic'd and happy with that frugal fare
Which Taste full Toil and hourly Danger [give]
  Hard is their Shallow Soil,   and ba[re]   170
Nor Ever Vernal Bee was hear'd to mu[rmur] there!

                        II.

Nor needst Thou blush that such false Themes [en]gage
  Thy gentle Mind of fairer stores possest
For not Alone they touch the Village Breast,
But fill'd in Elder Time th' Historic page   175
  There Shakespeare's Self with evry Garland crown'd
In musing hour his Wayward Sisters found
  And with their terrors drest the magic Scene!
[Fro]m them He sung, when mid his bold design
  Before the Scot afflicted and aghast   180
[Th]e Shadowy Kings of Banquo's fated line
  Thro' the dark cave in gleamy Pageant past
Proceed nor quit the tales which simply told
  Could once so well my Answring Bosom pierce

161 ragged] rugged *Transactions, Bell*   162 Prospect] prospects *Dobson*
164 Sainted] scented *Bell*   168 Suffic'd *above* Content *deleted*   169–71 *The
margin of the MS. is torn here; the words and letters in brackets are supplied from Transac-
tions on the assumption that they were then legible to Carlyle*   171 V *of* Vernal *cancels*
B[ee?]   172 [en]gage] *the first two letters, supplied by Carlyle, are torn away in the
margin of the MS.*   176 *This stanza has only 16 lines; a missing line would follow
this line (to rhyme with* Scene)   179, 181 *A tear in the MS. has removed some
letters from the beginning of these lines*

Proceed, in forcefull sounds and Colours bold   185
   The Native Legends of thy Land rehearse
To such adapt thy Lyre, and suit thy pow'rfull Verse

12

In Scenes like these which daring to depart
   From sober Truth, are still to Nature true
   And call forth fresh delights to Fancy's view   190
Th' Heroic Muse employ'd her Tasso's Art!
How have I trembled when at Tancred's stroke
   Its gushing Blood, the gaping Cypress pour'd
When Each live Plant with Mortal accents spoke
   And the wild Blast up-heav'd the vanish'd Sword.   195
How have I sate where-pip'd the pensive Wind
   To hear his harp by British Fairfax strung
Prevailing Poet, whose undoubting Mind
   Believ'd the Magic Wonders which He sung!
Hence at Each Sound Imagination glows   200
Hence his warm lay with softest Sweetness flows
   Melting it flows, pure num'rous strong and clear
And fills th' impassion'd heart, and lulls th' Harmonious Ear

---

185 Colours] colour *Bell*   190 fresh *cancels* new   delights] delight *Trans-*
actions, Bell   192–5 *These four lines are written above the following (deleted):*

     How have I trembled, when at Tancred's side
     Like him I stalkd and all his Passions felt
     Where Charmd by Ismen thro' the Forrest wide
     Barkd in Each Plant a talking Spirit dwelt!

193 Its gushing *above* The Cypress *deleted*   196 where] when *Transactions, Bell*
197 his *cancels* the   200–2 *These three lines are written above the following (deleted):*

     Hence sure to Charm his Early Numbers flow
     Tho faithfull sweet, tho' strong, of simple kind.
     Hence with Each Theme he bids the bosom glow
     While his warm lays an easy passage find

faithfull (*l. 2*) *above* strong yet *deleted*
200 *Because this stanza has only 16 lines, a missing line would follow this line (to rhyme
with* clear)   Hence at Each Sound *below* Hence with Each Strain (*last three words
deleted*)   201 softest] est *above* ness *of* softness *deleted*   202 num'rous]
murm'ring *Bell*   203 And fills th' impassion'd heart, and lulls *above* Pour'd
thro' Each inmost nerve, and win *deleted*   lulls] wins *Transactions, Bell*

13.

All Hail Ye Scenes that oer my soul prevail
   Ye   Firths and Lakes which far away   205
   Are by smooth Annan fill'd, or past'ral Tay
Or Don's Romantic Springs, at distance hail!
   The Time shall come, when I perhaps may tread
   Your lowly Glens oerhung with spreading Broom
Or o'er your Stretching Heaths by Fancy led   210
Then will I dress once more the faded Bow'r
   Where Johnson sate in Drummond's [x]   Shade
Or crop from Tiviot's dale Each
   And mourn on Yarrow Banks
Mean time Ye Pow'rs, that on the plains which bore   215
   The Cordial Youth, on Lothian's plains attend
Where'er he dwell, on Hill or lowly Muir
   To Him I lose, your kind protection lend
And touch'd with Love, like Mine, preserve my Absent
   Friend.

———

The End.

———

[x] Drummond of Hawthornden   See Heads of a Conversation &c

205 Firths] friths *Transactions, Bell*   206 Are *cancels* By   210 *This stanza
also has only 16 lines; a missing line would follow this line (to rhyme with* Broom)
213 Tiviot's dale] *Tiviotdale Bell*   214 Yarrow] *Yarrow's Transactions, Bell*
217 he] HOME *Bell*   dwell] dwells *Bell*   Muir] moor *Bell*   218 lose]
loose *Bell*

DRAFTS AND
FRAGMENTS OF
VERSE

Fragment 1

Yet this wild pomp so much in vain pursued,
The Courtly Davenant on our Thames renew'd.
For who can trace thro' Time's oer-clouded maze
The dawning stage of old Eliza's days?
What Critic search its rise, or Changes know,   5
With all the Force of Hollingshead ˣ or Stow ˣ ?
Yet all may gain, from many a worthless page,
Some lights of Charles and his Luxurious age.
Then, Thanks to those! who sent him forth to roam
Or equal Weakness! brought the Monarch home!   10
The Taste of France, her Manners and her Stile
(The Fool's gay Models) delug'd all our Isle:
Those courtly Wits which spoke the Nation's voice
In Paris learn'd their judgment and their choice
Vain were the Thoughts, which Nature's Passions speak,   15
Thy woes Monimia Impotent and weak!
Vain all the Truth of just Dramatic Tales!
—Nought pleas'd Augustus, but what pleasd Versailles!
His Hand of Powr outstretch'd with princely care
From his low state uprais'd th' instructive Play'r   20
And ev'n in Palaces, for never age
Was grac'd like Richlieus, plac'd his regal stage
To Those Proud Halls where Burgundy had vied
With all his Gallic Peers in Princely pride
The Muse succeeded like some Splendid Heir   25
And plac'd her Chiefs and favor'd Heroes there!
And could that Theatre, believe you, trust

[ˣ] Otway despis'd as a Writer while Dav'nant was in repute

---

1 pomp *cancels* scene   2 on *cancels* in   Thames *above* 'Isle' *deleted, and in*
right margin (underscored)   13 Those courtly *above* That Court of *deleted (except*
for Court, *expanded to* Courtly)   14 In *above* From *deleted*   learn'd their *above*
took its *deleted*   21 ev'n *cancels illegible word*   in *appears to cancel* on *or* an
22 plac'd *cancels* built   23 To *appears to cancel* In   27, 33 *Numerals placed*
before these lines appear to indicate the sequence of the lines in the MS., and not actual
stanzas, and therefore are not retained (see head-note)

To those weak Guides—the Decent and the just?
Ah no! could ought delight that modish Pit?
Twas but the Froth, and Foppery of Wit.   30
True Nature ceas'd; and in her Place, were seen
That Pride of Pantomime, the rich machine—
There, when some God, or Spirit pois'd in Air,
Surpris'd the scented Beau, or masking Fair
Think! with what Thunder, in so just a cause,   35
The Mob of Coxcombs swelld their loud applause!
These Witlings heeded nature, less than they
That rule thy taste, the Critics of to day:
Yet All could talk how *Betterton* was drest
And gave that Queen their Praise, who curtsied Best.   40
Thus Folly lasted long at Truth's expense
Spite of Just Nature, or reluctant sense—
Ask you what broke at last her Idle reign?
Wits Easy Villan could not laugh in vain.—

Fragment 2

['But why you'll Say to me this   Song
'Can these proud Aims to private Life belong
'Fair instances your Verse unbidden brings
'Th' ambitious Names of Ministers and Kings'
'Am I that Statesman whom a Realm obeys   5
'What ready Tributes will my Mandate raise
'Or like the Pontiff can my Word command
'Exacted Sums from every Pliant Land
'That all of which the Men of Leisure Read
'This Tast and Splendor must from me Proceed   10
'Tell me if Wits reprove or Fortune frown
'Where is my Hope but in th' uncertain Town
'Yet e'er you Urge weigh well the mighty Task
'Behold what Sums one Poet's Drama's Ask

33 There *cancels* Then   34 scented *also written in right margin*   35 with
cancels illegible word   39 talk *above* tell *deleted*   41 Thus *above* Such *deleted*
Folly *cancels* Follies   long at *above* till *deleted*

1-24 *These lines are not in Collins's hand (see head-note)*   7 will *deleted before* can

'When Shakespear shifts the place so oft to View   15
'Must each Gay Scene be beautifull and New
'Come you who Trade in Ornament appear'
'Come Join your Aids thro' all the busy Year'
'Plan Build and Paint thro' each laborious Day'
'And let us once produce this finish'd play'   20
Yes the Proud Cost allows some short Suspence
I Grant the Terrors of that Word Expence
Did Tast at once for full Perfection call
That sole Objection might determine all]
But such just Elegance not gain'd at Ease   25
Scarce wishd and seen, may come by slow degrees
To day   may one fair Grace restore
And some kind Season add one Beauty more
And with these aims of Elegant desire
The Critic's Unities, tis sure, conspire   30
And tho' no scenes suffice to deck the wild
           round their works on whom the Muse has smild
Some Scenes may still the fair design admit
Chast scenes which Addison or Phillips writ.
Is but our just delight in one increast   35
Tis something gain'd to Decency at least:
And what thy Judgement first by Nature plann'd
May find completion from some future Hand.
                    &c
The Pomp   40

Fragment 3

These would I sing—O Art for ever dear
Whose Charms so oft have caught my raptur'd Ear
O teach me Thou, if my unpolish'd lays

15 place *above* scene *deleted*   19 every *deleted before* each   26 Scarce
above Just *deleted*   27 *A word* (*probably* To day) *deleted above* To day   29 *Above*
With these amendments, what some yet admire *deleted* (*except for final three words*)
31 no scenes suffice to deck *above* your Arts can not attend *deleted*   32 *Above*
whom The Muse by Art untutor'd smild *deleted* (*the first word in each version has
been torn away*)   39–40 *Left incomplete*
   3 teach me *above* Scorn not *deleted*

Are all too rude to speak thy gentle praise
O teach me softer sounds of sweeter kind   5

Then let the Muse and Picture Each contend
This plan her Tale, and that her Colours blend
With me tho' both their kindred charms combine
No Pow'r shall emulate or equal thine!   10

And Thou the Gentlest Patron born to grace
And add new Brightness ev'n to Ashley's race
Intent like Him in Plato's polish'd style
To fix fair Science in our careless Isle
[Wh]ether thro' Wilton's Pictur'd halls you stray   15
Or o'er some speaking Marble waste the day
Or weigh each Sound its various pow'r to learn
Come Son of Harmony O hither turn!
Led by thy hand Philosophy will deign
To own me meanest of her votive train   20
O I will listen, when her lips impart
Why all my soul obeys her pow'rfull Art
Why at her bidding or by strange surprise
Or wak'd by fond degrees my Passions rise
How well-form'd Reed's my sure Attention gain   25
And what the Lyre's well-measur'd strings contain
The Mighty Masters too unprais'd so long
Shall not be lost, if Thou assist my Song
They who with Pindars in one Age bestow'd
Cloath'd the sweet words which in their numbers flowd 30

---

5 *Below* O Smile *deleted*   6 *Blank*   9 *Below* Ev'n these would I resign
deleted   11 *Two lines are deleted preceding this line*:

Ye too who living own'd her genial rule
The Sons and Daughters of her happy school

13 Intent *above* Whether *deleted*   14 To fix *above* Few form *deleted*   15 *Corner
of MS. missing*   18 Son of Harmony *above* Sweet Philosopher *deleted*   19 Philoso-
phy *written in a larger hand, but not underscored*   20 own *above* take (*original
reading, deleted*) *and after* aid *deleted*   21 when her lips impart *above* will thy
tongue reveals *deleted* (will *a mistake for* while?)   as thy *suggested above* when her
22 Why *below* The *deleted*   24 wak'd *above* gradual *deleted*   28 assist *above*
inspire *deleted*   30 numbers *above* their flowd *for insertion*

And Rome's and Adria's Sons—if Thou but strive
To guard their Names, shall in my Verse survive

Fragment 4

While You perhaps exclude the wintry gloom
In Jovial Jacob's academic Room
There pleas'd by turns in breathing paint to trace
The Wits gay Air or Poet's genial Face
Say happy Tonson, Say, what Great Design   5
(For warmest Gratitude must sure be thine)
What due return employs thy musing Heart
For all the Happiness their works impart
What taste directed monument which They
Might own with Smiles, and Thou with Honour pay?   10
  Evn from the Days when Courtly Waller sung
And tun'd with polish'd sounds our barbrous tongue
Eer yet the Verse to full perfection brought
With nicer Music cloath'd the Poet's thought
The Muse whose Song bespoke securest Fame   15
Made fair Alliance with thy favor'd Name
Dealt from thy press the Maid of Elder Days
Lisp'd the soft lines to Sacharissa's praise
Or the gay Youth for livelier Spirits known
By Cowleys pointed thought improv'd his own   20
Evn all the Easy Sons of Song who gain'd
A Poets Name when Charles and Pleasure reign'd
All from thy Race a lasting praise deriv'd
Not by Their toil the careless Bards surviv'd

---

1 *Below first version, deleted*: When oft in ease at lov'd Barn Elms you trace (in *appears to cancel* at)   exclude the wintry gloom *above* Ev'n now your hours consume *deleted*   5 Tonson, Say] Say *cancels* what   8 Happiness *cancels* Pleas[ure] 9 What *cancels* Some   taste] te *above* tefu *of* tastefu[l] *deleted*   10 Might] ight *above* ay *of* May *deleted*   Smiles *cancels* Poli[shed]   11 Evn *cancels* From   from *above* those *deleted*   Courtly *cancels* Poli[shed]   13 yet the Verse to *above* yet the chaste Expression *deleted*   17 Maid of Elder Days *above* Distant Lovers Eyes *deleted*   19 for *cancels* by   23 All *after* All *deleted*   24 by *above* from *deleted*   Their] ir (*followed by* toil) *above* mselves *of* Themselves *deleted*

You wisely sav'd the Race who   gay   25
But sought to wear the Mirtles of a day
At soft Barn Elms (Let evry Critic join)
You more than all Enjoy Each flowing line
Your's is the price whate'er their merits claim
Heir of their Verse and guardian of their Fame!   30

                              move
                        Luxury and Love

Fragment 5

Yes, Tis but Angelo's or Shakespear's Name
The Striking Beauties are in each the same
The s

Were Horace Dumb, Who knows Ev'n Fresnoy's Art   5
Might guide the Muse in some   Part
Or Searchfull Vinci, who his Precepts drew
For Tuscan Pencils, form the Poet too!

From these fair Arts,

                                                        (10)

Nor fear to talk of Numbers or of Oil
Tho' not quite form'd like Addison or Boyle
Defect in Each abound and more, you say
Than Sage Despiles instructs us how to weigh
Defects which glanc'd on those who finely feel   15
All Thornhills Colours would in vain conceal
Or all the Golden Lines howeer they flow
Thro' each soft Drama of unfruitfull Rowe
These too you sometimes praise to Censure loth
But fix the Name of Mannerist on both   20

27 At soft *cancels* Else had   30 Heir] *final* s *deleted*   31–2 *Blank*
33–4 *Blank except for concluding words*
   4 *Blank*   7 Precepts *cancels* Lessons   8 *A hiatus follows this line, perhaps*
a space for two more lines but probably to indicate a new stanza   9 which trust our
Critic Friends *deleted after* Arts,   10 Obtain one fair Ef[fect] *rubbed out*
13 Defect] *Collins probably meant* Defects (*as in l.* 15) *which would agree with his verb*

And should my Friend, who knew not Anna's age
So nicely judge the Canvas or the Page?
Still should his thought on some old Model plac'd
Reject the Briton with so nice a taste?
From each some forcefull Character demand   25
And but peculiar to his happy hand?
Some Sovereign Mark of Genius all his own

Ah where on Thames shall Gentle Dodsley find
The Verse contriv'd for so correct a Mind?   30
Or How shall Hayman trembling as you gaze
Obtain one breath of such unwilling praise?
Go Then in all unsatisfied complain
Of Time's Mistake in Waller's desprate strain
For Ah untimely cam'st Thou forth Indeed   35
With whom Originals Alone succeed! [x]
Go as Thou wilt, require the bliss denied
To call back Art and live e'er Carlo died
But O in Song the Public voice obey
There let Each Author   his   day   40
Abroad be Candid, reason as you will
And live at home a Chast Athenian still!

   For each correct design the Critic Kind
Look back thro' Age to Homer's godlike Mind
But Blackhall's self might doubt if all of Art   45
Were Self producd in one exhaustless Heart

[x] Waller to a very young Lady
                    Why came I so untimely forth
                    Into a world wch wanting Thee

---

26 And *cancels* But   28 *Blank*   29 on Thames *above* Eugenia where *deleted*
33 Then *cancels* Rather   34 Of *appears to cancel* On   36 n. *These lines are*
written beneath ll. 34–6 in the text, which occur at the bottom of 1^v   40 There *cancels*
And   46 *The rest of 2^r is blank following this line. The single word* These *appears*
at the beginning of 2^v

Fragment 6

On each new scene the Sons of   Vertú
Shall give fresh Objects to thy   view
Bring the grav'd Gem or offer as you pass
Th' Imperial Medal, and historic Brass
Then o'er its narrow surface mayst thou trace   5
The genuine Spirit of some Hero's face
Or see minutely touch'd the powrfull charms
Of some proud Fair that set whole realms in arms
The Patriot's Story with his look compare
And know the Poet by his genial air   10

Nor, for they boast no pure Augustan vein
Reject her Poets with a cold disdain
O Think in what sweet lays how sweetly Strong
Our Fairfax warbles Tasso's forcefull Song
How Spenser too, whose lays you oft resume   15
Wove their Gay   in his fantastic loom
That Cynthio prompted oft ev'n Shakespear's flame
And Milton valued ev'n Marino's name!

Fragment 7

The Moon with dewy lustre bright
    Her mild Æthereal radiance gave
On Paly Cloisters gleam'd her light
    Or trembled o'er th' unresting wave

T'was Mid night's hour—   5

1 On *cancels* In   Vertú] *final letter* (s?) *deleted*   2 thy *expanded from* the
5 bending *deleted after* Then   narrow *above* little *deleted*   6 genuine *above*
The Spirit *for insertion*   8 whole realms *above* the world *deleted*   9 Patriot's
above Sage's Story *for insertion* (*although* Sage's *is not deleted,* Collins *apparently did
not intend it to stand*)   Story *cancels* Writing   look *above* form *deleted*   10 *A
gap following this line suggests that a transitional couplet may have been omitted at this point
in the MS.*   13 O Think *above* Remember *deleted*   15 too *above* oft *deleted*
16 Colours *deleted after* Gay   17 *Below* How Shakespear's

   1 lustre *above* radiance *deleted*   2 radiance *above* lustre *deleted*

Long o'er the Spires and Glimmring Tow'rs
    The whispring Flood, and silv'ry sky   10
As One whom Musing Grief devours
    She glanc'd by turns her silent Eye!

Like Hers, The Fair Lavinias hand
    Once mix'd the Pallet's varied store
Blest Maid whom once Italia's Land   15
    In years of better Glory bore!

                                                          (20)

Like Her, O Death, O ruthless Powr
    O Grief of Heart remember'd well
In lovely Youth's untimely hour
    Like Her soft Tintoretta fell

Ev'n She, whose Science Philip sought   25
    To share his throne an envied Bride
Like Thee deplor'd, Ah fatal Thought
    By ev'ry Art lamented died

Thy draught where Love his hand employ'd
    Shall only please a shortliv'd day   30
And timeless like thy self destroyd
    In Each revolving year decay.

Yet soft and melting flow'd thy line
    As Ev'ry Grace had lent her aid

6–8 *Blank*   11 whom *after* whom *deleted*   17–20 *Blank*   24 Like
cancels The   28 Adorn'd with *deleted before* By   29 Thy draught where
above Yet thy sweet draught *deleted*   Love his *above* Gentle *deleted*

Bid each mild light unglaring shine   35
    And soft imbrown'd   melting shade

And when thy tints, ah fruitless Care
    With softest skill compounded lay
The Flaunting Bow'rs where Spring repairs
    Were not more bloomy sweet than They!   40

The Child of Them who now adore
    Thy tender tints and godlike Flame
Pass some few years on Adrias shore
    Shall only know thy gentle Name

Or when his Eyes shall strive in vain   45
    Thy Fairy Pencil's stroke to trace
The Faded Draught shall scarce retain
    Some Lifeless line or mangled Grace

Fragment 8

Ye Genii who in secret state
    Far from the wheaten field
At some throng'd Citie's antique Gate
    Your unseen sceptres wield

Ye Pow'rs that such high Office share   5
    Oer all the restless Earth
Who see Each day descend with care
    Or lost in senseless Mirth

36 soft] ly *of* softly *deleted*   imbrown'd *above* shed each *deleted* (*Collins may have intended* each *to stand*)   37 when *cancels* thy   46 Fairy *above* Mingling *deleted* 48 *There is space following this line for two additional stanzas, of which only the first line* (*49, deleted*) *and the last* (*56*) *have been written*:

What tho thy touch, belov'd of Art
. . . .
And but thy Grave be all forgot

In l. 49, What *cancels* Then *rubbed out*
    5 *Below* Take all who for the *deleted*   7 day *cancels* Sun

Take Them who know not how to prize
   The walks to Wisdom dear   10
The Gradual Fruits and varying skies
   That paint the gradual Year

Take all that to the silent Sod
   Prefer the sounding street
And Let your echoing squares be trod   15
   By their unresting feet

But me by   Springlets laid
   That thro' the Woodland chide
Let Elms or Oaks that lent their Shade
   To hoary Druids hide   20

Let me where'er wild Nature leads
   My sight Enamour'd look
And chuse my hymning Pipe from Reeds
   That roughen oer the Brook

Some times when Morning oer Plain   25
   Her radiant Mantle throws
I'll mark the Clouds where sweet Lorrain
   His orient Colours chose

Or when the Sun at Noon tide climbs
   I'll hide me from his view   30
By such green Plats and chearfull Limes
   As   Rysdael drew

Then on some Heath all wild and bare
   With more delight Ill stand
Than He who sees with wondring air   35
   The Works of Rosa's hand

---

19 Elms *cancels an illegible word*   25 the *apparently omitted after* oer (*cf. l.* 41)
29 at *cancels* to   33 all wild and bare *above* of all unseen *deleted*   34 With
more delight *above* In cooler hours *deleted*

There where some Rocks deep Cavern gapes
    Or in some tawny dell
Ill seem to see the Wizzard Shapes
    That from his Pencill fell   40

But when Soft Evning o'er the Plain
    Her gleamy Mantle throws
I'll mark the Clouds whence sweet Lorraine
    His   Colours chose

Or from the Vale I'll lift my sight   45
    To some
Where e'er the Sun withdraws his light
    The dying Lustre falls

Such   will I keep
    Till   50
The modest Moon again shall Peep
    Above some Eastern Hill

All Tints that ever Picture us'd
    Are lifeless dull and mean
To paint her dewy Light diffus'd   55

What Art can paint the modest ray
    So sober chaste and cool
As round yon Cliffs it seems to play
    Or skirts yon glimmring Pool?   60

The tender gleam her Orb affords
    No Poet can declare
Altho' he chuse the softest words
    That e'er were sigh'd in air.

38 Or *cancels* Oer   54 lifeless] ifeless *above* anguid *of* languid *deleted*   56 *Blank*
57 the *above* yon *deleted*   59 round *above* on *deleted*

Fragment 9

To Simplicity

1

O Fancy, Alter'd Maid
  Who now too long betrayd
To Toys and Pageant wed'st thy cheated Heart
  Yet once with Chastest thought
  Far nobler triumphs sought   5
Thrice Gentle Guide of each exalted Art!

2

  Too

No more, sweet Maid, th' enfeebling dreams prolong
  Return sweet Maid at length   10
  In all thy Ancient strength
And bid our Britain hear thy Græcian Song

3

  For Thee of loveliest Name
  That Land shall ever claim
And laid an Infant on her favor'd shore   15
  Soft Bees of Hybla's vale
  To Age attests the tale
To feed thy Youth   their s store

4

  From that   hour
  Thou knewst the gentle pow'r   20
To charm her Matrons chaste, and virtuous Youth
  For Wisdom learn'd to please
  By thy persuasive Ease
And Simplest Sweetness more ennobled Truth.

7 weakly *deleted after* Too   8 *Blank*   16 Soft *cancels* The   18 To feed
thy Youth *below* Around thy couch *deleted*   22 For Wisdom *cancels* From thy

5

Nor modest Picture less   25
　　Declin'd the wild Excess
Which frequent now distracts her wild design
　　The Modest Graces laid
　　Each soft unboastfull shade
While Feeling Nature drew th' impassion'd line!   30

6

O Chaste Unboastfull Guide
　　O'er all my Heart preside
And 'midst my Cave in breathing Marble wrought
　　In sober Musing near
　　With Attic Robe appear   35
And charm my sight and prompt my temprate thought

7

And when soft Maids and Swains
　　Reward my Native Strains
With flow'rs that chastest bloom and sweetest breathe
　　I loveliest Nymph Divine   40
　　Will own the merits thine
And round thy temples bind the modest wreath

Fragment 10

I

No longer ask me Gentle Friends
　　Why heaves my constant Sigh?
Or why my Eye for ever bends
　　To yon fair Eastern Sky

27 now *cancels* too   28 The *cancels* Thy   29 Each *cancels an illegible*
word   31 *Below* Come Gentle Goddess Sweet *deleted*   33 'midst my Cave
above ever near my view *deleted*   34 *Above* With lightest Attic lawn *deleted*
35 With *cancels* Or all   40 loveliest *cancels* Sweetest
　1 Gentle *above* Village *deleted*

Why view the Clouds that onward roll?   5
    Ah who can Fate command
While here I sit, my wandring Soul
    Is in a distant land.

                            2

Did Ye not hear of Delias Name?
    When on a fatal day   10
O'er Yonder Northern Hills she came
    And brought an Earlier May.
Or if the Month her bloomy store
    By gentle Custom brought
She ne'er was half so sweet before   15
    To my delighted thought

                            3

She found me in my Southern vale
    All in her converse blest
My   Heart began to fail
    Within my youngling Breast   20
I thought when as her
    To me of lowly Birth
There liv'd not ought so good and kind
    On all the smiling Earth

7 far off *suggested above* wandring   13 Or if the *above* Perhaps end *deleted*
13–16 *First version, deleted*:
                    She came and to my simple Mind
                        Improv'd the blossom'd Year
                    For She, Ye swains of all her kind
                        Is Damon's only Dear.

18 *Above* And *deleted, then* And scarce one thought exprest *deleted*   19 My *above*
Before my *deleted*   21–4 *First version, deleted*:
                    I thought to mark her gentle Mind
                        Tho born of lofty birth
                    And when She left my Cot methought
                        She mark'd my starting Tear

4

To Resnel's Banks, again to greet   25
    Her Gentle Eyes I strayd
Where once a Bard with Infant Feet
    Among the Willows play'd
His tender thoughts subdue the Fair
    And melt the Soft and Young   30
But mine I know were softer there
    Than ever Poet sung.

5

I shew'd her there the Songs of One
    Who done to Death by Pride
Tho' Virtue's Friend, and Fancy's Son   35
    In Love unpitied died
I hop'd when to that Shepherd's Truth
    Her Pity should attend
She would not leave another Youth
    To meet his luckless end.   40

6

Now tell me you who hear me sing
    and prompt the tender Theme
How far is Lavant's ˣ little Spring
    From Medway's mightier stream!

ˣ Dic quibus in terris &c

---

25 *Below* I saw her next by Resnel's side *deleted*   27 once a Bard *above* Otway
first *deleted*   29 His tender (tender *deleted*) *above* The   subdue the Fair
above which fill his tender scene *deleted* (*This revision suggests that* His tender *was meant
to stand*)   30 And melt *above* Subdue *deleted*   original opening (Then?) *deleted*
31–2 Collins *first left two lines blank except for the final two words of the second line* (I
hung), *and then added the present two lines*   31 But *above* But there *deleted*   entire
line *above* And yet my own were fond I ween (*first four words deleted*)   32 Than
above As *deleted*   33 her *cancels* here   there *expanded from the*   37 when
and that *cancel illegible words*   41–2 *These lines are written above the following version*
(*second line deleted*):

        But Ye who know what bounds divide'
        Our Shores or rightliest deem

43 is *above* remov'd is (remov'd *deleted*)   little Spring *above* side *deleted*

Confin'd within my Native dells   45
    The world I little know
But in some Tufted Mead she dwells
    Where'er those waters flow.

7

There too resorts a Maid renown'd
    For framing Ditties sweet   50
I heard her lips
    Her gentle lays repeat
They   how sweetly in her Bow'r
    A Greenwood Nymph complain'd
Of Melancholy's gloomy Pow'r   55
    And joys from Wisdom gain'd

---

45 Confin'd *cancels an illegible word*   49 And near her wonnes *suggested above*
There too resorts   53–6 *This is a heavily reworked passage. Collins began by draft-*
ing four lines which constitute a version of part of stanza 8 (see ll. 61–4 n.), and then
attempted to begin another stanza with these deleted lines:

From Wisdom whom she taught to please
She sootly sung how once she heard
    A Green-wood Nymph complain,
'Twas She that sung how soft and sweet
    A Green
To Wisdom first whose Love she gain'd
    The duteous Verse she paid

Partially interlined with this passage is the following version:

Ennobling Wisdom first she ownd
    And hail'd the Sacred Powr
Then like a Green wood Nymph bemoan'd

Of Melancholy last She tried
    To make the Virtues known
Ah Why? That Theme with Love allied
    Belong'd to me Alone!

In this passage Collins wrote bemoan'd *above* complain'd *deleted (l. 3)*   Of *cancels* And
(l. 4)   To save *is written (and deleted) twice in the margin following l. 4, perhaps as an*
alternative to the opening of the following line. Collins finally drafted the present reading in the
text, headed the passage with another '7', and placed a question mark at the beginning of each
line   53 They *expanded from* The   lays *deleted after* They   told *deleted above*
lays (*Collins may have intended to retain* told)   how *above* where of *deleted*   56 joys
above wreaths *deleted*

8

Sweet sung that Muse, and fair befall
  Her Life whose happy Art
What other Bards might envy All
  Can touch my Laura's Heart   60
Sweet Oaten Reeds for her I'll make
  And Chaplets for her Hair
If She for Friendly Pitys sake
  Will whisper Damon there.

9 and last —

Her strain shall dim if ought succeeds   65
  From my applauding tongue
Whateer within her Native Meads
  The Tunefull Thirsis sung
Less to my Love shall He be Dear
  Altho He earliest paid   70
Full many a soft and tender tear
  To luckless Collin's Shade!

---

57 Sweet sung that Muse *above* Yet sweet the Song *deleted*   sung that *above* flowd
her (flowd *deleted*)   60 my Laura's *above* Amanda's *deleted*   61–4 *First version*
(*at end of stanza 7; see ll. 53–6 n.*):

        I'll henceforth make with   Art
          Some Garland for her Hair
        That She who charms my Delia's heart
          May plead for Damon there!

That She who charms (*l. 3*) *above* Her Verse may touch *deleted*   May (*l. 4*) *above*
And *deleted. Four deleted lines are written in the right margin*:

        I will not soil with praise the lay
          Which soothly none can blame
        But count the Songs let all who may
          Divine the Writers name

65 ought *above* mine *deleted*

Fragment 11

Recitative Accompanied.

When Glorious Ptolomy by Merit rais'd
    Successive sate on Ægypt's radiant Throne
Bright Ptolomy, on whom, while Athens gaz'd
    She almost wish'd the Monarch once Her own
Then Virtue own'd one Royal Heart;   5
    For loathing war, humanely wise
For All the Sacred Sons of Art
    He bad the Dome of Science rise.
The Muses knew the festal day
    And call'd by Pow'r Obsequant came   10
With all their Lyres and Chaplets gay
    To give the Fabric ˣ its immortal Name
        High oer the rest in Golden Pride
        The Monarch sate, and at his side
        His Fav'rite Bards—His Græcian Quire   15
        Who while the Roofs responsive Rung
        To many a Fife and many a tinkling Lyre
Amid the Shouting Tribes in sweet succession Sung.

[ˣ] The Μουσειον

---

2 Successive sate on *above* Obtaind his Old *deleted*   Ægypt's] 's *cancels* ian *of*
Ægyptian   radiant *above* Ægypt's Throne *for insertion*   6 humanely *above* too
genrous and too *and after* too genrous (*both deleted*)   8 bad *cancels* bid   10 call'd
cancels an illegible word   12 To] o *above* hey *of* They *deleted* (*which cancels original
reading* Assign'd)   give *cancels* gave

LETTERS

To / John Gilbert Cooper Junr Esqr / at M^rs
Farmer's / in Leicester / There

London Tuesday Nov 10th
1747.

Dear Cooper,

Your obliging Paquet reach'd me last night, in an hour which
I had assign'd for the carrying on my design. I will not lose a line
in telling you how sensible I was of your kind promise. I hope our
Hearts are form'd so much alike, that Yours - will imagine the
force with w'ch such generosity must affect mine, without my   5
           recourse to those symptoms of vulgar Friendship
verbal acknowledgments—I had wrote to you by Saturday's post,
to tell you my thoughts of changing the title which I still think
should be = The Friendly Examiner, or Letters of Polémon and
Philèthus; or, the Plain Dealer, with the same Appendix. In regard 10
to the Clar—— I think it nimis fastuosum (to talk like Le Sage's
Salzedo) and apprehend it may be dislik'd by a *particular Body of
Jealous Literati*, at the same time that I concieve the above to be
more modest and equally comprehensive. You found by my last
that I propos'd the more literary papers should fall under the name 15
of Polémon, and the more lusory or Comic under that of Philethus.
In order to Hint this at the head of the Paper, I shall have a Medal-

lion engrav'd of two Elegant Heads al'antqiue thus

(Dont you think 'em a l'antique?) over the lower part of the Necks
of which there shall be a veil thrown, from under which a little *Art* 20
shall appear writing on a Roman scroll, and a *Satyr* either in contrast
holding up another, or writing on Part of the same   suppose

Address. Junr *written above the line in a smaller hand*   There] *Collins wrote* These,
apparently for There (*see the address of the following letter*)   1 last *above* Monday
deleted in cancels at   5 with w'ch *above* force such *for insertion*   6 *Word missing*
(having?) *where MS. is torn by seal*   10 Appendix *cancels blurred word*   17 the
Paper] the *cancels* my   19 over *above* over (*which cancels an illegible word*) lower
part of the *above the* Necks *for insertion*   22 *Word missing* (*probably* I) *where
MS. is torn by seal*

the veil be upheld by *Friendship*, who may at the same time point to the Relievo of the Medallion while she discovers the
25 ornaments of the base by supporting the veil. The Motto to the first Paper shall be with your approbation, Duo turba sumus. That to the second part, or the Paper of Philèthus, Idonea dicere vitæ or illustrans commoda vitæ, and that which shall appear at the head of the next of Polemon Usus vetusto genere, sed rebus novis.
30 Phædr: or Plus operis quanto veniæ minus or &c &c &c &c In the course of the Paper may be introduc'd New Characters such as, if it be not too ancient, Athenæus, from whom any Poetical fragments of our best writers, such as some MSS of Fairfax which I can procure, or any anecdotes of their lives &c might with the greatest propriety
35 come.

Thus far a desire of consulting you has carried me into a forgetfullness of the Essay, with which I have been so much charm'd till this half hour, when I began talking to You.

It is my sincere opinion that the subject could not have been
40 treated in a more Picturesque or forcible Allegory, and I am confident I am at least qualified to give the Public one Beautifull Paper. Allow me, Dear Cooper, to thank you from the sincerest Gratitude yet, before I leave you, for tho' I think it unnecessary, yet I feel it too natural to be resisted   Yours most aff[ly] and sinc[ly]:
45 WmCollins.

The Town has enough of Foote. He play'd Saturday at C Garden for the 3[d] time to almost an Empty House. There is a Song of Colley Cibber's perform'd to night at Drury lane, call'd, Tit for Tat, or the Sailors rendezvous at Portsmouth. Rich is to entertain the
50 Town with a New Actor in the Part of Pierre   Name is Sowden, a Man of great Pretence and some fortune. The Opera was crowded but went off, as the Musicians term, it ill. Frasi is engag'd for Ranelagh next Season with Beard——

23 who] *Collins first wrote* whos[e], *then deleted the* 's'   30 or *above* Plus operis
31 *Word obliterated following* Paper   be *above* may introduc'd *for insertion*
32 *Collins inadvertently wrote* whom *twice*   40–1 am confident *cancels* don't doubt
42 Paper *cancels* Essay   43 yet, *above* Gratitude before *for insertion*   unnecessary
expanded from necessary   46 on *deleted before* Saturday   50 *Word obliterated*
following Pierre

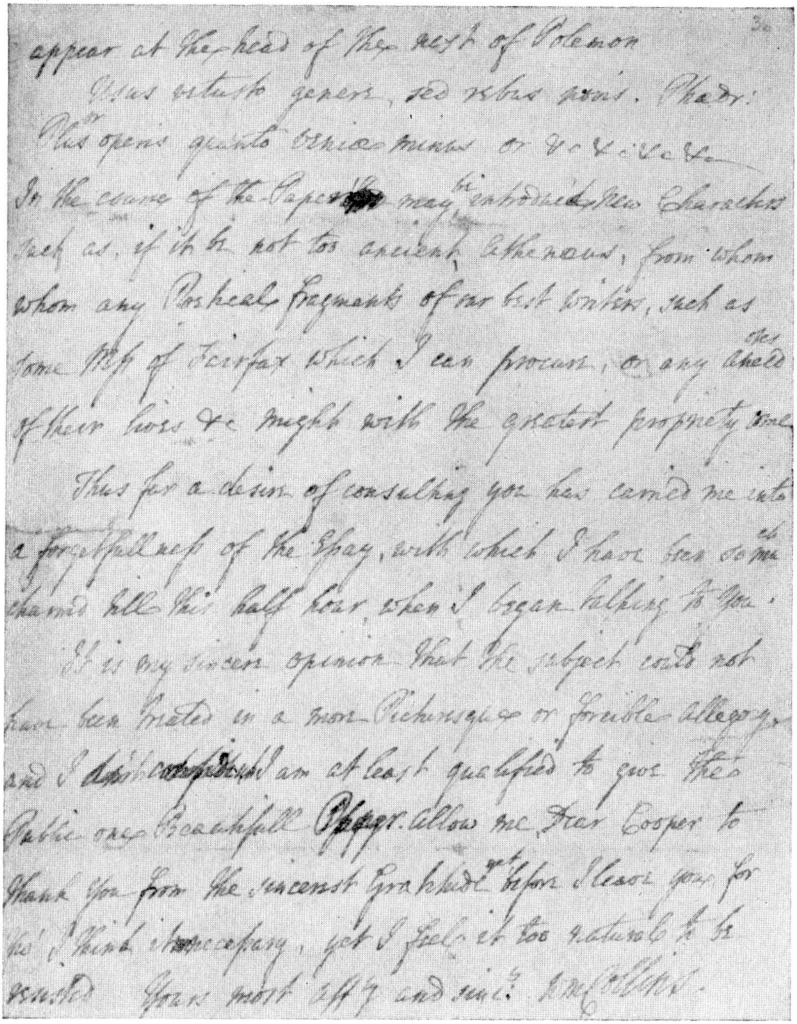

PLATE 2

The third page of Collins's letter to John Gilbert Cooper, which includes his signature
(BL Add. MS. 41178. I. f. 36ʳ). Reproduced by permission of the British Library Board.

To Dr Hayes / Professor of Music / in Oxford / There.

[Chichester
8 November 1750]

Sir

   Mr Blackstone of Winchester some time since inform'd Me of
the Honour You had done me at Oxford last Summer for which
I return You my sincere thanks. I have another more perfect Copy
of the Ode, which, had I known your obliging design, *I would* have
communicated to You. Inform me by a Line, If You should think   5
one of my better Judgment acceptable; In such Case I could send
you one written on a Nobler Subject, and which, tho' I have been
persuaded to bring it forth in London, I think more calculated for
an Audience in the University. The Subject is the Music of the
Græcian Theatre, in which I have, I hope, Naturally introduc'd the 10
Various Characters with which the Chorus was concern'd, as
Oedipus, Medæa, Electra, Orestes &c &c The Composition too
is probably more correct, as I have chosen the ancient Tragedies
for my Models, and onely copied the most affecting Passages in
Them.   15

   In the mean time You would greatly oblige me by Sending Me
the Score of the last—If you can get it written I will readily answer
the expence—If you send it with a Copy or two of the Ode, (as
printed at Oxford) to Mr. Clarke at Winchester, He will forward it
to Me here. I am   20

Sir

with great respect

Chichester, Sussex, Nov^{ber} 8th. 1750   Your Oblig'd humble Servt.

William Collins.

PS   25

   Mr Clarke past some days here, while Mr. Worgan was with Me
from whose Friendship I hope He will recieve some Advantage—

Address. Dr Hayes] Dr. William Hayes *Seward*   in Oxford] Oxford *Seward*
There] *omitted in Seward*   5 Inform me] *begins new paragraph in Seward*   12 **The**
Composition] *begins new paragraph in Seward*   16 Me] *omitted in Seward*

ORATIO AD PORTAS

[Oratio ad Portas]

Parum abfuit (Hosp: Doct:) quin lacrymis effusi, Silentio obruti ad vos salutandos prodiissemus, Has quippe Ædes dolori tanto nuper consecratas, Hos solennes conventus uti pristina deest et Gratia et Lætitia, Quis intueri potest istius Mæstitiæ vacuus, quæ Wiccamicorum omnium animos prægravat, Vultusque deformat? Nè vero ingrati quiddam sit in Silentio et Lacrymis, nè penuria quandam virtutum istarum egregiarum, videremus deflere, quibus desideratissimus noster Custos, jam ad Deum evectus, abunde præstitit: liceat nobis, ob conspectum vestrum aliquatenus gaudio indulgere. Et cum bene memores animis repetamus, quâ eruditione quâ benignitate quâ munificentia infantiles nostras et sustulit et aluit Musas, hoc etiam sit persuasum quod aureus alter non deficit, et quod Wiccamica arbor simili frondescit metallo. De te (Hosp: Dign:) Id mihi dicendum voluerunt socii, Ita in adventu tua, gaudere ut exoptarent etiam et annum fore. Te vero colere, amare, revereri, felicia omnia precari solummodo nobis relictum est, Laudes tuas efferre aut extendere non licet, quippe quæ passis velis ubique pervehuntur. Ex tanto virtutum Marum Cumulo unam tantum nobis impendas rogamus, unam maxime amabilem, et quâ præcipue præcellis, Candorem. Ad te vero doctissime Vir, festinat oratio; Ut juvat post multos dies te coram intueri! Ut lætatur Wiccamica Juventus tibi reduci in patriam gratulari! Cum in exteris regionibus In Italia tuâ diutius morabaris, non minus charus tuis, non minus his omnibus curæ eras. Quemcumque celebrem inter Romanos perlegimus Authorem, Tui meminerimus, te ante oculos posuimus, Cum Virgilii divinum et immortale opus animis manibusque versaremus, Hæc crede, diximus, Forsan ad hujusce tumulum jacet, et sacros veneratur manes. Ibi valeat, Ibi gaudeat, Musam hauriat amicam, Ejusque non dissimilem: Si ad Tullium verteremur, Ex Tusculo eundem in patriam amorem, easdem eloquentiæ virtutes referat, eâdem vi, at feliciori fortunâ, patriæ simul et ruentis religionis vindicet jura. Et Tu Vir colende licet Angliæ non abesses, iisdem

24 *Word obliterated following* Romanos

tamen, elegantibus studiis semper interfuisti; Ex rure tuô velut
ex altero Tusculo sapientiæ investigas fontes et ex veterum
35 præceptis vitam moresque effingis. Tuam vero erga omnes humani-
tate quâ maxime gloriaris, haud ita pridem experta est Wiccamica
pubes, detur et nobis eandem experiri. Accedite ergo, Viri insignis-
simi, optimè de Laribus hisce Meriti, Jucunda quædam est pietas ea
revisere cunabula, ex quibus Tanti prodiistis, ex quibus tot tantosque
40 viros vestrumque quam simillimos mox prodituros fore speramus.

Collins

Speech at the Gates
[Translation by John Baird]

How nearly, o learned guests, did we come forth to greet you
buried in silence and shedding tears! Who indeed can contemplate
this house lately consecrated to so great a sorrow, these annual
assemblies which want their former pleasantness and joy, and
5 remain untouched by that grief which weighs heavily upon the
minds and disfigures the countenances of all Wykehamists? But yet,
lest silence and tears may seem ungrateful, lest we may appear to
weep because we lack those very virtues in which our most lamented
Warden, already raised up to God, was abundantly pre-eminent,
10 we may properly allow ourselves some measure of joy upon your
appearance. And when right mindfully we recall with what learning,
with what kindness, with what generosity he both sustained and
nourished our infant Muses, we may indeed be persuaded that a
second golden bough will not fail to appear, and that the Wyke-
15 hamic tree still puts forth leaves of the same metal.

Concerning you, o worthy guest, my comrades have wished
me to say that they rejoice so greatly in your arrival that they
surely hope it will be repeated next year. To us, indeed, it remains
only to honour you, to love you, to revere you, and to wish you
20 every happiness; we cannot publish or extend your renown, which
in very truth is borne everywhere by full sails. From your great
treasury of manly virtues we ask that you lay out for us only one,
one particularly lovable, and in which you principally excel—
Candour.

To you, o most learned man, my speech hastens on! How I 25
rejoice after many days to behold you with my own eyes! How
Wykehamist youth delights to welcome you on your return to
your native land! You were not less dear to your friends, not less
the object of solicitude to all of us, while in foreign parts, in your
Italy, you were too long delaying. Whatever author celebrated 30
among the Romans we studied, we remembered you, we set you
before our eyes. When in our hands and minds we turned over the
divine and immortal work of Virgil, 'Believe you me,' we said,
'perhaps he is by this very funeral mound, and honours the sacred
shade. There let him be healthy, there let him rejoice; may he 35
drink in the favourable Muse, not unlike his own!' If we turned to
Cicero, 'May he derive from Tusculum the same love for his native
land, the same powers of eloquence; with the same force, but happier
fortune, may he at once defend the rights of his country and of his
endangered Church!'   40

And you, worthy Sir; though you have not been absent from
England, yet you have ever participated in the same elegant studies;
from your countryside as from another Tusculum you search out
the fountains of wisdom, and from the precepts of the ancients you
form your life and character. Indeed, not so long ago Wykehamist 45
youth knew your kindness to all, which is your special glory; may
it be given to us to experience the same!

Approach, therefore, o distinguished gentlemen, highly worthy
of the spirit of this house. Truly happy is the piety which brings
you to revisit the cradle from which you have emerged such great 50
men, and whence we hope will soon emerge as many men of equal
greatness and as much like yourselves as possible.

Collins

COMMENTARY

POEMS

TO MISS AURELIA C——R, ON HER WEEPING AT HER SISTER'S WEDDING

This short poem first appeared in the *Gentleman's Magazine*, 9 (Jan. 1739), 41, above the name 'AMASIUS'. In his brief sketch of Collins's life in the *Poetical Calendar* (1763), xii. 107–8, James Hampton reprinted the poem as Collins's: 'The following epigram, made by him while at Winchester-school, discovers a genius, and turn of expression, very rarely to be met with in juvenile compositions.' The poem was later appended to Samuel Johnson's 'Life of Collins', where Johnson stated that Collins 'first courted the notice of the publick by some verses *To a Lady weeping*, published in *The Gentleman's Magazine*' (*Lives*, iii. 334). The poem was subsequently included in most editions of Collins's poetry until Christopher Stone's in 1907.

Stone's rejection of the poem was based on evidence supplied in G. B. Hill's edition of the *Letters of Samuel Johnson* (Oxford: Clarendon Press, 1892), ii. 130–1. In a letter to John Nichols early in 1780, Johnson wrote that 'Dr. Warton tells me that Collins's first piece is in the G. M. for August, 1739. For August there is no such thing. *Amasius* was at that time the poetical name of Dr. Swan, who translated Sydenham. Where to find Collins I know not.' In his note Hill argues that the author of this piece must have been Dr Swan: 'Johnson, I conjecture, mentions *Amasius* in his Letter, because in the August number there are some lines signed with that name which Nichols might have attributed to Collins.' And Hill suggests that Collins's first piece was in fact the 'Sonnet' appearing in the October issue of the magazine: 'It, too, is about a Lady's tears; hence perhaps the confusion between the two poems.'

Hill's argument has been adopted by Lonsdale, who points out that Johnson had been working for the *Gentleman's Magazine* in 1739 and would therefore have been in a position to know that 'Amasius' was the pseudonym of Dr John Swan, who edited Thomas Sydenham's *Works* in 1742. Lonsdale also draws attention to the numerous poems signed 'Amasius' which appeared in the magazine between 1739 and 1743, claiming that 'it is impossible to believe that C. was also responsible for these mediocre pieces' (p. 561). The most probable explanation, Lonsdale suggests, is the following: Johnson's source of information, Joseph Warton, told him that Collins's first published poem appeared in the *Gentleman's Magazine*, that it concerned a lady weeping, and (possibly) that it was included in the August issue (where another poem signed 'Amasius', presumably by Swan, appears). But apparently Nichols, or someone else, discovering the attribution in the *Poetical Calendar* or the poem itself in the January issue of the *Gentleman's*, appended the poem to Johnson's 'Life of Collins'. 'The matter is still far from clear,' Lonsdale concludes, 'but the fact that the lines are signed "Amasius" seems to prevent their acceptance as C.'s.'

If this fact is the only major barrier to our acceptance of the poem as Collins's, then the following information would appear to make that acceptance much more certain. In a note at the end of the poetical essays in the January 1739 issue of the *Gentleman's*, the editor indicates that '*The two Poems sign'd* Amasius *in this* Mag. *are from different Correspondents*' (p. 43). This note was first pointed out by Donald F. Bond, 'The Gentleman's Magazine', *MP*, 38 (1940), 93. The other poem signed 'Amasius' in this issue is entitled '*Left in Dr* Shaw's *Translation of my Lord* Bacon's *Works, belonging to a Friend*', a poem which closely corresponds in subject with Swan's interest in translation and which is stylistically similar to many of the other poems in the magazine written above his name or pseudonym (cf. especially the poem '*To Miss* CARTER, *On her Translation of Sir* ISAAC NEWTON's *Philosophy explain'd for the Use of the Ladies*', signed 'J. SWAN' in the June 1739 issue, p. 322).

This editorial note appears to obviate Johnson's objection as well as any suggestion that Collins must be held responsible for any of the other poems submitted by 'Amasius' to the magazine (both Dyce and Bronson in their editions point out the comparative mediocrity of these other poems). This information should also strengthen the possibility that Joseph Warton informed Johnson that Collins's first published poem was signed 'Amasius' (and perhaps that it dealt with marriage); it is otherwise difficult to explain why Warton would have mistakenly referred Johnson to the August issue, where he would have found a poem '*To a Friend on his* MARRIAGE' printed above this pseudonym. And if Warton did inform Johnson that the piece involved a lady weeping, his description more accurately fits 'To Miss Aurelia C——r, on her Weeping at her Sister's Wedding' than it does Collins's 'Sonnet'. Close attention should also be paid to the original attribution by James Hampton in the *Poetical Calendar*. Hampton was a contemporary of Collins at Winchester and Oxford (and later the translator of Polybius), who in fact remarked in his sketch of Collins that 'His Latin exercises were never so much admired as his English.' There is no reason to doubt Hampton's attribution, nor is there anything in the poem itself to suggest that it was not written by Collins at the time of the 'Sonnet'.

The poem is therefore cautiously reintroduced here into the body of Collins's work, and its text printed from the *Gentleman's Magazine*. Although C. L. Carlson, *The First Magazine* (Providence: Brown Univ., 1938), p. 251, refers to the poem as 'To Miss Aurelia Cibber', Aurelia herself, and the occasion on which the poem was written, remain unknown (if in fact they existed at all). It is possible that Collins used, as a model for his poem, Matthew Prior's 'To Leonora. Encore' ('Cease, LEONORA, cease to mourn'), published posthumously in his *Miscellaneous Works* (1740). This would imply, however, that Collins had seen Prior's poem in manuscript before it was included among his published works. A more likely conclusion is that Collins modelled this short lyric, like his 'Sonnet', on Pope's early imitations of Waller and Cowley (see the following head-note). Collins's poem echoes the opening line of Pope's 'Of a Lady singing to her Lute. [In imitation of Waller.]' ('Fair charmer cease, nor make your voice's prize'); but Collins, like Pope, only broadly modelled his imitation on an actual poetic source.

SONNET

This poem was first published over the signature 'DELICATULUS' in the *Gentleman's Magazine*, 9 (Oct. 1739), 545. A head-note to this and the two preceding poems reports that '*The three next were sent us in one Letter.*' The poem was attributed to Collins by Joseph Warton in a memorandum reprinted in John Wooll's *Biographical Memoirs of the late Revd. Joseph Warton, D.D.* (1806), p. 107 n.: 'Sappho's Advice was written by me, then at Winchester school; the next by Tomkyns; and the sonnet by Collins.' Tomkyns was apparently Richard Tomkins, later a fellow of New College, Oxford (T. F. Kirby, *Winchester Scholars* (1888), p. 241). Wooll reprinted Collins's poem, as did Dyce and subsequent editors. The present text follows the *Gentleman's Magazine* as copy.

A correspondent in the November issue of the *Gentleman's*, commending the poetical essays of the preceding month, claimed of Collins's poem: '*The least, which is a Favourite of mine, carries a* Force *mix'd with* Tenderness, *and an uncommon* Elevation' (*GM*, 9 (1739), 601). Wooll (p. 109) contended that this criticism had been written by Samuel Johnson, but Chalmers, in his *English Poets* (1810), xviii. 145, pointed out Wooll's error, and his conclusion is corroborated by W. P. Courtney and D. N. Smith, *A Bibliography of Samuel Johnson* (Oxford: Clarendon Press, 1915; rpt. 1968), p. 11. Further notice was given to the three poems in the verse epistle '*To Mr* URBAN, *On the Poetical Essays in his last* MAGAZINE' (*GM*, 9 (1739), 600–1).

The three schoolboy authors apparently read each other's poems, for Collins's closing line closely parallels the conclusion of the second poem, 'Beauty and Innocence', by Tomkins ('Auramantulus'): 'Thus *Aura* justly was confess'd / The brighter queen of love'. But Collins also had clearly in mind Pope's early 'Verses in imitation of Cowley. By a Youth of thirteen.' The 'Sonnet' is modelled on Pope's 'Weeping', a three-stanza lyric that is based on Cowley's poem 'Weeping' in *The Mistress* (*Poems*, ed. A. R. Waller (Cambridge: Cambridge Univ. Press, 1905), pp. 136–7). Pope's imitation of Cowley, first published in *Poems on Several Occasions* (1717) and then reprinted with revisions in Pope's *Works* (1736), vol. iii, was thus easily accessible to Collins in 1739.

Title. A 'sonnet' could indicate any 'small poem' (*Dict.*).

1. *wanton*: 'Frolicksome; gay' (*Dict.*).

7. *teeming*: both 'to be full' and 'to be pregnant; to engender young' (*Dict.*).

ORIENTAL ECLOGUES

Collins's *Oriental Eclogues* presents editorial problems of considerable complexity. The difficulties include not only the determination of authorial revision but the choice of a copy-text as well. To some extent the problems here are biographical: we must ask ourselves if Collins was in fact capable of revising his poetry in the 1750s, a question which entails a full survey of the nature of his illness. This issue is examined in detail in the Introduction to this edition; the following discussion summarizes the findings reached there, and pursues parallel problems in the presentation of the text.

Collins's *Persian Eclogues* was published anonymously in January 1742: 'London: Printed for J. Roberts, in Warwick-Lane. 1742. (Price Six-pence)'. Notice of publication was given in January in both the *Gentleman's* and the *London Magazine*. An entry in the printer Henry Woodfall's ledger records the following information concerning printing for 'Mr. Andrew Millar, Dr.': 'Dec. 10, 1741. Persian Eclogues, 1 1/2 shts., No. 500. Reprinting 1/2 sht.' (P.T.P., 'Woodfall's Ledger, 1734–1747', *N&Q*, 1st ser., 11 (1855), 419).

Joseph Warton, in his edition of Pope (1797), provides an account of the poem's composition:

> Mr. Collins wrote his Eclogues when he was about seventeen years old, at Winchester School, and, as I well remember, had been just reading that volume of Salmon's Modern History, which described Persia; which determined him to lay the scene of these pieces, as being productive of new images and sentiments. (i. 61 n.)

Although this early work met with success (or perhaps because it was so successful), Collins later became dissatisfied with his schoolboy production. Warton continues:

> In his maturer years, he was accustomed to speak very contemptuously of them, calling them his Irish Eclogues, and saying they had not in them one spark of Orientalism; and desiring me to erase a motto he had prefixed to them in a copy he gave me; ---- quos primus equis oriens afflavit anhelis. Virg. He was greatly mortified that they found more readers and admirers than his Odes. (i. 61–2 n.; see also Johnson's 'Life of Collins'.)

The copy given to Joseph Warton contained, in addition to the revised motto, a number of other corrections in Collins's hand (the book was given to Warton when he and his brother visited Collins at Chichester, presumably in September 1754; it is preserved in the Dyce Collection of the Victoria and Albert Museum). In 1757 a new edition of the poem was published under the title *Oriental Eclogues* ('London: Printed for J. Payne, at Pope's Head, in Paternoster-Row. M DCC LVII.') and advertised in the monthly catalogues for

January and February in the *London Magazine*. The text of the *Oriental Eclogues*, with a different title-page only, was published three years later: 'The Second Edition. London: Printed for Tho. Hope, at the Bible and Anchor, the Corner of Bartholomew-Lane, Threadneedle-Street. M.DCC. LX.'

The *Oriental Eclogues* contains many changes in accidentals, some substantive variants, the addition of a couplet to the third eclogue, and a revised title and motto. Some of these revisions were made in Collins's hand in the copy of the *Persian Eclogues* he gave to Joseph Warton (referred to here as *Dyce 1742*); other substantive changes, however, are found in the 1757 edition only, and it is these changes which have been questioned by recent editors. Although all eighteenth- and nineteenth-century editors chose the revised edition of 1757 as their text, twentieth-century editors have for the most part retained the earlier readings, usually on biographical grounds. Thus Christopher Stone (1907) prints the 1742 text because the second edition, containing 'negligible' differences, was published in 1757 'when Collins was mad'. Austin Lane Poole (2nd edn., 1927) follows Stone's text as well as his reasoning, arguing that 'the second edition appeared in 1757, when Collins was mad and unable to give his mind to the work of editorship.' And Roger Lonsdale (1969) suggests that if, 'as seems likely, Joseph Warton superintended the 1757 edn, he may well have made these well-meaning "improvements" himself, on behalf of his friend who was now thought to be insane.'

These arguments raise several objections. It appears in the first place that Lonsdale is offering unsupported conjecture—revision by Warton—in place of the more likely possibility that the changes were made by Collins himself. In addition to Thomas Warton's testimony that the odes bore 'marks of repeated correction', we have the evidence of revision in Collins's *An Epistle: Addrest to Sir Thomas Hanmer*, 'The Passions' (see his letter of 1750), and the drafts and fragments presented to Joseph Warton. We know, moreover, that Collins had revised part of his *Eclogues* by 1754 (when he presented a copy to the Wartons), and that even then he was not satisfied with it, as Joseph Warton's account suggests. It thus seems probable that, a new edition being called for in 1756, Collins would have added further corrections. The revisions themselves support this view. Some tend to rework images; others change the point of view of a supposedly 'Asiatick' poem. Even the change in the title, from the specific 'Persian' to the more general 'Oriental' eclogues, reinforces this sense of Collins's continuing dissatisfaction with his early attempt to produce (in Warton's phrase) 'new images and sentiments'.

Finally, Stone, Poole, and Lonsdale accept a version of Collins's illness which is not consistent with the facts left by those friends and biographers who knew the poet in his last years. We know that his illness was, at its worst, of an intermittent nature. We know that Collins's interest in literature remained unabated, even though he was not, apparently, writing poetry in the mid and late 1750s. It is true, as Lonsdale says, that Collins 'was now thought to be insane', but it was Joseph Warton who best understood the truth about his friend, and it was he who suggested that as late as 1756 Collins was still contemplating his vast historical project, *A History of the Revival of Learning*. The encounter with James Smith, the anecdote from Shenton, and the meeting with Thomas Warton 'not many months before his death' (incidents documented in the Introduction) all point to the probability that Collins was able and eager to perform additional revision as late as 1756. Such testimony, taken with the nature of the revisions themselves, should therefore authorize the acceptance of all the substantive variants in the *Oriental Eclogues*.

The determination of a copy-text for the *Eclogues* presents a problem of similar complexity. Under normal circumstances a work with this kind of printing history would prompt a straightforward textual decision to follow the first edition as copy-text (assuming that, in the absence of a manuscript or corrected proof, this presentation of the text would most closely conform to the author's intentions regarding accidentals). The edition would then incorporate authorial revisions from the later printing into the base text, and these revisions would be modified, if necessary, to conform to the style of the text chosen as copy. (These procedures are taken from W. W. Greg, 'The Rationale of Copy-Text', *SB*, 3 (1950), 19–36, and Fredson Bowers, 'Current Theories of Copy-Text, with an Illustration from Dryden', *MP*, 48 (1950), 12–20.)

But the *Persian* and *Oriental Eclogues* (published in 1742 and 1757) pose a special problem in the modification of revisions, standing as they do on opposite sides of the 'Great Divide' in eighteenth-century printing practice (the phrase is Bertrand Bronson's, 'Printing as an Index of Taste', in his *Facets of the Enlightenment* (Berkeley and Los Angeles: Univ. of California Press, 1968), p. 339). As Bronson has pointed out, little research has been done, and little reaction has been recorded, concerning this major change in the presentation of literary texts. Almost exactly at mid-century, printers began to abandon the capitalization of every noun and the italicization of proper names. The impact on the reader is enormous: 'The whole visual effect of a page of type is transformed by it' (Bronson, p. 340). The difference in the visual texture of the poetry can be gauged in the opening of Collins's *Eclogues*.

> 1742: Ye *Persian* Maids, attend your Poet's Lays,
>   And hear how Shepherds pass their golden Days:
> 1757: Ye Persian maids, attend your poet's lays,
>   And hear how shepherds pass their golden days.

What effect this change had on Collins we do not know. Poets continued, as Bronson points out concerning Gray, to write out their manuscripts in traditional fashion, employing capitals for every noun. None of Collins's finished manuscripts survives, although the Aldouri manuscript of the 'Ode to a Friend on his Return &c' demonstrates Collins's pervasive use of capitals

as late as 1749–50. But even if Collins had accepted this new presentation of
his text, we must assume that earlier he had accepted the original printing
of 1742. From the evidence provided by J. Smith in *The Printer's Grammar*
(London, 1755), it seems possible that authors could exert some influence on
printing style:

> Before we actually begin to compose, we should be informed, either by the Author,
> or Master, after what manner our work is to be done; whether the old way, with
> Capitals to Substantives, and Italic to proper names; or after the more neat practice,
> all in Roman, and Capitals to Proper names, and Emphatical words. (p. 201.)

But it is doubtful if Collins, removed from the centre of the publishing world,
could have had as much influence here as the master (or compositor) of the
printing house.

The problem inherent in the modification of an eclectic, 'amalgamated'
text in this case lies in the fact that it would not note the radical departures
in stylistic presentation occurring within the author's own lifetime. Nor do
the substantive changes in the text warrant separate printings of the two
editions; the two editions do not embody different 'versions' of the same
poem. But the disadvantages of choosing the later edition as copy are, on the
other hand, even greater. Such an edition, following the 1757 text for both
substantives and accidentals, would impose a 'tyranny of the copy-text' by
allowing the choice of substantives to rule the accidentals (instead of dis-
tinguishing between what Greg considered two entirely separate textual
decisions). The choice of the second edition would also place the text even
further along in a line of possible textual corruption, including (as it would)
punctuation which, when it differs from the 1742 text, is only questionably
Collins's. As Bowers has argued, an editor 'is only playing the correct odds
when, as a general proposition, he retains the texture of the original edition'
instead of adopting a general system still further removed from the original
form ('Current Theories of Copy-Text . . .', p. 16). The full acceptance of this
later edition would also further remove the poem from its early prominence
in Collins's career; it would, in effect, more completely become a poem of
1757.

The text printed here therefore follows *Persian Eclogues* (*1742*) as copy-text
and incorporates substantive revisions from *Oriental Eclogues* (*1757*). Revisions
found both in *1757* and in the annotated copy of *Persian Eclogues* (*Dyce 1742*)
are noted in the textual apparatus. Revisions from the later edition are modi-
fied to conform to the presentation of accidentals in the copy-text. Changes
in punctuation, spelling, and format in the 1757 edition are recorded in the
textual notes, but not differences in capitals or italics. Substantive variants
in other early printings of the poem have been noted as well.

The formats of the two editions are as follows:

Persian Eclogues (*1742*): 8º (1/2 shts.): A² B–C⁴ D²; *i–iii* iv, 5–24; *i* title, *ii* blank, *iii* preface, iv preface, 5–24 text. *Dyce 1742* (annotated copy) lacks A2 (preface). Foxon C298; Williams, p. 108; Rothschild 653; Tinker 727.

Oriental Eclogues (1757): 4⁰ (1/2 shts.): π^2 A–G^2; *i–iv* v–viii, 1–23, *24*; *i* half-title, *ii* blank, *iii* title, *iv* blank, v–viii preface, 1–23 text, *24* advert. Dyce lacks πι (half-title). Williams, p. 112; Rothschild 654; Tinker 728.

Copies of these editions are rare. The following copies are known to us:

Persian Eclogues: L, LVA-D (2), O, CSmH, CtY, NN-B, TxHR, Rothschild, Taylor.

Oriental Eclogues: L (2), LVA-D, O, OM, CtY, DLC, MH, MB, TxFTC, Rothschild, Sparrow, A. Houghton.

Oriental Eclogues ('Second Edition', 1760): O.

More popular than his *Odes*, Collins's *Eclogues* was even more successful after its second edition in 1757. The poem was immediately extracted in the *London Chronicle* (13–15 Jan. 1757), and Eclogue IV was reprinted in the *Gentleman's Magazine*, 27 (Feb. 1757), 81. All four eclogues were reprinted in the *Weekly Amusement*, 1 (30 June and 15 Sept. 1764), 447–8, 623–4; 2 (9 Mar. 1765), 159–60; and 4 (5 July 1766), 451–2; in Goldsmith's *Poems for Young Ladies* (1767), pp. 228–41, as well as in *The Beauties of English Poesy* (1767), i. 239–53, and in the collections of Moses Mendez (1767) and George Pearch (1768). As Woodhouse notes, Eclogue II (ll. 18–28) was set to music by Callcott ('Collins in the Eighteenth Century', *TLS* (16 Oct. 1930), p. 838). The poem was reviewed by James Grainger in the *Monthly Review*, 16 (June 1757), 486–9, and Langhorne included 'Observations on the Oriental Eclogues' in his edition of Collins (1765). Goldsmith added a brief comment on the poem in *The Beauties of English Poesy* (i. 239): 'The following eclogues, written by Mr. Collins, are very pretty: the images, it must be owned, are not very local; for the pastoral subject could not well admit of it. The description of Asiatic magnificence, and manners, is a subject as yet unattempted amongst us, and, I believe, capable of furnishing a great variety of poetical imagery.' William Shenstone, on the other hand, found the poem unsatisfactory: 'The Orientals afforded a new, & very fertile subject for eclogues. Poor Collins did not wholly satisfy me; having by no means sufficiently availd himself of their many local peculiarities' (*Letters*, ed. M. Williams (Oxford: Blackwell, 1939), p. 552).

Collins's general source for his poem was, as Joseph Warton recorded and Collins mentioned in a note (iii. 17), Thomas Salmon's *Modern History*, published in 31 volumes between 1725 and 1738. Lonsdale suggests that it is possible that Collins's poem was connected with the appearance of a much more accessible collected edition of three volumes in April 1739. If this is true, it would narrow the possible date of first composition from the time of Collins's seventeenth birthday (25 December 1738) to the appearance of this new edition four months later. The *Eclogues* was presumably finished before Collins went up to Oxford in March 1741, but it may have been revised prior to publication later that year.

The scope of Salmon's work is indicated in the full title he gave to the collected edition: *Modern History: Or, The Present State Of All Nations. Describing Their respective Situations, Persons, Habits, Buildings, Manners, Laws and Customs, Religion and Policy, Arts and Sciences, Trades, Manufactures and Husbandry, Plants, Animals and Minerals.* The history was, he claimed in the 'Introduction', 'an attempt to distinguish truth from fiction, and to discover the certainty of those accounts we have received of distant nations' (1739 edn., i. ix). Collins's probable debts to Salmon, first documented by Ainsworth, have been pointed out in the notes.

A more exact source has been claimed for the third eclogue. John Mitford, in his edition of *The Poems of Thomas Gray* (1814), p. 36, claimed that Collins was indebted to the *Free-Thinker*, Nos. 128–9 (12 and 15 June 1719, reprinted in collected editions in 1722–3, 1733, and 1737). One of the editors of the periodical was Ambrose Philips, and Johnson (in his 'Life of Philips') records that it had 'been reprinted in volumes, but is little read; nor can impartial criticism recommend it as worthy of revival' (*Lives*, iii. 322). Dyce rejected the 'charge of plagiarism' as ill-founded, but the parallels are worth noting. In '*The History of* ALIBEZ', a 'curious Piece of *Persian* History', Cha-Abbas, King of Persia, makes a progress through his dominions in order to see 'the simple, natural Life of the Peasants'. In the course of his travels the king encounters the young shepherd Alibez, and, charmed by the youth's intelligence and natural graces, offers to have him educated at the court. Alibez assents, and soon 'The Sheep-Hook, the Pipe, and the Shepherd's Garb, were laid aside; he was now cloathed in a Purple Robe, and a Turban sparkling with Jewels; and his Beauty was the Admiration of the Court.' In spite of his post as keeper of the royal jewels, Alibez nevertheless remains faithful to the 'Days of Innocence' he has left behind. And when the king's successor, Cha-Sephi, accuses him of misconduct in office, Alibez shows the new ruler the contents of his own treasure-vault: 'And all the Wealth he found there, was a Sheep-Hook, a Pipe, and a Shepherd's Habit, which *Alibez* had worn; all which, he often took a Pleasure in visiting privately, to remind him of his former Condition.' To the last, even as he was further elevated at the court, Alibez esteemed the condition of shepherds 'the most desirable State of Life' (1722–3 edn., iii. 172–85). E. G. Ainsworth, *Poor Collins*, pp. 202–3, suggests the stories of Nour Mahal and Cha Selim recounted by Salmon in his 'Present State of Proper India' (*Modern History* (1739 edn.), i. 242–4) as further sources for the third eclogue, but the parallels are less striking.

Motto. Collins's quotation is taken from Virgil's *Georgics*, i. 250–1: 'nosque ubi primus equis Oriens adflavit anhelis, / illic sera rubens accendit lumina Vesper' ('and when on us the rising Sun first breathes with panting steeds, there glowing Vesper is kindling his evening rays'). The motto for the 1742 edition is from Cicero's *Pro. A. Licinio Archia Poeta Oratio*, the speech on behalf of Archias the poet: 'But let us for the moment waive these solid advantages; let us assume that entertainment is the sole end of reading; even so, I think you would hold that no mental employment is so broadening to the sympathies or so enlightening to the understanding' (vii. 16).

Preface 4–5. These national characteristics were commonly pointed out in travel literature of the period. Jean Gailhard, in *The Compleat Gentleman* (1678), p. 178, described the Spanish as 'lordly' in behaviour and 'troublesome' in conversation. Addison thought young Frenchmen to be full of 'Fire and Levity' (*The Letters of Joseph Addison*, ed. Walter Graham (Oxford: Clarendon Press, 1941), p. 8). See John G. Hayman, 'Notions on National Characters in the Eighteenth Century', *HLQ*, 35 (1971), 1–17.

Preface 7–9. Salmon (1739 edn.) claims that 'the antient philosophers in the east were all poets' whose 'invention is fruitful and lively' and whose figures contain an 'abundance of hyperbole' (i. 398). Lonsdale points out earlier statements to the same effect in Thomas Rymer's 'Preface to the Translation of Rapin's *Reflections on Aristotle's Treatise of Poesie*' (Spingarn, ii. 165).

Preface 14, 16. Salmon, i. 367, describes Tauris as 'esteemed little inferior to Babylon it self, either for its antiquity or magnificence', and as 'a place of very great trade' (i. 375); among the richest commodities were silk and carpets.

Preface 19. The exploits of 'the great Shaw ABBAS' are recorded at some length by Salmon, i. 405–6. The king, 'having reigned about forty years, died anno 1628'. Collins's poet celebrates a king who, according to Salmon, 'somewhat above a hundred years ago, drove the Turks out of this part of Persia' (i. 375).

Preface 23–4. Cf. Salmon, i. 406: having succeeded to the throne in 1664, 'This Prince changed his name, and took that of SOLYMAN instead of SEFI. . . . he died on the 29th of July 1694, and was succeeded by his son Shaw Sultan HOSSEIN.'

I. Heading: 'TIME, *the* MORNING.' Collins's four pastorals, like Pope's, are set during the four stages of the day: morning, noon, evening, and night.

I. 30–2. Lonsdale claims that 'This revision may seem too clear and pointed to have been made by C. himself', but, apart from its revision away from the influence of Pope, the change also mirrors revisions in Thomson's *The Seasons* which would have been known to Collins. Cf. 'Summer', ll. 147–8:

> At thee the ruby lights its deepening glow,
> A bleeding radiance grateful to the view. (1727–38)

> At thee the ruby lights its deepening glow,
> And with a waving radiance inward flames. (1744)

Thomson's addition of a line in 1744 ('The lively diamond drinks thy purest rays', l. 142) is also closely paralleled in Collins's change.

I. 30 n. Cf. Salmon's account of the pearl-fishery in the Persian Gulf '. . . of which they are very jealous, it being reckoned the best in the world. . . . The pearl fishery lyes near the island of Baharem' (i. 369; see also i. 396).

I. 38. *Ermin*: 'The fellmongers and furriers put upon it little bits of Lombardy lambskin, which is noted for its shining black colour, the better to set off the whiteness of the ermine' (*Dict.*, quoting Trevoux).

I. 46. Collins's substitution of 'Immortal' for 'The fair-eyed' Truth may have been thought more acceptable for a male personification (Bronson, p. 85 n.).

II. 1 ff. Cf. Salmon's account of the desert regions of southern Persia: 'The winds blow over large sandy deserts, heated like an oven, and especially between the mountains, which reflect the heat from one side to the other, and there are no refreshing breezes or showers to cool the air, as there generally are near the line' (i. 368). Salmon also describes a suffocating 'pestilential blast'. Collins seems to ignore other sections of Salmon's history, however: 'People usually travel in this country with the caravan, consisting of four or five hundred camels, besides other beasts, and there is no place where they travel with greater security. . . . a traveller seldom meets with any difficulties but what are easily surmounted' (i. 381).

II. 3. *Cruise*: 'A small cup' (*Dict.*).

II. 4. *Scrip*: 'A small bag; a satchel' (*Dict.*).

II. 12. *strook*: 'The preterite of *strike*, used in poetry for *struck*' (*Dict.*).

II. 14. Cf. Salmon, i. 373: 'Schiras, or Sheraz, as we pronounce it . . . is usually reckoned the second city of the kingdom. It is the capital of the province of Fars, or the antient Persia.' Collins disregards Salmon's notice that 'There are no walls about the place.'

II. 37. *tempt*: used here, and in II. 67, to mean 'To try; to attempt' (*Dict.*). Collins uses the verb in its commoner sense in II. 35 and IV. 31.

II. 44. *Pride*: 'Ornament; show; decoration' (*Dict.*).

II. 51-8. Cf. Salmon, i. 394: 'In Hyrcania and Curdistan, the woody parts of the country, wild beasts abound, such as lions, tygers, leopards, wild-hogs, jackalls, &c.' These animals are not, however, creatures of the desert.

II. 61-4. Cf. Salmon, i. 394: 'That part of the country which lyes upon the Caspian or Hyrcanian sea is full of serpents, toads, scorpions, and other venomous insects. . . . Scorpions particularly there are of an immoderate size, whose sting is mortal, it is said, if proper remedies be not immediately applied, and at best a person stung by one of them is in such torture, that he becomes raving mad for some time.'

III. 1. Salmon (i. 367, 376) describes 'Tefflis, or Cala, the capital of Eastern Georgia', with its fourteen Christian churches, cathedral, and castle (perhaps the towers of Collins's line).

III. 5-6. Although Collins added these lines later, he could have found descriptions of the rice crops in Salmon, i. 390.

III. 15-18 (15 n.). Cf. Salmon, i. 392: 'about Ispahan and some other towns jonquils grow wild: they have also daffodils, lilies, violets and pinks in their season, and some flowers which last all the year round; but what they have the greatest quantity of are lilies and roses.'

III. 26. The absoluteness of the Persian monarchy is described by Salmon, i. 406–7.

IV. 8. *wild'ring*: to 'wilder' is 'To lose or puzzle in an unknown or pathless tract' (*Dict.*).

IV. 26. Salmon mentions the Persians' custom of destroying the countryside as they retreated, but no such practice on the part of their enemies; see i. 424.

IV. 31–8. Cf. Salmon, i. 381, who describes the reign of the Shah Hossein: 'This Prince chose to live an indolent unactive life among his women in the haram, leaving the administration of the government entirely to his ministers, who placed and displaced whom they saw fit, oppressed the subjects with taxes and impositions', etc. Salmon then chronicles the resulting Persian civil war and the invasions by Turks, Tartars, and Arabs. Collins, as Lonsdale suggests, may also have been influenced by a later passage (i. 421–2): 'The Persian Kings have given themselves up to a luxurious indolent life, and so neglected the discipline of their troops, as well as the government of the state, that we have seen a little despicable rebel undertake a march from the borders of Usbeck Tartary, six or seven hundred miles, with no more than five or six thousand men, depose the King, and make himself master of the capital city of the kingdom . . . and the Turk and Muscovite have seized those towns on the frontiers which lay next them.'

IV. 44–6. Cf. Salmon, i. 367: 'Erivan, or Irvan', lies in the province of Shirvan, 'upon the river Sargi, near the borders of Armenia'; Tarku is the capital of Dagistan; Aly lies near Tefflis and appears on the map of Persia facing i. 365.

IV. 51. Cf. Salmon, i. 391: 'Dates are reckoned one of the most delicious fruits in this country: they are no where so good as in Persia.'

AN EPISTLE: ADDREST TO SIR THOMAS HANMER, ON HIS EDITION OF SHAKESPEAR'S WORKS

Collins's *Verses Humbly Address'd to Sir Thomas Hanmer. On his Edition of Shakespear's Works. By a Gentleman of Oxford.* was published in December 1743 by M[ary] Cooper ('Price Six Pence.'). The poem was mentioned in the list of newly published books and pamphlets in the December issue of the *Gentleman's Magazine*, 13 (1743), 672. At the end of the poem Collins himself added the date-line 'Oxford, Dec. 3. 1743.' A much revised second edition of the poem, no longer anonymous ('By Mr. WILLIAM COLLINS, of *Magdalene*-College in OXFORD'), appeared on 9 May 1744. This later edition, published by both Robert Dodsley and Mrs Cooper, included his 'Song from Shake-spear's *Cymbelyne*', and sold for a shilling (Straus, p. 327).

Despite the ostensible occasion of the poem, its origins remain uncertain. Hanmer's stately six-volume edition of Shakespeare, published at the Claren-don Press in Oxford, was to be purchased by subscription only, and thus the details of its publication are vague. Hanmer had delivered his copy to the press in 1742 (Nichols, v. 589); the title-page to each volume was dated 1744, but the plays themselves were dated 1743 (vols. i–iv) and 1744 (vols. v–vi). The imprimatur was signed by the Vice-Chancellor of the University on 26 March 1744. It thus appears that Collins's *Verses* appeared before the edition it was meant to celebrate, perhaps while the poet was himself still in Oxford (he graduated on 18 November 1743). It is possible, as Lonsdale suggests, that Collins was either courting Hanmer's patronage as he left Oxford for London, or hoping that his role in an important Oxford event would bolster his chances for a fellowship there. If so, he was successful in neither enterprise.

Sir Thomas Hanmer (1677–1746), educated at Christ Church, had been Speaker of the House of Commons in 1714–15, where he played an important role in the Protestant succession on the death of Queen Anne. He later joined the Tory opposition, but upon the succession of George II in 1727 he retired to his country seat of Mildenhall in Sussex, devoting his remaining years to the edition of Shakespeare. As a dull celebrity, and through his quarrel with William Warburton, he gained a place as Montalto in the *Dunciad* of 1742–3 (iv. 105). His attitude towards the edition is revealed in a letter of October 1742:

As to my own particular, I have no aim to pursue in this affair: I propose neither honour, reward, or thanks, and should be very well pleased to have the books continue upon their shelf, in my own private closet. If it is thought they may be of use or pleasure to the publick, I am willing to part with them out of my hands, and to add, for the honour of Shakespeare, some decorations and embellishments at my own expence. It will be an unexpected pleasure to me, if they can be made in any degree profitable to the University, to which I shall always retain a gratitude, a regard, and reverence. (Quoted by Nichols, v. 589.)

Although the edition was handsomely printed, it suffered (like its pre-decessors) from arbitrary emendations and a lack of close textual collation. Samuel Johnson, in his *Miscellaneous Observations on the Tragedy of Macbeth: With Remarks on Sir T. H.'s Edition of Shakespear* (1745), declared that 'its pomp recommends it more than its accuracy' (Johnson, vii. 45); but later, in the 'Preface' to his edition (1765), he spoke of the editor as 'a man, in my opinion, eminently qualified by nature for such studies' (vii. 97). The print-ing of the 'Oxford Edition' was supervised by Joseph Smith, Provost of Queen's College, and Robert Shippen, Principal of Brasenose; its subscribers were largely from the University. Hanmer's was also the only edition be-tween Rowe's (1709) and Johnson's not to be printed by the firms of Tonson and Wellington, who considered this publication a piracy of literary property traditionally in their copyright. (See Giles E. Dawson, 'Warburton, Hanmer, and the 1745 Edition of Shakespeare', *SB*, 2 (1949–50), 35–48.)

Collins made substantial revisions for the second edition of his poem, but not enough to warrant a reading of the two versions as essentially different poems, nor to justify printing the editions separately (as Stone and Poole, and Arthur Johnston do). The original 160 lines were cut to 148, largely by omitting the fanciful description of the Isis, perhaps an indication of Collins's failure in finding preferment in Oxford. This omission enables the poem to fit more squarely into the genre of the verse epistle, and also tightens the construction of the traditional progress motif in the poem (see John R. Crider, 'Structure and Effect in Collins' Progress Poems', *SP*, 60 (1963), 57–72). Most of the other changes in the poem reflect Collins's attempt to clarify images, to free his lines of any unnecessary repetition of words, and often to revise his phrasing away from Pope's. Thus in l. 63, for instance, Collins substituted '*Smiles* and *Graces*' for 'Loves and Graces', which, in the 1743 edition, closely mirrored Pope's 'In these gay Thoughts the Loves and Graces shine' ('Epistle to Miss Blount, With the Works of Voiture', l. 1). And in l. 111 Collins substituted 'some free Design' for 'fair', which he had also used three lines later and in l. 148 of the 1743 edition. Two copies of the 1743 edition demonstrate Collins's immediate dissatisfaction with the 'fair Design': in copies in the Harvard and Folger libraries, 'fair' has been deleted and 'just' substituted above the word (apparently in Collins's hand). 'Just', however, had appeared three times in the first edition—and was to appear twice in the second—and thus the adjective finally settled upon was 'free'.

The two editions are remarkably close in their treatment of accidentals. Accidental variants were introduced into only seven lines of the second edition; four of these are reworked lines, and thus their accidentals seem to have been altered only as the substantives themselves were changed. It is uncertain, however, whether these changes in accidentals were made by the printer or by Collins himself. But such careful reproduction in the rest of the edition—to the extent of duplicating a mistakenly italic 's' in '*Maro's*' (l. 74) —suggests that Collins may have annotated a copy of the first edition and presented this to his publishers as copy for the second edition. A previously unknown letter by the antiquarian William Oldys suggests that 'Mr Collins' was in London by 22 February 1744 (five months earlier than previous evidence disclosed), and implies, in its description of his activities and 'Subscription', that he may have been in town even earlier (this letter is in the possession of Mrs Donald F. Hyde). Further evidence that Oldys is speaking of William Collins during his search for patronage is provided by an earlier, unknown advertisement for the second edition of Collins's verses to Hanmer (discovered by Mary Margaret Stewart): '*In a few Days will be publish'd, The* SECOND EDITION *of* AN Epistle to Sir THOMAS HANMER, on his Edition of Shakespear's Works. To which will be added a Song, from the

Cymbeline of the same Author. Printed for M. Cooper, in Pater-noster-Row'
(*Daily Advertiser*, Friday, 6 Apr. 1744). Both pieces of evidence indicate that
it is at least possible that Collins was in close touch with his publishers early
in 1744 and thus was able to assist in the preparation of the second edition
before its publication on 9 May.

The present text follows the first edition (*Verses*, referred to as *1743*) as
copy, and adopts the substantive revisions from the second edition (*An
Epistle*, referred to as *1744*). Because of the close similarity in accidentals
between the two editions, however, the present text virtually reproduces
1744. All variant readings from *1743* have been noted in the textual apparatus,
as well as variant accidental readings from *1744*. Substantive variants from
later editions of the poem have also been included in the textual notes.
Because Collins supplied two additional notes to the revised poem, the
devices indicating notes in *1744* have been adopted here for the sake of con-
sistency and clarity.

The formats of the two editions are as follows:

Verses (1743). 2⁰: A^1 B–C^2 D^1; *1–3* 4–12; *1* title, *2* blank, *3* 4–12 text.
Foxon C299; Williams, pp. 108–9; Rothschild 655.

An Epistle (1744). 2⁰: A–D^2; *1–2* 3–15 *16*; *1* title, *2* blank, 3–12 text, 13–15
'A Song from Shakespear's *Cymbelyne*', *16* blank. Foxon C300; Tinker 729;
Williams, p. 109; Rothschild 656.

Copies of both editions are rare; only the following have been located:

Verses: L, LVA-D, C, MH, DFo, Rothschild, Taylor.
An Epistle: LVA-D, CtY, MB, DFo, Rothschild, Ryskamp.

An Epistle was reprinted in Dodsley's *Collection* (1755), iv. 64–70, and in the
Poetical Calendar (1763). Lines 93–100 were included in Samuel Derrick's
Poetical Dictionary; or, The Beauties of the English Poets (1761), ii. 23, under the
heading 'Fancy' (accompanied by Theseus' speech from *A Midsummer Night's
Dream*, v. i). G. B. Hill, *Letters of Samuel Johnson* (1892), ii. 131 n., cites an
entry in *The Orders of the Delegates of the Clarendon Press*: 'February 8, 1769.
Mr. Collins's Copy of Verses to Sir. Thos. Hanmer to be inserted after the
Preface.' Collins's revised poem was included in this 'Second Edition' of
Hanmer (1770–1), edited by Thomas Hawkins.

In spite of his revisions for the 1744 edition, Collins's poem—a verse epistle
written in heroic couplets—continues to indicate the substantial influence of
Pope, and some of Collins's changes (especially in ll. 35–6) reveal the addi-
tional influence of Pope's revised *Dunciad* (1742–3). Collins's obvious sources
would have been the *Essay on Criticism* and the two important verse epistles
dealing with the sister arts, Dryden's 'To Sir Godfrey Kneller' and Pope's
'Epistle to Jervas'. Another probable model is Ben Jonson's 'To the Memory
of . . . Mr. William Shakespeare'. It is also important to note Lonsdale's dis-
covery that Collins, while recommending scenes from Shakespeare's plays as

subjects for future paintings, was at the same time drawing upon actual engravings of those scenes in Rowe's edition of 1709 (reprinted, with some new engravings by Du Guernier, in 1714). Some additional sources in Rowe's edition have been noted below.

1 ff. The Muse of the opening lines is the Muse of poetry in general, but in ll. 5–8 she is particularly the Muse of the youthful poet. Hanmer, by means of his edition of Shakespeare, acts as guardian to a Muse who is both blossoming in his care and yet hesitant about this youthful production.

9–16. These lines, more appropriate to a verse epistle, replace a much longer and more fanciful passage in the 1743 edition. Collins exaggerates the critical disregard of Shakespeare, perhaps as a compliment to Hanmer (cf. ll. 139–40). There had been three major editions of Shakespeare earlier in the century: by Rowe (1709), Pope (1725), and Theobald (1733).

10. *Science*: knowledge.

19. *Rage*: afflatus, poetic inspiration.

22. *Phædra*: the wife of Theseus, who (in Euripides' *Hippolytus*) is tortured by her love for her own stepson. Lonsdale suggests that 'C. would also know Racine's *Phèdre* (1671) and Edmund Smith's adaptation, *Phaedra and Hippolitus* (1707).'

23–4. As Collins's note points out, this is an allusion to Sophocles' *Oedipus Tyrannus*, in which the king discovers that he has murdered his father and married his mother. Cf. 'Ode to Fear', ll. 38–41.

27–34. Collins, while praising the comic dramatists Terence and Plautus, Roman successors to Greece's Menander, points out that no Roman tragedian was able to challenge the Greeks.

33. *Ilissus*: a river near Athens, hence Greek tragedy in general.

36. Goths, priests, and Vandals were commonly held to be medieval 'Learning's Foes'. Cf. Dryden, 'To the Earl of Roscommon', ll. 15–16: 'But *Italy*, reviving from the trance, / Of *Vandal*, *Goth*, and *Monkish* ignorance'; and Pope, *Essay on Criticism*, l. 692: 'And the *Monks* finish'd what the *Goths* begun', and the revised *Dunciad* (1742–3), especially iii. 83–112.

37 (n.). Julius II, Pope from 1503 to 1513, was the friend of both Raphael and Michelangelo. Cf. *Essay on Criticism*, ll. 697 ff., in which Pope describes the revival of the sister arts under the pontificate of Leo X. Collins's great historical project, for which he reputedly wrote an introduction, was described by James Hampton (*Poetical Calendar*, xii. 109) as a 'history of the revival of learning in Italy, under the pontificates of Julius II. and Leo X.'

each exiled Maid: the Muses.

38. *Cosmo*: Cosmo de' Medici (1389–1464), the great Florentine patron of the arts.

Etrurian Shade: Florence, on the banks of the Arno (l. 40), in old Etruria.

39–42. Collins's chronology is perhaps knowingly confused: the French troubadours emigrated to Italy in the early thirteenth century. Bronson suggests that Collins wished 'to pass directly, for purposes of contrast, from Provençal poetry to Shakspere' (p. 92 n.). Provençal poetry could be didactic or heroic, but Collins, here and in his 'Ode to Simplicity' (ll. 37–42), insists that 'Love was all [they] sung'.

48. *Tuscan*: Florence lies in modern Tuscany.

55. *Johnson*: Ben Jonson. The contrast with Shakespeare is a conventional one; cf. *Dunciad*, ii. 224: 'With Shakespear's nature, or with Johnson's art'.

57. *Fletcher*: John Fletcher (1579–1625), often a collaborator with Francis Beaumont. Fletcher is the next in order (l. 58) because he began writing for the stage a decade after Jonson.

63. *Smiles and Graces*: Collins revised away from Pope's 'In these gay Thoughts the Loves and Graces shine' ('Epistle to Miss Blount, With the Works of Voiture', l. 1).

63 n. See Dryden's 'The Grounds of Criticism in Tragedy', prefixed to *Troilus and Cressida* (1679): the excellency of Shakespeare was 'in the more manly passions; Fletcher's in the softer: Shakespeare writ better betwixt man and man; Fletcher, betwixt man and woman: consequently, the one described friendship better; the other love: yet Shakespeare taught Fletcher to write love' (Watson, i. 260).

67 n. *Hardy*: Alexandre Hardy (1569?–1630). See Fontenelle's *Vie de M. Corneille*, *Avec L'histoire Du Theatre François Jusqu'a Lui*, in *Œuvres* (Paris, 1742), iii. 73.

67–70. A conventional evaluation of French correctness; cf. *Essay on Criticism*, ll. 711–12: 'Thence Arts o'er all the *Northern World* advance; | But *Critic Learning* flourish'd most in *France*', and Collins's Fragment 1, in which he deplores the influence of France on the Restoration stage.

71 (n.). Pierre Corneille (1606–84) based his *La Mort de Pompée* on the *Pharsalia* of Lucan (A.D. 39–65), an epic poem on the war between Pompey and Caesar.

74. *Maro*: Virgil.

78. *the Manners*: 'General way of life; morals; habits' (*Dict.*); cf. Collins's 'The Manners'.

81. The battle of Agincourt was described in *Henry V* and depicted in Rowe's frontispiece to the play, vol. iii (1709).

83–92. The young Edward V was murdered with his brother in the Tower by his uncle, Richard III (formerly the Duke of Gloucester). In *Richard III*, v. iii, the king dreams that the ghosts of his victims appear before him, promising defeat at Bosworth Field on the following day. This scene is illustrated in the frontispiece to the play in Rowe's edition, vol. iv (1709), vol. v (1714).

87 n. Slightly misquoted from *Aeneid*, x. 503–4: 'Turno tempus erit . . .' ('To Turnus shall come the hour when for a great price will he long to have bought an unscathed Pallas').

90–1. 'Thy' in these lines refers to Edward.

96–8. Lonsdale points out that 'Fairies' and a 'circled Green' are depicted in the frontispiece to *A Midsummer Night's Dream* in Rowe's edition, vol. ii (1709, 1714); cf. also the frontispiece to *As You Like It*, vol. ii (1709), for Collins's 'rural Grove' and 'quiet Scene'.

100. *th' enchanted Isle*: a reference to *The Tempest*; in the adaptation by Dryden and Davenant (staged in 1667) the sub-title reads '*or The Enchanted Island*'.

113. *Lights*: 'The part of a picture which is drawn with bright colours, or in which the light is supposed to fall' (*Dict.*). Cf. Dryden, 'To Sir Godfrey Kneller', ll. 69–70: 'Where Light to Shades descending, plays, not strives; / Dyes by degrees, and by degrees revives.'

115–20 (115 n.). A reference to *Julius Caesar*, III. ii; this scene is depicted in the frontispiece to the play in Rowe's edition, vol. v (1709), vol. vi (1714).

121–32 (121 n.). A reference to *Coriolanus*, V. iii, a scene depicted in this manner in Rowe's edition, vol. iv (1709). Collins's note refers to Joseph Spence's *An Essay on Pope's 'Odyssey'* (1726), p. 84: 'And certainly what makes so beautiful a Figure in the finest Poets, might deserve the imitation of the best Painters. . . . If our *Shakespear* can give us the struggle of Passions in the Breast of *Coriolanus*, *Thornhill* might trace the same, and speak them as well with his Pencil.' (Sir James Thornhill (1675–1734) painted the cupola of St. Paul's; cf. Fragment 5, l. 16.)

137. The Sibyl wrote her prophecies on leaves which were disordered by the wind; see *Aeneid*, iii. 445–51, and vi. 75.

141–6. According to tradition, Pisistratus, tyrant of Athens, was responsible for collecting and ordering Homer's scattered works. See Cicero, *De Oratore*, iii. 137; and Sir William Temple, 'Of Poetry' (1690), in Spingarn, iii. 107, where the credit is bestowed upon Lycurgus.

A SONG FROM SHAKESPEAR'S *CYMBELYNE*

This poem was first published with *An Epistle: Addrest to Sir Thomas Hanmer* ('The Second Edition', 1744), pp. 13–15. The date of composition would thus presumably lie between the publication of the first edition of the verse epistle without the 'Song' (December 1743) and the publication of the second edition on 9 May 1744; but, as Lonsdale cautions, there is no factual evidence to support this conclusion. Echoes of James Hammond's *Love Elegies* (1743, published December 1742), which are recorded in the explanatory notes, may, however, suggest a *terminus a quo* for the poem.

The poem was reprinted under the title 'Elegiac Song' in the *Gentleman's Magazine*, 19 (Oct. 1749), 466–7. The variations were apparently the work of the editor, Edward Cave. Sir John Hawkins, in *The Life of Samuel Johnson, LL.D.* (1787), pp. 48–9, wrote of a visit to Cave:

I remember that, calling in on him once, he gave me to read the beautiful poem of

Collins, written for Shakespeare's Cymbeline, 'To fair Fidele's grassy tomb,' which, though adapted to a particular circumstance in the play, Cave was for inserting in his Magazine, without any reference to the subject: I told him it would lose of its beauty if it were so published: this he could not see; nor could he be convinced of the propriety of the name Fidele: he thought Pastora a better, and so printed it.

The text was restored to its original state (but with changes in accidentals) when the poem was reprinted in Dodsley's *Collection* (1755), iv. 71–2. The text of the poem's original publication in *An Epistle* is followed here as copy-text, and substantive variants are noted from contemporary editions.

As Woodhouse pointed out in 'Collins in the Eighteenth Century', *TLS* (16 Oct. 1930), p. 838, Collins's lyric enjoyed immense popularity later in the century. Thomas Arne set it to music in *The Second Volume of Lyric Harmony* (1746), and it later appeared in *Clio and Euterpe or British Harmony* (vol. ii, 1759, with variants), and in *The Vocal Magazine* (1781). The Harding Collection in the New Bodleian Library also lists its inclusion in *The Bullfinch* (1748). The *Vocal Enchantress* (1783) printed the variant 'glassy' for 'grassy' (l. 1), as did *Calliope: or, the Musical Miscellany* (1788), the *Edinburgh Musical Miscellany* (1792), and several later miscellanies. The poem was reprinted as 'To fairest Delia's grassy tomb' in *Elegies, Composed by William Jackson of Exeter* (1785). A later version of Arne's setting abbreviated the poem and rearranged the stanzas: see *A Second Set of Glees . . . Harmonized by Thomas Billington* (London, n.d.). A translation into Latin was printed in the *GM*, 73 (Sept. 1803), 860.

In a note to the text of *Cymbeline* in his 1765 edition of Shakespeare (vii. 358 n.), Samuel Johnson remarked: 'For the obsequies of *Fidele*, a song was written by my unhappy friend, Mr. *William Collins* of *Chichester*, a man of uncommon learning and abilities. I shall give it a place at the end in honour of his memory.' Johnson then printed the poem in vol. vii. 403–4. Dyce claimed that 'All succeeding editors of Shakespeare have followed his [Johnson's] example in subjoining it to the tragedy' (p. 194).

Cymbeline was 'adapted' by Thomas D'Urfey at Covent Garden in February 1737: 'Not Acted these Sixteen Years. Revis'd with Alterations.' By 1744, Arthur H. Scouten reports, only six Shakespearean plays had not been recently revived in their original form, *Cymbeline* among them. But in the autumn of 1744 the play was adapted by Theophilus Cibber, played to crowded houses in the New Haymarket, and 'Cibber followed this success by restoring the original *Cymbeline*' (Scouten, ed., *The London Stage, 1660–1800, Part 3: 1729–1747* (Carbondale: Southern Illinois Univ. Press, 1961), i. cli). Shakespeare's dirge for Imogen was set to music by Arne in a 1759 version of *Cymbeline* by William Hawkins. A later review of the play in the *London Chronicle*, 30 (28 Sept.–1 Oct. 1771), 316, suggests that Collins's dirge was also used in stage productions:

This piece [*Cymbeline*] was revived some years ago with great alterations, consisting chiefly of a removal of the most glaring absurdities, with respect to time and place, an omission of some characters and scenes not necessary to the general design . . . The learned and ingenious Mr. William Collins, of Chichester, wrote a very elegant song for the obsequies of *Fidele*, in the room of the old one, and we believe it was introduced on the revival of the piece, but is now omitted. We do not think the Managers blameable in this, as the performance of it must rather retard the action, for which reason, part of the old one is repeated by Guiderius and Arviragus with more propriety.

The context of Collins's poem is derived from *Cymbeline*, IV. ii, where the brother shepherds Guiderius and Arviragus lament the apparent death of Imogen, disguised as 'Fidele' and drugged by a powerful potion. Shakespeare's own dirge—'Fear no more the heat of the sun'—is the major source for the poem, but (as Lonsdale notes) Collins's dirge should also be viewed against Pope's influential 'Elegy to the Memory of an Unfortunate Lady' and Tickel's 'Colin and Lucy'.

3–4. Cf. *Cymbeline*, IV. ii. 218–20:

> With fairest flowers
> Whilst summer lasts and I live here, Fidele,
> I'll sweeten thy sad grave.

5–6, 9–10. Cf. *Cymbeline*, IV. ii. 276–9:

> No exorciser harm thee.
> Nor no witchcraft charm thee.
> Ghost unlaid forbear thee.
> Nothing ill come near thee.

11–12. Cf. *Cymbeline*, IV. ii. 217–18:

> With female fairies will his tomb be haunted,
> And worms will not come to thee.

13. Cf. *Cymbeline*, IV. ii. 224–9:

> The raddock would,
> With charitable bill (O bill, sore shaming
> Those rich-left heirs that let their fathers lie
> Without a monument!), bring thee all this,
> Yea, and furr'd moss besides. When flow'rs are none,
> To winter-ground thy corse—

The ruddock was another name for the robin; Lonsdale suggests the *Spectator*, No. 85, as an eighteenth-century source.

17–18. Cf. Hammond's *Love Elegies* (1743), xiii. 17–20:

> What Joy to hear the Tempest howl in vain,
> And clasp a fearful Mistress to my Breast?
> Or lull'd to Slumber by the beating Rain,
> Secure and happy sink at last to rest?

18. *cell*: 'Any small place of residence' (*Dict.*).

21–2. Cf. Hammond, *Love Elegies*, iii. 11–12.

> And, when thou dy'st, may not one Heart be griev'd,
> May not one Tear bedew the lonely Tomb.

23. Fidele 'will be loved until life ceases to exercise its power of bewitching us, until it releases us from its magic spell' (Johnston, p. 149 n.).

SONG. THE SENTIMENTS BORROWED FROM SHAKSPEARE

This Shakespearean imitation was first printed in the *Gentleman's Magazine*, 58 (Feb. 1788), 155. Its publication was pointed out by A. D. McKillop, 'A Bibliographical Note on Collins', *MLN*, 38 (1923), 184–5 (see also 'A Poem in the Collins Canon', *MLN*, 37 (1922), 181). The poem was preceded by the following introduction, signed 'C—T—O' and dated 2 February: 'In turning over your Magazine, for May, 1765, I observed a copy of most elegant verses by Collins, which are not to be found in any edition of his poems. The following lines are to the best of my knowledge in the same predicament, and I believe have never yet appeared in print.'

The correspondent was Henry Headley (1765–88), a former scholar of Trinity College, Oxford, a friend of Thomas Warton, and a frequent contributor to the *Gentleman's Magazine*. In 1786 Sir Herbert Croft wrote to the editor, John Nichols:

C. T. O., in your Magazine, I find, stands for *Coll. Trin. Oxon.* The author is Mr. Headly, of Trinity, who had published 'Invocation to Melancholy', and some Miscellaneous Poems, in 4to, a promising young man, but poetical from top to toe. The magnetism of Tom Warton draws many a youth into rhymes and loose stockings, who had better be thinking of prose and propriety; and so it is with his brother Joe. (John Nichols, *Illustrations of the Literary History of the Eighteenth Century* (1828), v. 210.)

Headley had mentioned Collins in his *Select Beauties of Ancient English Poetry* (1788) and had closely imitated the 'Ode to Evening' in his 'Invocation to Melancholy'.

The 'Song' was claimed for Headley himself, however, by his friend William Beloe in *The Sexagenarian* (1817), i. 178–9: 'A few specimens of this young man's taste and talents will be found in the Appendix, but the following Song, which is not printed with his works, seems to merit insertion here.' Beloe's claim has been supported by P. L. Carver, who argues that Headley may have mentioned Collins's name as a ruse to promote his own poem's publication; see *NQ*, 177 (1939), 272–4, and 180 (1941), 407–8, and *The Life of a Poet*, pp. 183–5. But Beloe's book was vigorously attacked in its own time by Samuel Parr, who had been Beloe's tutor (*Bibliotheca Parriana* (1827), p. 393), as well as in the *Monthly Review*, 85 (Feb. 1818), 203:

. . . were we to disprove all the 'questionable evidence' of these volumes, we must write two of equal magnitude; for we are persuaded that they contain scarcely a page which would not require refutation, if it were necessary, after the specimens already given, to spend more time on a book which for presumption, mis-statement, and malignity, has rarely within our knowledge been exceeded, or even equalled.

More recently Earl Wasserman has defended the attribution by arguing that if Headley were referring to himself, 'we should have to postulate an amazingly self-confident and arrogant young poet who, in 1788, could say, "If you consider an unpublished poem by Collins worthy of appearance in your columns, then here is one of mine which also, I believe, has not previously been published," as, in effect, Mr. Carver understands the letter to say' ('Collins's "Young Damon of the Vale is Dead"', NQ, 178 (1940), 194). Wasserman also notes that Henry Kett, who knew Headley more intimately than did Beloe, did not include this poem in his 1810 edition of Headley's *Select Beauties*, even though he did include the poem 'Sickness', which had also appeared anonymously. Considering the lengthy interval between the poem's appearance and that of Beloe's book, Beloe's general untrustworthiness, and the access that Headley may have had to Collins's unpublished material through his friend Thomas Warton, it seems reasonable to conclude with Wasserman that Headley's identity as the contributor to the *Gentleman's* merely explains why Beloe later made his error.

Moy Thomas, furthermore, added the following note in his edition of Collins (1858): 'A manuscript copy in the collection recently belonging to Mr. Upcott, and now in the British Museum, is headed, "Written by Collins when at Winchester School. From a Manuscript "' (p. 101 n.). Bronson, in his edition, wrote that a 'recent search at the British Museum by the present editor failed to discover any trace of such a manuscript' (p. 80), and the manuscript remains untraced to this day. Dyce, noting that the poem was not included in Park's *British Poets* (1805), but that it was apparently added in a later edition, informs us that 'Mr. Park (who inserted it on an additional leaf) observes to me, that he has now forgotten on what authority he gave it as the production of Collins, but that he must have been satisfied of its genuineness at the time he reprinted it, else he would not have done so' (p. 208).

Although the attribution to Collins cannot be conclusively proven, the evidence at hand—Headley's note, his access to Warton, and the mention of the manuscript—and Wasserman's argument point to its probability. The text of the *Gentleman's Magazine* (1788) is followed here as copy-text, and substantive variants have been noted from later printings: Beloe's *Sexagenarian* (1817, cited as *Beloe*); the *General Evening Post* (4–6 Mar. 1788); and the *Public Advertiser* (7 Mar. 1788). The poem is printed here with the similarly imitative 'Song from Shakespear's *Cymbelyne*', although Moy Thomas's note suggests an earlier date ('at Winchester School') and A. D. McKillop has suggested a later. McKillop, PQ, 36 (1957), 353, has linked the song with Fragment 10, another 'Damon' lyric (c. 1745–6), but it seems reasonable to associate this with the more easily datable poem from this period, and echoes from Hammond's *Love Elegies* (1743), recorded in the notes below, may support this earlier date.

Collins's editors have noted the probable source in Ophelia's mad-scene in *Hamlet*, IV. v, especially 'He is dead and gone, lady, / He is dead and gone', and Lonsdale also mentions the possible influence of David Mallet's popular *William and Margaret* (1723?).

3. Cf. Hammond, *Love Elegies*, iii. 23-4:

> Then Home returning drop the pious Tear,
> And bid the Turf lye easy on her Breast.

9-12. Cf. Hammond, *Love Elegies*, iii. 21-2:

> With flowry Garlands, each revolving Year
> Shall strow the Grave where Truth and Softness rest.

11-12. Dyce re-punctuates these lines:

> Bestrew'd the boy, like him to waste
> And wither in their prime.

15. *bell of peace*: Cf. '*some simpler Bell*' in 'The Bell of Arragon' (Lost Poems).

WRITTEN ON A PAPER, WHICH CONTAINED A PIECE OF BRIDE CAKE GIVEN TO THE AUTHOR BY A LADY

This poem was first printed in the *Gentleman's Magazine*, 35 (May 1765), 231, and ascribed to '*the late Mr* COLLINS'. This was noted by A. D. McKillop, 'A Bibliographical Note on Collins', *MLN*, 38 (1923), 184-5, who suggested that its publication in 1765 may have been prompted by 'the revival of interest in Collins occasioned by the appearance of Langhorne's edition in March of that year'. Bronson, following Dyce, had mistakenly ascribed the first appearance of the poem to George Pearch's *A Collection of Poems* (1768), ii. 46-7, a continuation of Dodsley's successful miscellany which included many of Collins's poems. The text printed here follows the *Gentleman's Magazine* as copy-text, and notes a substantive variant from Pearch.

The attribution to Collins has been challenged by Carver alone, *NQ*, 177 (1939), 274, who claimed that there were insufficient grounds for attribution; Carver, however, later retracted his objection in *The Life of a Poet*, p. 166 n. While the details of the poem's provenance and publication remain unknown, the poem may have been one of those occasional pieces mentioned by Collins's friend John Ragsdale in *The Reaper*, No. 26: 'I had formerly several scraps of his poetry, which were suddenly written on particular occasions, these I lent among our acquaintance, who were never civil enough to return them, and being then engaged in extensive business, I forgot to ask for them, and they are lost.'

There is likewise no evidence for dating the poem, but there is little reason to agree with Carver (*The Life of a Poet*, p. 167) that it was written in 1753 in connection with the wedding of Thomas Barrow, the 'cordial Youth' of the 'Ode to a Friend' (the 'Superstitions' ode). Carver cites this wedding as the only known occasion on which Collins might have written such a poem, but doubtless there were others that have not been recorded. The similarity of diction with several of the *Odes*, as well as with James Hammond's *Love Elegies* (1743), may safely place the poem in the period 1744-6.

The bride cake of the title refers to the practice of placing a slice of wedding cake under a pillow in order to dream of a lover, an old custom debunked in the *Spectator*, No. 597 (22 Sept. 1714):

A letter dated *September* the Ninth acquaints me, That the Writer being resolved to try his Fortune, had fasted all that Day; and that he might be sure of dreaming upon something at Night, procured an handsome Slice of Bride-Cake, which he placed very conveniently under his Pillow. In the Morning his Memory happened to fail him, and he could recollect nothing but an odd Fancy that he had eaten his Cake; which being found upon Search reduced to a few Crums, he is resolved to remember more of his Dreams another Time, believing from this that there may possibly be somewhat of Truth in them. (v. 41.)

6. *shepherd's*: i.e., the poet's.

9. *The Cypryan queen*: Venus, the 'fabled queen of love' of Collins's 'Sonnet'. See note to l. 14, below.

11-12. Lonsdale cites *Rape of the Lock*, iv. 84-6, for these 'manifestations of female temperament':

> Sighs, Sobs, and Passions, and the War of Tongues.
> A Vial next she fills with fainting Fears,
> Soft Sorrows, melting Griefs, and flowing Tears.

but also compare Hammond, *Love Elegies*, i. 41-4:

> Hence all the Blame that LOVE and VENUS bear,
> Hence Pleasure short, and Anguish ever long,
> Hence Tears and Sighs, and hence the peevish Fair.

14. According to one legend, Venus was born in Cyprus and travelled to Cythera (Hesiod, *Theogony*, 192-8); in another account she is said to have travelled to Paphos (Hesiod, *Homeric Hymns*, v. 58-9).

16. Bronson re-punctuates the end of this stanza with a semi-colon.

24. Cf. 'Ode to Evening', l. 2.

ODES ON SEVERAL DESCRIPTIVE AND ALLEGORIC SUBJECTS

Collins's major volume of poetry was published in December 1746. The details concerning this publication are not entirely clear, but the general background at least is known. In late spring of 1746 (probably 20-2 May),

Collins and Joseph Warton, his close friend and fellow student at both Winchester and Oxford, met at Guildford Races in Surrey. In a letter to his brother, Joseph described their projected joint venture:

Dear Tom,

You will wonder to see my name in an advertisement next week, so I thought I would apprize you of it. The case was this. Collins met me in Surrey, at Guildford Races, when I wrote out for him my Odes, and he likewise communicated some of his to me: and being both in very high spirits we took courage, resolved to join our forces, and to publish them immediately. I flatter myself that I shall lose no honour by this publication, because I believe these Odes, as they now stand, are infinitely the best things I ever wrote. You will see a very pretty one of Collins's, on the death of Colonel Ross before Tournay. It is addressed to a lady who was Ross's intimate acquaintance, and who by the way is Miss Bett Goddard. Collins is not to publish the Odes unless he gets ten guineas for them.

I returned from Milford last night, where I left Collins with my mother and sister, and he sets out to-day for London. I must now tell you that I have sent him your imitation of Horace's Blandusian Fountain, to be printed amongst ours, and which you shall own or not as you think proper. I would not have done this without your consent, but because I think it very poetically and correctly done, and will get you honour.

- - - - - - - - - - - - - - - - -

You will let me know what the Oxford critics say. (John Wooll, *Biographical Memoirs of the late Revd. Joseph Warton, D.D.*, pp. 14–15 n.)

Wooll describes this letter as 'Without a date of time or place', but the most likely date is after 20–2 May (when the most important of the Guildford Races were held), and in 1746 (as witnessed by the impatience of the two young writers to publish their work 'immediately'). The advertisement mentioned by Warton has never been located, and the joint venture—anticipating the collaborative format of the *Lyrical Ballads*—was at some point replaced by a decision that the two poets should submit their manuscripts to Robert Dodsley at the same time but separately.

It is uncertain why Dodsley agreed to publish Warton's volume of poems and not Collins's, but his choice proved to be a sound one. Warton's *Odes on Various Subjects* was published on 4 December 1746 (price one shilling and sixpence), and a second edition of the quarto volume had been called for by 9 January 1747. Collins's *Odes*, meanwhile, was published by Andrew Millar on 20 December 1746 (but was dated 1747, as was common with publications late in the year); it appeared in octavo format and sold for a shilling (*General Advertiser*, 20 Dec. 1746). In addition to the comparative difficulty of Collins's work, two other reasons why Dodsley may have been more sympathetic to Warton's poetry are suggested in a letter the publisher wrote to Thomas Warton on 29 January [1747], discussing Thomas's 'Pleasures of Melancholy': 'As to the Terms, I believe I shall rather chuse to print as I did your Brothers for so very few Poems sell, that it is very hazardous purchasing almost any thing' (BL Add. MS. 42560, f. 13). If the publication of poetry was thought to be this hazardous, the publisher may have felt that one venture at a time was called for; and Dodsley appears unlikely to have been sympathetic to Collins's intention 'not to publish the Odes unless he gets ten guineas for them'.

Little is known of Collins's acquaintance with his bookseller, although Millar was James Thomson's publisher and a member of the circle of friends which Collins was later to join. John Langhorne, in his edition of Collins's poetry (1765), pp. xi–xii, claimed that Millar, 'a favourer of genius, *when once it has made its way to fame*', published Collins's odes 'ON THE AUTHOR'S ACCOUNT.—He happened, indeed, to be in the right not to publish them on his own; for the sale was by no means successful; and hence it was that the author, conceiving a just indignation against a blind and tasteless age, burnt the remaining copies with his own hands.' This appears to be the first account of Collins's action, and it was corroborated by Ralph Griffiths, who reviewed Langhorne's edition in his *Monthly Review*, 32 (1765), 294. Griffiths disagreed, however, with Langhorne's description of the publication of the *Odes* by Millar:

[he] is here said to have warily publish'd them ON THE AUTHOR'S ACCOUNT. This we are assured, was by no means the case; for the bookseller actually *purchased* the copy, at a *very handsome price* (for those times) and, at his own expence and risk, did all in his power to introduce Mr. Collins to the notice of the Public. In this instance, therefore, Mr. Millar ought by no means to be pointed out as 'a favourer of genius, *when once it has made its way to fame.*'——The *sequel* of this little anecdote, is greatly to the honour of our Poet's memory.—At the time when he sold his Odes to Mr. Millar, his circumstances were too narrow to have allowed him to print them at his own expence; and the copy-money was then, to him, a considerable object. Afterwards, when he came to the possession of an easy fortune, by the death of his uncle, Colonel Martin,—he recollected that the publisher of his poems was a *loser* by them. His spirit was too great to submit to this circumstance, when he found himself enabled to do justice to his own delicacy; and therefore he desired his bookseller to balance the account of that unfortunate publication, declaring he himself would make good the deficiency: the bookseller readily acquiesced in the proposal, and gave up to Mr. Collins the remainder of the impression, which the generous, resentful Bard, immediately consigned to the flames.

Griffiths's account of the burning of the *Odes* appears to be trustworthy: he was an intimate of Dr William Rose, literary adviser to Millar (Nichols, iii. 386, 506). Langhorne, who was one of Griffiths's reviewers, removed his statement in later editions.

Collins's volume was entered in the ledger of the printer Henry Woodfall: 'Mr. Andrew Millar, Dr. Dec. 15, 1746. Mr. Collins's Odes, 8vo., No. 1000, 3 1/2 shts.' (P.T.P., 'Woodfall's Ledger, 1734–1747', *NQ*, 1st ser., 11 (1855), 419). The *Stationers' Registers*, ii (1746–73), f. 7, records the receipt of nine volumes from Millar on 19 December 1746.

The format of the *Odes* is as follows:

8°: A^2 B–G⁴ H²; *i–iv* 1 2–52; *i* title *ii* blank *iii* contents *iv* errata 1 2–52 text. Williams, p. 110; Rothschild 657; Tinker 730.

In spite of Collins's reputed burning of the remaining volumes, the book is not as rare as commonly thought. There appears to be at least one surviving presentation copy, a copy in its original marbled paper wrappers inscribed 'From the Author' and sold at Sotheby's on 8 November 1965 for £500. A copy in the Dyce collection (LVA-D) bears the inscription 'Mrs Mulso'.

Because several of the odes were later reprinted in collections of poetry, the copy-text for each ode has been determined separately in this edition and discussed in individual head-notes. In actual practice, however, the text of the *Odes* has proven to be the best choice of copy-text even for those poems printed in altered form in Dodsley's *A Collection of Poems* or his *Museum*, which imposed a rigid house-style on Collins's accidentals (for a full discussion, see Richard Wendorf, 'Robert Dodsley as Editor', *SB*, 31 (1978), 235–48). The dating of each poem is also discussed in the head-notes; the ordering of the odes follows Collins's scheme, which is not chronological. In several of the odes, the spacing between lines is irregular and occasionally misleading (in that it suggests the division of a poem into additional stanzas). But it appears that these gaps have no formal significance and, although they have been pointed out in the notes, they have not been retained in the text. No attempt has been made to alter inconsistencies in spelling, capitalization, or italicization in the 1747 *Odes*.

Considerable attention has been focused on the possibility that Collins did have a scheme in mind in ordering the odes in this volume. Thus S. Musgrove, 'The Theme of Collins's Odes', *NQ*, 185 (1943), 214–17, 253–5, has claimed that the book is about 'the nature of the True Poet', and that each poem is 'descriptive of one of the qualities or circumstances essential to the attainment of the Poet's true stature'. And Ricardo Quintana, 'The Scheme of Collins's *Odes on Several . . . Subjects*', in *Restoration and Eighteenth-Century Literature*, ed. Carroll Camden (Chicago: Univ. of Chicago Press, 1963), pp. 371–80, has elaborated this argument by pointing out the volume's division of poems into those 'exploring the resources of poetry' and those patriotic odes 'expressing the hopes and desires of a civilized community'. This division had also been noticed by H. W. Garrod who, in *Collins* (1928), pp. 46–7, suggested that 'The *Ode to Peace* betrays by a false catchword that it has been misplaced; and, the catchword apart, it quite clearly belongs to the series of Odes of patriotic theme which forms the central section of the volume of 1746: the continuity of this section is interrupted by the *Ode to Evening*.' Plausible as this suggestion is (and although the catchword at the foot of p. 40 should read 'The' instead of 'Ode'), there is no other evidence to support a mistaken ordering here. Lonsdale, moreover, has suggested that the 'Ode to Evening' may have been given its position in the volume in order to maintain a scheme in which 'no two poems with the same metrical form are juxtaposed' (p. 413).

While Collins appears to have had some thematic scheme in mind, his title also specifies that the odes are based on 'Several Descriptive and Allegoric

Subjects'. Johnson defined 'several' in this context as 'Different; distinct; unlike one another', and it was this use of the word which Collins was surely familiar with in the titles of Milton's *Poems, &c. upon Several Occasions* (1673) and Akenside's *Odes on Several Subjects* (1745). Similarly, Warton entitled his volume *Odes on Various Subjects*, and his poems, like Akenside's, cover a broad range of topics. Langhorne attempted to define Collins's descriptive and 'allegorical imagery' in his edition (1765), pp. 137–46, where he noted that both description and allegory were rooted in the sister art of painting. See also A. S. P. Woodhouse, 'Collins and the Creative Imagination', pp. 59–130, and 'The Poetry of Collins Reconsidered', in *From Sensibility to Romanticism*, ed. F. W. Hilles and Harold Bloom (New York: Oxford Univ. Press, 1965), pp. 93–137; and Quintana's study, cited above.

Our only account of the composition of the odes is that by John Ragsdale in *The Reaper*, No. 26:

To raise a present subsistence he set about writing his *Odes*, and having a general invitation to my house, he frequently passed whole days there, which he employed in writing them, and as frequently burning what he had written, after reading them to me. Many of them which *pleased me*, I struggled to preserve, but without effect; for pretending he would alter them, he got them from me and thrust them into the fire.

And William Hymers, in a note in his annotated edition of Langhorne, p. 194, wrote in 1783: 'On what occasion was it ['The Manners'] written? Mr Ragsdale will inform me—Many of the Odes were written at his house—' Although there is no surviving manuscript of any of these poems, Thomas Warton remarked that he had seen all of Collins's odes 'in his own hand-writing, they had the marks of repeated correction: He was perpetually changing his Epithets.—I had lately his first manuscript of the *Ode on the Death of Colonel Ross*, with many interlineations and alterations' (*The Reaper*, No. 26).

The publication of the *Odes* seems to have raised little comment except from Thomas Gray who, writing to his friend Thomas Wharton (*Correspondence*, i. 261), asked:

Have you seen the Works of two young Authors, a Mr Warton & a Mr Collins, both Writers of Odes? it is odd enough, but each is the half of a considerable Man, & one the Counter-Part of the other. the first has but little Invention, very poetical choice of Expression, & a good Ear. the second, a fine Fancy, model'd upon the Antique, a bad Ear, great Variety of Words, & Images with no Choice at all. they both deserve to last some Years, but will not.

And in the *Gray's Inn Journal*, 62 (23 Dec. 1753), 2nd edn., 1756, Arthur Murphy wrote that 'a Treatise on *Cribbidge*, or a Calculation of the Chances at Whist, is sure of being better received at present, than the Odes of a *Collins*, or any Performance of distinguished Genius.' Joseph Warton noted in his edition of Pope's *Works* (1797), ii. 345–6, that Collins believed his own poems to be ridiculed in the parodic 'Ode to Horror. In the Allegoric, Descriptive, Alliterative, Epithetical, Fantastic, Hyperbolical, and Diabolical Style of our modern Ode-Wrights, and Monody-Mongers', a poem first published in *The Student* (1751), ii. 313-15, and possibly by Thomas Warton himself (see A. S. P. Woodhouse, 'Thomas Warton and the "Ode to Horror"', *TLS* (24 Jan. 1929), p. 62; (23 May 1929), p. 420).

It is difficult to determine how much influence Joseph Warton's odes had on Collins's; according to Warton's letter to his brother, he had written out his odes for his friend at the races and had sent him a copy of one of Thomas's poems. Collins, in turn, 'communicated some of his' own to Warton, and this suggests that Collins, before May/June 1746, had already written more than his 'Ode, to a Lady', the only poem mentioned in Warton's letter. But without more precise knowledge of which poems the two authors showed each other, the question of influence (and dating) remains vexed. For a discussion of the possible influence of Warton's ode 'To Fancy' on Collins's volume, see the introduction to his *Odes on Various Subjects*, ed. Richard Wendorf (Los Angeles: Augustan Reprint Society, 1979). Later in the decade Warton borrowed at least once from Collins's work in rewriting (and often writing) his father's posthumous poems; see David Fairer, 'The Poems of Thomas Warton the Elder?', *RES*, n.s., 26 (1975), 287-300, 395-406; n.s., 29 (1978), 61-5.

Joseph Warton prefixed the following 'Advertisement' to his own publication, which appears to be applicable to his friend's volume as well:

The Public has been so much accustom'd of late to didactic Poetry alone, and Essays on moral Subjects, that any work where the imagination is much indulged, will perhaps not be relished or regarded. The author therefore of these pieces is in some pain least certain austere critics should think them too fanciful and descriptive. But as he is convinced that the fashion of moralizing in verse has been carried too far, and as he looks upon Invention and Imagination to be the chief faculties of a Poet, so he will be happy if the following Odes may be look'd upon as an attempt to bring back Poetry into its right channel.

The motto Collins chose for his own volume is from Pindar's *Olympian Odes*, ix. 80-3: 'Would I could find me words as I move onward as a bearer of good gifts in the Muses' car; would I might be attended by Daring and by all-embracing Power!' (for a discussion of the epigraph, see Musgrove's article, cited above). The emblem below the epigraph on the title-page, engraved by Van der Gucht, had been previously used by Millar in editions of Thomson's *The Seasons*; see the *Book Collector*, 1 (1952), 195; 2 (1953), 157.

Ode to Pity

The dating of this and the following two odes, often considered its companion pieces on Greek drama, rests largely on Collins's projected translation of and commentary on Aristotle's *Poetics*, itself an enterprise of uncertain date. Johnson, in his *Life of Collins*, relates that he was one day 'admitted to him when he was immured by a bailiff that was prowling in the street. On this

occasion recourse was had to the booksellers, who, on the credit of a trans-
lation of Aristotle's *Poeticks*, which he engaged to write with a large com-
mentary, advanced as much money as enabled him to escape into the country.
He shewed me the guineas safe in his hand' (*Lives*, iii. 336).

A similar incident is related by Collins's friend John Mulso in a letter
dated 28 May 1746:

I can't help telling You, tho' tis a little uncharitable, that Collins appears in good
cloaths & a wretched carcass, at all ye gay Places, tho' it was with ye utmost Diffi-
culty that He scrap'd together 5 pound for Miss Bundy at whose Suit He was
arrested & whom by his own confession He never intended to pay. I don't beleive
He will tell ye Story in Verse, tho' some circumstances of his taking would be bur-
lesque enough. The Bailiff introduc'd himself with 4 Gentlemen who came to drink
Tea, & who all together could raise but one Guinea. The ἀναγνώρισις (a word He is
fond of) was quite striking & ye catastrophe quite poetical and interesting. (*Letters
to Gilbert White of Selborne from . . . the Rev. John Mulso*, ed. R. Holt-White [1907],
p. 14.)

Although Sigworth (pp. 40–2) assigns these incidents to different years—1745
and 1746—there is good reason to believe that the two accounts describe
the same embarrassing situation at Miss Bundy's house, and Collins's refer-
ence to the Aristotelian 'anagnorisis' (recognition scene) and 'catastrophe'
strengthens this conclusion. It therefore appears that the most probable
period in which Collins would have been composing odes to Pity and Fear
(the two emotions Aristotle claimed were aroused and purged in tragedy),
as well as to Simplicity, would have been *c.* May 1746. Joseph Warton's
account of their joint venture projected at Guildford Races is contemporary
with Mulso's letter, and the races may have been one of the 'gay Places' to
which Mulso refers. Again, it seems probable that Collins, in agreeing to the
venture, would have had other poems besides his 'Ode, to a Lady' in mind,
if not already down on paper.

Thomas Warton claimed that 'In the *Ode to Pity*, the idea of a *Temple* of
Pity, of its situation, construction, and groupes of painting, with which its
walls were decorated, was borrowed from a Poem, now lost, entitled, the
Temple of Pity, written by my brother, while he and Collins were school-
fellows at Winchester College' (*The Reaper*, No. 26). Warton's account of the
poem is confirmed by J. S. Cunningham, 'Thomas Warton and William
Collins: A Footnote', *Durham University Journal*, 46 (1953), 22–4). Joseph,
moreover, in a letter of March/April 1745, told his brother: 'You know I had
entirely laid aside the Temple of Pity: but I have now begun to write an Ode
to Pity: which I will make as correct as I can' (BL Add. MS. 42560, f. 4).
Thomas replied enthusiastically: 'I am glad you have laid aside the Temple of
Pity, for that of writing an ode to it, in which you may not only mention her
temple with all its' attendants, but likewise bring in several of the unfortunate
Characters' (BL Add. MS. 42560, f. 5). At the foot of this letter, dated 19
April [1745], Joseph then wrote out a fragment of his intended ode, beginning

'Daughter of pining, pale-ey'd Woe'. A rough draft of this poem, apparently unnoticed in one of Joseph's notebooks at Trinity College, Oxford, indicates that Joseph did in fact take his brother's advice, especially in his survey of human misery (Thomas's 'unfortunate Characters'). But this ode, entitled 'To Pity' and filling five heavily-revised pages, seems to bear little resemblance to Collins's poem.

Lonsdale has also pointed out that 'Joseph Warton's lost poem, as described by Thomas, bears a suspicious resemblance to a fragment of a poem quoted by John Wooll, in his *Memoirs of Joseph Warton* (1806), pp. 91–95, describing the "Temple of Love", which may well have been the work Thomas had in mind and which, in a general way, probably did influence C.' (p. 415). It should be noted, however, that Collins could have drawn upon numerous sources for Pity's temple, especially Pope's 'Temple of Fame' (see the Twickenham Pope, ii. 209–13, for a discussion of the popularity of temple poems, and the note to ll. 27–36 below). Pity, moreover, would have been associated by Collins's readers with their contemporary regard for compassion and benevolence as well as with the Aristotelian notion of catharsis in drama. See the account of the good Samaritan in Luke 10: 25–37 (the source for both *Joseph Andrews*, i. xii, and Sterne's sermon on philanthropy), and the *Spectator*, No. 397 (Addison) and No. 588 (Henry Grove). The 'Ode to Pity' was set to music by Callcott (1785?).

7 (n.). Euripides died at Pella, the ancient capital of Macedonia. Collins's note refers to *Poetics*, xiii. 10, where Aristotle claims that Euripides is 'certainly the most tragic of the poets'. The implicit 'Comparison' with Sophocles lies in Aristotle's juxtaposed remarks on Oedipus (xiii. 5, and xiv. 2).

14. *Ilissus*: a river running near Athens, where Euripides' tragedies were performed. Cf. *An Epistle: Addrest to Sir Thomas Hanmer*, l. 33.

16 (n.). Thomas Otway (1652–85) was, like Collins, a native of Sussex (the village of Trotton), a Wykehamist, and an Oxonian. 'W.C.' and 'J.W.', apparently Collins and Joseph Warton, erected a monument to the dramatist in the Sixth Chamber at Winchester College. Collins also mentions Otway in Fragment 1, ll. 15–16, and Fragment 10, ll. 25–30. Collins's opinion that Otway was 'unspoil'd by Art' (l. 23) is consistent with Johnson in his 'Life of Otway': he 'conceived forcibly and drew originally by consulting nature in his own breast' (*Lives*, i. 246).

19. *Wren*: sometimes associated with pity, as in Shakespeare, *Cymbeline*, IV. ii. 303–5: 'if there be / Yet left in heaven as small a drop of pity / As a wren's eye.'

Myrtles: sacred to the goddess of love and used for wreaths for bloodless victors.

21. *Cell*: 'The cave or little habitation of a religious person' (*Dict.*).

24. *Thy Turtles*: 'The turtle dove, the bird of Venus by reason of its talent in courtship, may also be claimed by Pity for its gentleness. Collins is creating

a new Pantheon in these odes, and his deified abstractions perforce filch from the old gods' (Bronson, p. 97 n.).

27–36. Thomas Warton claimed his brother Joseph's 'Temple of Pity' as the inspiration for these lines (see head-note). But compare Pope's 'Temple of Fame' (ll. 178–243), in which 'pompous Columns' illustrate scenes from prominent classical authors. The southern site of Pope's temple describes the priests of Egypt (ll. 109–18); in describing the 'Southern Site' of Pity's temple, designed to raise a 'wild Enthusiast Heat', Collins may have been echoing his remarks on the Persian philosopher-poets in *Oriental Eclogues*, 'Preface', ll. 7–10.

27. *Pride*: 'Ornament' or 'Splendour' (*Dict.*).

34. *Buskin'd Muse*: the Muse of Tragedy, whose buskins were the high shoes worn 'by the ancient actors of tragedy, to raise their stature' (*Dict.*).

39. The conclusion here and in the 'Ode to Fear' is modelled on 'Il Penseroso', ll. 175–6 ('These pleasures *Melancholy* give, / And I with thee will choose to live'), and 'L'Allegro', ll. 151–2 ('These delights, if thou canst give, / Mirth with thee, I mean to live').

42. *Shell*: 'used for a musical instrument in poetry . . . the first lyre being said to have been made by straining strings over the shell of a tortoise' (*Dict.*). See Benjamin Boyce, 'Sounding Shells and Little Prattlers in the Mid-Eighteenth-Century Ode', *ECS*, 8 (1975), 245–64.

Ode to Fear

For an approximate dating of this poem *c.* May 1746, see the head-note to the preceding ode. A. S. P. Woodhouse, 'Collins in the Eighteenth Century', *TLS* (16 Oct. 1930), p. 838, points out that the poem was set to music by William Lindley in 1800. Arthur Johnston, in his edition of Collins (p. 154), remarks that 'Collins does not accurately repeat the metrical pattern of the strophe in the antistrophe; in place of l. 9 he substitutes, at ll. 54–55, a couplet.' It is possible that a line was dropped before or after l. 9, thus shortening the strophe to 25 lines while the antistrophe comprises 26 (this was first pointed out by Garrod, *Collins* (1928), p. 58). Odes of similar construction ('Poetical Character', 'Mercy', and 'Liberty') have a strophe and antistrophe of equal length. No copy of the *Odes*, however, contains any written additions at this point in the 'Ode to Fear'.

16–19. Woodhouse, 'Collins and the Creative Imagination', p. 105 n., suggests as a source the spirits who 'dwell in the elements and preside over storm and earthquake as well as over human violence' in Thomas Nashe's *Pierce Penniless his Supplication to the Devil*, an Elizabethan pamphlet which Collins might have known. For this entire section of the poem (ll. 9–23),

Arthur Johnston (p. 155 n.) singles out Robert Burton's treatment of the 'objects that, traditionally, are thought to produce terror' in the *Anatomy of Melancholy*, ed. H. Jackson (London: Dent, 1932), Pt. 1, Sec. 2, Mem. 4, Subsec. 3; and Pt. 1, Sec. 3, Mem. 1, Subsec. 2. For a possible visual source, see the frontispiece to *The Tempest* in Rowe's edition of Shakespeare (1709), vol. i.

22 (n.). Collins quotes from the chorus in *Electra*, ll. 1385–8: 'Breathing out blood and vengeance, lo! / Stalks Ares, sure though slow. / E'en now the hounds are on the trail; / Within, the sinners at their coming quail.' Bronson conjectures that Collins changed the order and case of the Greek words in order to adapt the phrase into the grammar of his English sentence.

26–45. *EPODE*: 'The epode should have been called a mesode, as it comes between strophe and antistrophe instead of after the latter. In the extant odes of Pindar there are no mesodes, but they sometimes occur in the choral odes of the Greek dramas' (Bronson, pp. lxix–lxx).

30–3 (30 n.). Aeschylus (525–456 B.C.) fought at the battle of Marathon in 490 B.C.

34. *He*: Sophocles (496–406 B.C.), a generation younger than Aeschylus.

35. *Hybla*: a city and mountain in Sicily, famous for its thyme, flowers, and honey. Sophocles was called 'the Attic bee' because of the sweetness of his verse.

37. *baleful Grove*: the scene of *Oedipus at Colonus* is the entrance to a grove dedicated to the Furies (Eumenides). Collins seems to be mistakenly suggesting that this was the harshest of Sophocles' plays. See also Michael Gearin-Tosh, 'Obscurity in William Collins', *Studia Neophilologica*, 42 (1970), 30–2.

38–41 (38 n.). In his note Collins quotes from *Oedipus at Colonus*: ll. 1621–5: '[but when at last] / Their mourning had an end and no wail rose, / A moment there was silence; suddenly / A voice that summoned him; with sudden dread / The hair of all stood up and all were 'mazed.' The 'sad Call' was in fact one of many, and not from Jocasta (Oedipus' wife and mother) but from the god, who spoke out of a thunderstorm (Collins's 'cloudy Veil').

47. Strutt (1796), p. 11 n., suggested that 'Io, and her miseries, . . . seem to have been the prototype of the distresses of this fugitive nymph'; cf. Aeschylus, *Prometheus Bound*, ll. 561–5.

48. *shroud*: 'To harbour; to take shelter' (*Dict.*).

50–1. In the *Odes* these lines are not indented to match ll. 5–6.

55. *awak'ning Bards*: i.e., poets who arouse their listeners; cf. 'The Passions', l. 83.

56. *my blasted View*: Johnson defines 'blast' in this sense as 'To confound; to strike with terrour' (*Dict.*).

59. *that thrice-hallow'd Eve*: numerous dates have been suggested for this night, which is probably Hallowe'en, 31 October, 'when fairies, imps, and witches are supposed to be especially active' (Bronson, p. 99 n.). But cf. Langhorne, p. 154 (St. Mark's Eve, 24 April); Mrs Barbauld, p. xxi, and

Dyce, p. 173 (Midsummer Eve or St. John's Eve, 23 June); and Crowe, p. 23 (Christmas Eve). Arthur Johnston further suggests that 31 October is 'thrice-hallow'd' because 'it is the day of three saints, St. Quintin, St. Foillan and St. Wolfgang' (p. 158 n.).

68. *Fury*: both fear and inspiration (Collins also uses 'Rage' in this sense).

70. *Cypress Wreath*: the traditional crown for a tragic poet.

71. Collins's conclusion here, as in the 'Ode to Pity', is modelled on 'L'Allegro', ll. 151–2, and 'Il Penseroso', ll. 175 6.

Ode to Simplicity

This poem is linked to the previous two odes by a similarity of literary subject and by its reference to Sophocles in l. 18 (there are additional Greek references in ll. 11, 14, and 19), as well as by its placement immediately after them in Collins's volume. Dating, however, remains tentative: the most reasonable period seems to be the spring or summer of 1746, when Collins was promising his edition of the *Poetics* and presumably composing the odes to Pity and Fear. Lonsdale has suggested a *terminus a quo* of July 1744, when a revised edition of Thomson's *The Seasons* included the first recorded use of the word 'unboastful'. Collins's ode adopts the word (l. 12), as does the fragment 'To Simplicity' (ll. 29, 31), which appears to be a draft of the final ode and with which it should be compared.

'Simplicity', Joseph Warton wrote in No. 26 of the *World* (28 June 1753), 'is with justice esteemed a supreme excellence in all the performances of art, because by this quality they more nearly resemble the productions of nature: and the productions of nature have ever been accounted nobler, and of a higher order, in proportion to their SIMPLICITY' (1782 edn., i. 159–60). In addition to its affinity with nature (which Collins reflects in his opening and closing lines), simplicity was associated with unity, clarity, elegance, and universality in literature (especially classical literature). See Raymond D. Havens, 'Simplicity, A Changing Concept', *Journal of the History of Ideas*, 14 (1953), 3–32; and John R. Crider, 'Structure and Effect in Collins' Progress Poems', *SP*, 60 (1963), 62–9.

5–6. Fancy is the child of either Simplicity or Pleasure, although Langhorne's emendation makes Fancy the offspring of their union. Cf. *Guardian*, No. 22 (6 Apr. 1713) on the first age of the world: 'it was a State of Ease, Innocence and Contentment; where Plenty begot Pleasure, and Pleasure begot Singing, and Singing begot Poetry, and Poetry begot Pleasure again' (quoted by Crider, p. 66; see head-note).

9. *Gauds*: a gaud is 'An ornament; a fine thing' (*Dict.*).

10. *decent*: 'Becoming; fit; suitable' (*Dict.*).

14. *Hybla*: see the note to 'Ode to Fear', l. 35.

16 (n.). Cf. Sophocles' *Oedipus at Colonus*, ll. 668–93, describing 'the haunt of the clear-voiced nightingale, / Who hid in her bower, among / The wine-dark ivy that wreathes the vale, / Trilleth her ceaseless song'.

18. *Electra's Poet*: although Milton spoke of Euripides as 'sad *Electra's* Poet' (Sonnet VIII, l. 13), Collins refers to Sophocles, who described the nightingale in his *Electra*, ll. 147–9.

19. *Cephisus*: because there were at least two major Greek rivers known by this name, Collins's reference has caused some confusion among his commentators. One river Cephisus ran near Athens, and was mentioned in Sophocles' description of the nightingale's bower (*Oedipus at Colonus*, l. 687; see the note to l. 16). The other river Cephisus, to which Collins apparently refers here, ran through Phocis and Boeotia and was the site of the battle of Chaeronea (338 B.C.) in which Philip of Macedon ended the independence of Thebes and Athens. Cf. Milton, Sonnet X, ll. 6–7: 'that dishonest victory / At *Chæronéa*, fatal to liberty'. The Boeotian Cephisus was a favorite haunt of the Graces, and thus would have provided Simplicity with a 'green Retreat' (l. 21).

20. *Sweep*: 'The compass of any violent or continued motion' (*Dict.*), hence the river's motion or course.

22. *enamel'd*: 'variegated with colours inlaid' (*Dict.*, s.v. 'Enamel').

26. *To*: into.

27. *native*: artless, 'natural' (*Dict.*).

31. *While*: as long as.

34. *staid*: ceased (*OED*, s.v. 'Stay', 2b).

35. *one distinguish'd Throne*: that of Augustus, whose emperorship succeeded the Roman Republic. Cf. Sir WilliamTemple, 'Of Poetry': '*Augustus* was not only a Patron, but a Friend and Companion of *Virgil* and *Horace*, and was himself both an Admirer of Poetry and a pretender too, as far as his Genius would reach or his busy Scene allow. 'Tis true, since his Age we have few such Examples of great Princes favouring or affecting Poetry, and as few perhaps of great Poets deserving it' (Spingarn, iii. 107–8).

39. *her*: Collins continues to refer to Rome (or Italy), but now to her medieval or modern literature; cf. *An Epistle: Addrest to Sir Thomas Hanmer*, ll. 40–4.

Ode on the Poetical Character

Although there is no external evidence for dating this ode, its marked boldness argues for a relatively late date, probably in 1746. It is possible, as Lonsdale points out, that occasional echoes of Akenside's *The Pleasures of Imagination* (January 1744) and *Odes* (March 1745) may suggest a *terminus a quo* for the poem, but in fact these echoes are much fainter than those of

Spenser and Milton. For a stimulating discussion of Milton's influence on the poem, see Earl Wasserman, 'Collins' "Ode on the Poetical Character"', *ELH*, 34 (1967), 92–115.

1–16 (5 n.). Spenser described the cestus of Venus in the *Faerie Queene*, IV. v. 3. 1–5: 'That girdle gaue the vertue of chast loue, / And wiuehood true, to all that did it beare; / But whosoeuer contrarie doth proue, / Might not the same about her middle weare, / But it would loose, or else a sunder teare.' Florimel's loss of the girdle is described in *F.Q.*, III. vii. 31, and III. viii. 2, 49; the competition for the girdle is mentioned in IV. ii. 25–7, and described in IV. v. 1–20. Amoret assumes the girdle only briefly in Book IV (although Collins specifies Florimel in his note, she was not present at the competition). The false Florimel, who won the competition, wore the girdle until she melted (v. iii. 24–5), after which it was placed on the true Florimel, its rightful owner (v. iii. 27–8). Cf. also *Iliad*, XIV. 214–21.

1. *Regard*: attention.

4. *Elfin Queen*: Spenser describes her thus in *F.Q.*, II. i. 1. 6.

8–9. In the *Odes* there is a slight gap between these lines which has not been reproduced here (see the general head-note to the *Odes*).

9. *applied*: brought into contact.

12. *Band*: the girdle.

16. *Zone*: 'A girdle' (*Dict.*).

19. *Cest*: 'The girdle of Venus' (*Dict.*, s.v. '*CESTUS*').

22. *gaze*: gaze upon.

24. *that creating Day*: here, the fourth day of Creation. See Genesis 1: 14–19, and *Paradise Lost*, vii. 339–56 (describing the creation of the sun).

26. *tented*: 'Formed or shaped like a tent or pavilion' (the first recorded usage under this definition in the *OED*).

laughing: '[In poetry.] To appear gay, favourable, pleasant, or fertile' (*Dict.*, s.v. 'Laugh').

27. *drest*: adorned, embellished.

29. *Enthusiast*: Fancy. Wasserman (see head-note) suggests that the model for Collins's Fancy is the female figure of Wisdom ('Sapientia') pictured in Proverbs (8: 22–30), and in the apocryphal Ecclesiasticus (1: 1–10) and Wisdom of Solomon (Wisdom 8: 3). Wasserman and Lonsdale also suggest prototypes in Spenser's 'Hymne of Heavenly Beautie', ll. 183–266 ('Sapience'), and in Milton's *Paradise Lost*, vii. 8–12. The etymology of 'enthusiasm' corroborates Collins's suggestions of both poetic and divine inspiration (cf. l. 74).

32–4. Collins appears to be modelling God's throne on Ezekiel 1:26 and 10:1, and Milton's 'At a solemn Musick', ll. 7–13.

37. Cf. Jocasta's 'cloudy Veil' ('Ode to Fear', l. 38).

38. For the punctuation here, see the following note.

39. *rich-hair'd Youth of Morn*: the sun. Cf. 'bright-hair'd Sun' in the 'Ode

to Evening', l. 5, and Spenser's description in the *Faerie Queene*, I. v. 2. 3–5: 'And *Phœbus* fresh, as bridegrome to his mate, / Came dauncing forth, shaking his deawie haire: / And hurld his glistring beames through gloomy aire.' The sun is associated here both with God's creation of the universe and with his creation of the poet's cestus (Apollo was the god of prophecy, poetry, and music). Cf. Sir William Temple, 'Of Poetry', who, writing of Apollo, speaks of 'that Cœlestial Fire which gave such a pleasing Motion and Agitation to the minds of those Men that have been so much admired in the World, that raises such infinite images of things so agreeable and delightful to Mankind. . . . [it] is agreed by all to be the pure and free Gift of Heaven or of Nature, and to be a Fire kindled out of some hidden spark of the very first conception' (Spingarn, iii. 80). The youth has also been identified, however, as the poet himself, the offspring of a liaison between God and the female Fancy: see Garrod (p. 69); Northrop Frye, *Fearful Symmetry* (Princeton: Princeton Univ. Press, 1947), pp. 169–70; and Harold Bloom, *The Visionary Company* (New York: Doubleday, 1961), pp. 3–10. E. L. Brooks, 'William Collins's "Ode on the Poetical Character" ', *College English*, 17 (1956), 403–4, suggests that this interpretation would not hold up if l. 38 were re-punctuated with a comma instead of a colon. It should be noted, though, that a colon, in eighteenth-century pointing, did not always have the force that Brooks attributes to it; it was often used in place of a comma or semicolon. Cf. Collins's use of the colon in ll. 42 and 44, directly following this construction.

40. *subject Life*: 'The golden-tressed Apollo, and his subject divinities, the inferior orbs that encircle him' (Strutt, (1796), p. 7 n.).

42. *sainted*: 'Holy; sacred' (*Dict.*).

46. *Tarsel*: tercel, a male hawk.

54. *This hallow'd Work*: the girdle.

55–62. Collins's description of an Eden like Milton's own is closely modelled on *Paradise Lost*, iv. 132–8.

60. *embrown*: 'To make brown; to darken; to obscure; to cloud' (*Dict.*, s.v. 'Imbrown').

63. *that Oak*: cf. 'th' accustom'd Oke' and the 'monumental Oake' of 'Il Penseroso', ll. 60, 135; and *Paradise Regained*, i. 305: 'Under the covert of some ancient Oak'. Ainsworth, Wasserman, and Lonsdale also suggest the oak tree of the oracle at Dodona, where the future was interpreted from its rustling leaves.

65. *drop'd*: dripped.

66. *its*: Garrod (p. 66) claims that this refers back to Milton's ear (l. 64), but surely it is Milton's ear which hears heaven's native strains.

67. *Trump*: Wasserman (p. 111) notes that the trumpet was the ancient instrument of prophecy.

69. Collins associates the myrtle (sacred to Venus, and thus an emblem of love) with the amorous verse of Edmund Waller (1606–87). Waller was

well known for his poems to Sacharissa and (appropriately) for his poem 'On a Girdle'. See also Akenside, *The Pleasures of Imagination*, iii. 546–67, in which he draws a sharp contrast between Waller and Shakespeare.

Ode, Written in the beginning of the Year 1746

Collins's deliberate dating of the poem in his title would suggest a time of composition following the battle between the English army and the Scottish rebels at Falkirk on 17 January 1746. But when the poem was inserted in the second edition of Dodsley's *A Collection of Poems* (1748), i. 330, it was described as an 'Ode, Written in the same Year' as his 'Ode, to a Lady' (which was dated May 1745). Although Collins seems to have been responsible for the substantive variants appearing in his poems in the *Collection*, it is possible that the re-titling (and re-dating) of the ode was the work of the editor Dodsley, who perhaps desired a convenient format linking the two odes. Even if this later dating of the poem is the poet's own work, it is possible, as Lonsdale suggests, that Collins was being deliberately misleading by implying that the poem celebrated his country's losses against the French rather than the Scottish rebels (who by 1748 were no longer a cause for anxiety). And Collins was, Lonsdale continues, later a member of the Richmond group largely composed of Scottish expatriates, whom he would not wish to offend.

The battle of Falkirk (like that at Prestonpans, 21 September 1745) was a setback for the English troops in Scotland. Although the rebels celebrated the Young Pretender's victory in their French publications, the English press tended to minimize the defeat. Dispatches quoted in the *Gentleman's Magazine* in January suggested that the confrontation had resulted in a draw, but by April the history of the rebellion carried in Dodsley's *Museum* (to which Collins was a contributor) drew a more accurate picture. Although 'the Men did not behave so well as might have been expected', the *Museum* reported, 'their Officers shew'd themselves to great Advantage, and gave glorious Examples of Intrepidity, tho' they were but ill copied' (i. 115). Nevertheless, the number of casualties among the officers was large, and when 'the News of this Battle reached *London*, it made it necessary to provide for the immediate Extinction of so dangerous a Flame' (i. 117). The Duke of Cumberland himself took charge of the English troops, and the rebellion was crushed on 16 April at the battle of Culloden.

The composition of the 'Ode, to a Lady' does indicate that the two poems are closely linked. The present ode appears to be, in part, a reworking of ll. 7–20 of an early version of the 'Ode, to a Lady', which in turn, in its revised form in the *Odes* (especially in ll. 19–24), seems to have been influenced by this ode.

Edmund Burke's later reprinting of the ode in Dodsley's *Annual Register* (1768) is discussed by Regina Janes and Robert Mahony, 'A Newly Discovered Reprinting of Collins's "How Sleep the Brave"', *NQ*, 221 (1976), 355–7. To A. S. P. Woodhouse's account of the musical settings for the ode (*TLS* (16 Oct. 1930), p. 838), should be added James Oswald's in *The Musical Magazine. By Mr. Oswald, And other Celebrated Masters* (1761–2?), p. 60, and Francis Ireland's in John Bland, *The Ladies Collection, of Catches, Glees . . . &c.* (1790?), ii. 182–3. The most important setting was Thomas Arne's at the end of Act II of *Alfred the Great, A Drama for Music* (1753), pp. 24–5, where the ode appeared as '*A* NEW FUNERAL DIRGE, *in Honour of the Heroes who die in the Service of their Country, supposed to be sung to* ALFRED *by Aerial Spirits*'. This publication of *Alfred*, a revised version of the original masque written by James Thomson and David Mallet in 1740, introduced variants in ll. 5, 7, and 8 of Collins's ode. It is possible that these variants were authorized by Collins, who was apparently a friend of Mallet and (in 1755) a witness to his will (see David Mallet, *Ballads and Songs*, ed. Frederick Dinsdale (1857), p. 54). But there seems to be no obvious justification for the slight changes introduced in this version, and Collins did not revise his poem in any of the numerous editions of Dodsley's *Collection*. The present text therefore follows the *Odes*, while noting these substantive variants.

5–6. Johnson misquotes these lines in his *Dict.*, s.v. 'Sod'.

Ode to Mercy

According to Langhorne, 'The ode written in 1746, and the ode to Mercy, seem to have been written on the same occasion, viz. the late rebellion; the former in memory of those heroes who fell in the defence of their country, the latter to excite sentiments of compassion in favour of those unhappy and deluded wretches who became a sacrifice to public justice' (p. 161). Collins's poem does in fact reflect the continuing debate in England during the summer months of 1746 over whether George II should pardon Lord Balmerino and the Earls of Kilmarnock and Cromartie, three noblemen who had participated in the recent rebellion. Following a trial for high treason on 29 July 1746, in which all three had pleaded guilty and been sentenced to death, a plea for mercy was made to the king by Kilmarnock and Cromartie. The noblemen's case was closely and often sympathetically followed in the *General Evening Post*; the *Gentleman's Magazine* juxtaposed columns 'For Mercy' and 'Against Mercy' (16–19 Aug. 1746). Even after the king's pardon of Cromartie only and the execution of Kilmarnock and Balmerino on 18 August, the *Gentleman's Magazine* continued to follow the debate into its October issue. The most likely date for composition of the poem is therefore during the height of the 'Mercy' debate in July or August.

5. *fatal*: 'Deadly; mortal; destructive' (*Dict.*).

14–22. Although Collins may be referring here to the invasion of England in 1745 by the Young Pretender, the *'Fiend of Nature'* (l. 15) is probably war in general or 'a principle of evil prompting man to war and other cruel deeds' (Bronson, p. 105 n.). Lonsdale points out that Collins draws upon classical descriptions of Venus in his treatment of disarmed cruelty; cf. Lucretius, *De Rerum Natura*, i. 31–40, and Statius, *Thebaid*, iii. 263–70.

15. *join'd his Yoke*: yoked his steeds.

19–20. There is a slight gap between these lines in the *Odes*, apparently of no formal significance, which has not been reproduced here.

21. *Salvage*: 'It is now spoken and written *savage*' (*Dict.*).

26. Bronson argues that 'Queen' is predicate nominative; Johnston and Lonsdale suggest that Mercy shall rule *'as* our Queen', although Collins then seems to refer literally to George II ('our Monarch's Throne').

Ode to Liberty

This poem has been dated September or October 1746 by Lonsdale, who cites as evidence the allusion in l. 49 to Genoa's plight in the allied campaign against the French in Italy, and the plea in the concluding lines (129–44) which expresses a widely-held contemporary hope for peace. Collins in fact returned in August 1746 from the Netherlands where he had witnessed the ravages of war. His friend John Mulso wrote to Gilbert White on 1 August 1746 that he had just received a letter from Collins from Antwerp:

He gives me a very descriptive Journal of his Travells thro' Holland to that Place, which He is in Raptures about, & promises a more particular Account of: He is in high Spirits, tho' near ye French. He was just setting out for ye Army, which He says are in a poor way, & He met many wounded & sick Countrymen as He travell'd from Helvoet-Sluys. (*Letters to Gilbert White of Selborne from . . . the Rev. John Mulso*, ed. R. Holt-White [1907], p. 15.)

To this evidence should be added the close parallel in the ode's closing line which links this poem with the preceding 'Ode to Mercy', probably written in the late summer of 1746.

Both Ainsworth and Lonsdale have pointed out possible sources for passages in this poem in Salmon's *Modern History*, which Collins had used as his poetical quarry for the *Oriental Eclogues*. Although Collins's use of Salmon here, at least four years later, is not explicitly stated, references to probable sources in the *Modern History* have been provided in the notes.

1–2. Collins's source is probably Thucydides, v. 70; but cf. *Paradise Lost*, i. 550–3: 'the *Dorian* mood / Of Flutes and soft Recorders; such as rais'd / To highth of noblest temper Hero's old / Arming to Battel'.

3–4. Herodotus, vii. 208–9, describes the Spartans' ritual of combing their hair before the battle of Thermopylae.

7–12 (7 n.). In his note Collins quotes from a drinking song preserved in Athenaeus, *Deipnosophistae*, xv. 695 (secs. 10–13, omitting ll. 3–4, 7–8, 15–16). The entire song may be translated:

10

In a myrtle-branch I will carry my sword, as did
Harmodius and Aristogeiton, when they slew the
tyrant and made Athens a city of equal rights.

11

Dearest Harmodius, thou art not dead, I ween,
but they say that thou art in the Islands of
the Blest, where swift-footed Achilles lives,
and, they say, the brave son of Tydeus, Diomed.

12

In a myrtle-branch I will carry my sword, as did
Harmodius and Aristogeiton, when at the Feast of
Athena they slew the tyrant Hipparchus.

13

Ever shall your fame live in the earth, dearest
Harmodius and Aristogeiton, for that ye slew the
tyrant, and made Athens a city of equal rights.

This scolion was attributed, in part at least, to Callistratus, although the attribution to Alcaeus was common in the eighteenth century. Carver, *The Life of a Poet*, p. 117, points out that when the text of this song was printed in Causaubon's folio edition of Atheneaus (Lyons, 1657), it confusingly faced the italicized quotation '*Ex Alceo et Anacreonte scolion quoddam sumptum mihi cane*' (which Lonsdale identifies as Aristophanes'). Harmodius and Aristogeiton planned to assassinate both Hippias and Hipparchus at the Panathenea (the festival of Athena, goddess of wisdom) in 514 B.C. Although only Hipparchus was murdered, the assassins were regarded as liberators by the Athenians. See Herodotus, v. 55, and vi. 123; and Thucydides, vi. 54–7.

15. *Shell*: see the note to 'Ode to Pity', l. 42.

15 n. Collins quotes from Callimachus, 'Hymn to Demeter', l. 17: 'Nay, nay, let us not speak of that which brought the tear to Deo [Demeter]!'

26. *the least*: i.e., of the fragments (l. 25).

26–63. In this section Collins, as Lonsdale and Arthur Johnston point out, generally follows Thomson's description of the progress of Freedom in *Liberty* (1736), iv. See also A. D. McKillop, *The Background of Thomson's 'Liberty'*, Rice Institute Pamphlets, 38 (1951), No. 2.

34–7 (36 n.). Florence was ruled by the Medici family, powerful patrons of the arts, throughout most of the fifteenth century. Collins's attitude toward the Medici seems more ambivalent here than in *An Epistle: Addrest to Sir Thomas Hanmer*, l. 38.

38-9. Pisa was annexed by Florence in 1406, regained its freedom in 1494, but was finally defeated in 1509.

40 (n.). In describing San Marino, Salmon (*Modern History*) quotes from Addison's *Remarks on Several Parts of Italy* (1705): 'Nothing, says Mr. AD-DISON, can be a greater instance of the natural love mankind have for liberty, and of their aversion to an arbitrary government, than to see such a savage mountain cover'd with people, when the Campania of Rome (under a Monarch) in the same country, is destitute of inhabitants' (1739 edn., ii. 434). The independence of this tiny republic in northern Italy had been threatened in 1739, but restored in 1740.

43 (n.). Salmon, ii. 364, attributes the decline of the Doges' power in Venice to the rise of the 'leading men of the republick. . . . the sovereign power became vested in the most substantial citizens; the Doge retain'd no more than the shadow of his antient authority.'

44-5 (44 n.). Salmon, ii. 369, describes how the Doge of Venice was symbolically wedded each year to the sea when, on Ascension Day, he threw a gold ring into the Adriatic from his gilded vessel, the Bucentaur; cf. also Shaftesbury's *Characteristicks* (1737-8 edn.), ii. 396.

47. *Lydian*: 'one of the modes in ancient Greek music, characterized as soft and effeminate' (*OED*). Milton and Pope had employed the term to describe soft and pleasing music; Collins's usage here does not appear to characterize this entire passage.

48-9 (49 n.). Lonsdale points out that 'proud' Genoa's fate in the War of the Austrian Succession was documented in the *Gentleman's Magazine*, where the public was characterized as 'at present very attentive to the critical situation of the *Genoese* republick' (16 (Sept. 1746), 471). See also *GM*, p. 498, describing the 'thorough humiliation of that proud city, which has been forc'd to submit upon very hard terms to the conqueror'.

50-5. Collins is recalling the role of the archer William Tell in the Swiss insurrection against the Austrians (whose insignia was an eagle); cf. Salmon, ii. 286-7.

56. *willow'd*: 'Bordered or grown with willows' (*OED*, where the earliest usage is ascribed to Thomas Warton, 'Ode to Morning', l. 14, written 1745, published 1750).

57 n. Cf. Salmon, ii. 234, and Thomson, 'Autumn', ll. 849-61. Collins had visited his uncle in the Netherlands in 1745 and 1746.

58-9. The Duke of Alva was infamous for his butchery while Spanish governor of the Netherlands (1567-73). Queen Elizabeth declined an offer of the Dutch crown by the revolting provinces in 1575. Cf. Salmon, ii. 151-4.

66-9 (67 n.). This legend is discussed in Holinshed's *History* (1577) and Camden's *Britannia* (1586), ed. Gibson (1695), p. i. Poetical use had in fact been made of this material by Spenser, *Faerie Queene*, II. x. 5. 5; Drayton, *Poly-Olbion*, xviii. 718–20; and Thomson, *Liberty*, iv. 460–3. Collins's note was parodied in a note to the 'Ode to Horror', l. 39 n., which is concluded: 'I don't remember that any poetical use has been made of this story' (*The Student* (1751), ii. 314).

68. *hoary*: here, 'White; whitish' (*Dict.*).

72. *Orcas*: the Orkney Islands, discussed in Camden's *Britannia*, ed. Gibson, pp. 1073–87.

wolfish: full of wolves.

73. *banded West*: Woodhouse (p. 106 n.) suggests that 'Collins is thinking of a group of spirits associated with the West and banded together for the production of storm and earthquake', whom Nashe had described in his *Pierce Penniless his Supplication to the Devil* (see the note to 'Ode to Fear', ll. 16–19).

75. The Giants of Albion are described in Camden's *Britannia* and in Geoffrey of Monmouth's *Historia Regum Britanniae*, i. 16.

76–9. The separation of England from the continent is discussed in Camden's *Britannia*, ed. Gibson, pp. i, 206–7.

82 n. Collins is apparently fusing two stories—one of a mermaid's love for a young man, and another of the blue mist shrouding the island—in George Waldron's *A Description of the Isle of Man* (1726), in his *Works* (1731), ii. 176–7 (Lonsdale notes that a new (third) edition in 1744 would have made this book accessible to Collins). Langhorne claimed that Mona was usually identified as Anglesey: 'Both those isles still retain much of the genius of superstition, and are now the only places where there is the least chance of finding a faery' (p. 166).

90. *Navel*: the centre, Arthur Johnston suggests, as in the Latin 'umbilicus', although Lonsdale notes a discussion of a druid temple in a grove on Anglesey in Henry Rowlands's *Mona Antiqua Restaurata* (Dublin, 1723), pp. 69, 91–2 (see also the note to *Ode Occasion'd by the Death of Mr. Thomson*, l. 19).

91. For Collins's 'Shrine' see Thomson's *Liberty*, iv. 626–31, and the note to l. 90.

93. *painted Native*: Camden, ed. Gibson, p. cx, notes the 'fashion of painting and dawbing themselves with colours' common to both the Britons and the Picts.

97–8. Drawing upon Tacitus, Camden describes the Roman conquest of Mona (ed. Gibson, pp. 673–4). The Danish invasion is portrayed in Thomson's *Liberty*, iv. 709–21.

107. *Islands blest*: perhaps a reference to the song Collins quoted in his note to l. 7. Lonsdale points out, however, that England was sometimes thought to have been the blessed islands (in Camden's *Britannia*, ed. Gibson, p. iii (iv)), as were Anglesey and the Isle of Man (in Rowlands's *Mona Antiqua Restaurata*).

108. *Hebe*: the goddess of youth.

111. The druids were traditionally considered sacred bards; cf. Caesar, *Gallic Wars*, VI. xiv; Camden's *Britannia*, ed. Gibson, p. iii (iv); and Thomson, *Liberty*, iv. 630–1.

118. For the role of the Gothic in political thought, see Samuel Kliger, *The Goths in England* (Cambridge, Mass.: Harvard Univ. Press, 1952). Gothic architecture was being championed, Lonsdale notes, in Batty Langley's *Ancient Architecture Restored* (1742) and *Gothick Architecture Improved* (1747).

123. *Mold*: 'Earth; soil; ground in which any thing grows' (*Dict.*, 1756 edn.).

124. *emblaze*: 'adorn with glittering embellishments' (*Dict.*).

127. *grav'd*: engraved.

133–6. Cf. 'Ode to Mercy', ll. 17–22.

144. Cf. 'Ode to Mercy', l. 26.

Ode, to a Lady on the Death of Colonel Ross in the Action of Fontenoy

Because Collins's 'Ode, to a Lady' exists in four different forms, it provides both textual difficulties and our clearest glimpse of Collins's poetical workmanship. The poem was first published as an 'Ode to a Lady, On the Death of Col. Charles Ross, in the Action at Fontenoy. Written May, 1745' in Dodsley's *Museum: Or, The Literary and Historical Register* (7 June 1746), i. 215–17, a periodical edited by Mark Akenside. The battle of Fontenoy had been fought on 11 May 1745; the Duke of Cumberland, directing the allied forces, had been defeated by the French. Among the fatalities was Capt. Charles Ross, whom the *Gentleman's Magazine* called 'a fine young gentleman, member for the shire of *Ross*' (15 (May 1745), 276).

When the poem appeared in Collins's *Odes* (1747), the fourth stanza had been revised, two stanzas added (augmenting the sentiments of the original fourth stanza, and celebrating the Duke of Cumberland, who had been the victor in the battle between the British forces and the Scottish rebels at Culloden in April 1746), and the title shortened so that it no longer carried the date of composition or Ross's Christian name. The ode was subsequently reprinted in this form as 'An Ode to the Memory of Colonel Charles Ross of Balnagown, who was killed in the Action at Fontenoy', but with no substantive changes in the text, in the *British Magazine: or, the London and Edinburgh Intelligencer* (July 1747), i. 354.

Still further changes occurred when the poem was reprinted in the second edition of Dodsley's *A Collection of Poems by Several Hands* (1748), i. 327–9. In this version of the ode, the title followed the first edition in Dodsley's *Museum* and the stanzas added in the *Odes* were now dropped from the poem.

These changes, and some details in punctuation, suggest that here Dodsley was simply following as copy his earlier publication of the poem. But the fourth stanza was again revised in this version, and Dodsley's addition of the full 'Harting's' in l. 58 and other details in punctuation prove that in fact this third version is derived from both previous printings. There is no external evidence to prove that these final changes were actually made by Collins, but they are consistent with the poem's history of repeated correction. Thomas Warton, in *The Reaper*, No. 26, pointed out that he had seen Collins's original manuscript of the poem, and it too varied in some respects from the first printing: 'I had lately his first manuscript of the *Ode on the Death of Colonel Ross*, with many interlineations and alterations. . . . In the first Stanza, my manuscript *sunk in grief* for *stain'd with blood*. . . . Many variations I have forgot.'

Thus there are difficulties in determining Collins's final intentions in the poem. Surely Lonsdale is right in arguing that the removal of the additional two stanzas in the version in Dodsley's *Collection* 'was the result of political rather than literary considerations' (p. 456), the Duke of Cumberland having been defeated by the French at Laeffelt in July 1747. But even if these two stanzas are incorporated in the poem, there remains the matter of determining whether Collins's later revisions in the fourth stanza represent his final thinking about that stanza, or whether they merely compensate for the removal of the two others later in the poem. Lonsdale does not include these revisions, arguing that 'the various changes in stanza 4 were made to accommodate this insertion [of stanzas 7 and 8] and then its eventual removal' (p. 460 n.). But this stanza of the ode, as it stands in Dodsley's *Collection*, appears much closer to the version in the *Odes* than in the original *Museum* reading, and in fact seems to be an independent refinement of the previous version. Lonsdale argues as much in speculating that 'C. may have decided not to revert to the original *Museum* text of stanza 4 because its pair of personifications were now too close to the *Ode, Written in the Beginning of 1746* 9–12, where Freedom and Honour also appear, no doubt in imitation of the earlier poem', the 'Ode, to a Lady' as it appeared in the *Museum* (p. 458 n.). What Collins's revisions in effect supply then, independent of the removal of the other stanzas in the poem, is a partial corrective to the close similarity between this poem and the 'Ode, Written in the beginning of the Year 1746' as they appeared together in the 1747 *Odes*. And as Bronson pointed out in his enthusiastic approval of the stanza as it stood in the *Collection*, these revisions also supply an appropriate address to the lady herself in the mention of 'thy Virtues' in l. 19.

The copy-text followed in the present edition is Collins's *Odes* (1747), on the assumption that this version more closely approximates Collins's preference in the treatment of accidentals than either of Dodsley's two versions, both of which appear in the characteristic house-style of the *Museum* and *Collection*. (For a full discussion of Dodsley's influence on the accidentals of Collins's text, see Richard Wendorf, 'Robert Dodsley as Editor', *SB*, 31 (1978), 235–48.) Substantive revisions from the later version in the *Collection* (in stanza 4 but not in l. 58, which seems to be a compositor's error, corrected in some editions) are therefore incorporated in the text and modified to conform to the style of the copy-text. Substantive variants from all four versions are noted in the textual apparatus.

Collins's relation to Ross, to the lady addressed in the poem, and even to the Sussex village of Harting has produced much speculation but little concrete fact. Capt. (not Col.) Charles Ross was the second son of George, thirteenth Lord Ross, three times Commissioner of Customs and Salt. Born in 1721, young Ross had become owner of the estate of Balnagown in 1732, was commissioned in the Scots Guards in 1739, and elected a Member for the County of Ross in 1741. Horace Walpole, writing to Sir Horace Mann (16 December 1741), spoke of Ross as a 'son to a commissioner of the Customs, and saved from the dishonour of not liking to go to the West Indies when it was his turn, by Sir R[obert]'s giving him a lieutenancy' (*Correspondence*, ed. W. S. Lewis (New Haven: Yale Univ. Press, 1954), xvii. 244). In a letter following the battle of Fontenoy, Col. John Munro wrote that 'Poor Charles Ross of Balnagown was shot with a musket ball through the belly, I believe early in the action; my Servants found him in a Ditch, and I sent him away to our head Quarters, where he died that night' (*Culloden Papers* (1815), p. 200). More information concerning Ross is included in Carver's *The Life of a Poet*, pp. 75–7. As Carver suggests, it is unlikely that Collins was acquainted with Ross, whose rank he had mistaken and whom he presumably had not met after Ross's departure from England in 1743.

'The *lady* to whom this Ode is addressed was Miss Elizabeth Goddard, who then lived at or near Harting, in Sussex', Thomas Warton wrote in *The Reaper*, and Warton seems to have received his information from the late William Hymers, who had intended to publish a full edition of Collins's poems. In Hymers's annotated copy of Langhorne's edition, now in the Osborn Collection at Yale, is the following account of the poem (preceding p. 67):

The Lady to whom this Ode was addressed was a Miss Elizabeth Goddard who died within the present year [1783] at Paradise Row Chelsea—It originated in love—Collins at the time he wrote it had no knowledge of Col. Ross and but little of Miss Goddard—He had fallen into her company and wished to recommend himself to her—The event was recent—and he used it for that purpose. With what success I have not learned—

And in Joseph Warton's letter to his brother describing the projected publication of his odes with those of Collins, he added: 'You will see a very pretty one of Collins's, on the death of Colonel Ross before Tourney. It is addressed to a lady who was Ross's intimate acquaintance, and who by the way is Miss Bett Goddard.'

The manuscript version of l. 49 recorded by Thomas Warton ('If drawn by all a Lover's Art') has stimulated discussion of Collins's relationship with the mysterious Miss Goddard, whom William Seward, in his *Supplement to Anecdotes of Some Distinguished Persons* (1797), p. 125, identified as the young lady to whom Collins was 'extremely attached' but who 'did not return his passion with equal ardour'. Sir Harris Nicolas, in Brydges's edition of Collins (1830), p. xxxviii, reported that 'It is said that Collins was extremely fond of a young lady who was born the day before him, and who did not return his affection; and that, punning upon his misfortune, he observed, "he came into the world a day after the fair." '

Apparently Collins mentions Harting not as the young lady's home but, as Lonsdale suggests (p. 456), 'as a place of some obscurity, known both to himself and the lady' (Collins points out that 'even' humble Harting's vale will learn the 'sad repeated Tale'). H. D. Gordon, *History of Harting*, (1877), pp. 166–9, presents some information about the Collins family and connections living in the village, but little trace of the Goddards. Most important is the fact that Harting is located on the route between Chichester and Winchester, and that Collins's fellow Wykehamist, Lord Tankerville, lived at Up-Park in Harting until 1745. These few facts, and the account presented by Hymers, are thus consistent with the explanation offered in Brydges's edition (p. xxxviii) by Nicolas:

The lady is supposed to have been Miss Elizabeth Goddard, the intended bride of Colonel Ross, to whom he addressed his beautiful Ode on the death of that officer at the battle of Fontenoy, at which time she was on a visit to the family of the Earl of Tankerville, who then resided at Up-Park, near Chichester, a place that overlooks the little village of Harting, mentioned in the Ode.

There is no evidence to support J. S. Cunningham's remarks in *William Collins: Drafts & Fragments of Verse* (1956), p. 31, that Ross was Elizabeth Goddard's uncle, nor that she was also the subject of Fragment 10.

1. *lost to*: deprived of.

13. The river Scheldt actually flows slowly through the flat land of Belgium near Fontenoy; cf. Goldsmith's *The Traveller*, l. 2: 'Or by the lazy Scheld, or wandering Po'.

13-24. Cf. 'A Song from Shakespear's *Cymbelyne*', ll. 1-4, and 'Ode, Written in the beginning of the Year 1746'.

25-36. Cf. *Aeneid*, vi. 477-93 and 637-65.

26. *fair recording Page*: cf. 'The Passions', l. 108.

31. In fact only the eldest son of Edward III, known as the Black Prince, fought at the battle of Crécy in 1346 (almost exactly 400 years before the publication of this poem in the *Museum*).

38. Cf. 'Ode to Mercy', l. 9.

39. *Impatient*: 'Vehemently agitated by some painful passion' (*Dict.*).

46. *William*: the Duke of Cumberland, who had led the English forces to a decisive victory over the Scottish rebels at Culloden in April 1746 and who was expected to return to lead the British troops in Flanders. For the addition and removal of these two stanzas (ll. 37–48), see the head-note to the poem.

54. *insulting*: 'With contemptuous triumph' (*Dict.*, s.v. 'Insultingly').

58. *Harting*: see the head-note to this poem.

cottag'd: the first use of the word in this sense recorded in the *OED*.

Ode to Evening

The 'Ode to Evening' was first published in Collins's *Odes* (1747). When it was reprinted in the second edition of Dodsley's *Collection* (1748), i. 331–2, it contained revisions affecting much of the poem: five lines were rewritten, substantive variants appeared in seven other lines, and there were numerous changes in accidentals. There is no surviving evidence to prove that these substantive changes were in fact Collins's, and, knowing Robert Dodsley's editorial practice, there is always the chance that Dodsley himself was responsible for the revisions in the poem when it appeared in his miscellany (for details of Dodsley's practice, see Richard Wendorf, 'Robert Dodsley as Editor', *SB*, 31 (1978), 235–48). The cautious acceptance of these revisions rests on two factors: the frequency with which Collins revised his other poems (e.g., 'Ode, to a Lady', *An Epistle: Addrest to Sir Thomas Hanmer*, *Oriental Eclogues*, and the fragments), and Thomas Warton's decision to adopt these substantive changes in his publication of the poem in *The Union: Or Select Scots and English Poems* (Edinburgh—D. Nichol Smith, *RES*, 19 (1943), 263–5, points out that it was actually printed in Oxford—1753; London, 1759), pp. 39–41.

A detail in punctuation (in l. 44) and the acceptance of 'thy' for 'the' in l. 49 suggest that Warton, the anonymous editor of *The Union*, actually followed as his text the so-called 'fourth volume' of Dodsley's *Collection*, issued in 1749 to provide purchasers of Dodsley's first edition with the additional poems which had been inserted in the second edition. At the same time, Warton seems to have corrected a misprint in Dodsley's 1749 volume ('fallow' for 'sallow', l. 45), and to have introduced an accidental variant of his own into the text which seems to have no authority. Because Warton would presumably have followed a text of the poem which he believed to be Collins's, the substantive revisions in the *Collection 1748* appear to be legitimate. They have been incorporated in the present edition and modified to match the presentation of accidentals in the copy-text. The text of the *Odes* has been chosen as copy on the assumption that this earlier printing has a greater probability of reflecting Collins's preference in accidentals than

Dodsley's text in the *Collection*, which conforms to a distinctive house-style. Substantive variants from all early editions of the poem (including the rare first state of *The Union*, cited as *Union 1753a*) are noted in the textual apparatus. The division of the ode into stanzas dates only from the *Poetical Calendar* (1763), and has not been preserved here.

The evidence which has been collected for dating the poem is very slim, and is largely based on the possible influence of Thomas and Joseph Warton. It is not certain, however, which of Joseph's odes Collins saw at the Guildford Races in May 1746, whether he had begun his own ode by that time, or (if he did see the Wartons' poems) whether he was actually influenced by them in his own compositions. Joseph Warton, in a note appearing in his brother's edition of Milton's *Poems upon Several Occasions* (1785), p. 368 n., pointed out that 'In this measure, my friend and school-fellow Mr. William Collins wrote his admired Ode to EVENING; and I know he had a design of writing many more Odes without rhyme.' The ode is written in the unrhymed metre of Milton's translation of Horace's 'Pyrrha' (1. v), and could have been influenced by Thomas's 'Ode to a Fountain', which Joseph sent to Collins following the races and which was included among Joseph's *Odes* (1746). Also written in this metre is Joseph's 'The Happy Life', which replaced Thomas's poem in the second edition of the *Odes* (1747); and there are further similarities between Collins's poem and Joseph's 'Ode to Evening' and 'Ode to Fancy'. Thomas Warton commented on his brother's note in the edition of Milton: 'Dr. J. WARTON might have added, that his own ODE to EVENING was written before that of his friend Collins' (p. 369 n.). There is, however, no actual evidence to suggest that Collins saw (or imitated) these particular poems by his friends. A. D. McKillop, on the other hand, has suggested that the ode may have had its origins in the second part of Collins's Fragment 8; see 'Collins's *Ode to Evening*—Background and Structure', *Tennessee Studies in Literature*, 5 (1960), 73–83, and the head-note to this fragment. The similarities between the two poems suggest the possibility that Collins may have been meditating his ode before his meeting with Warton, although the fragment itself could conceivably have been written as late as May 1746.

The 'Ode to Evening' was set to music by John Callcott in 1785. For an index to the poem's popularity, see A. S. P. Woodhouse, 'Imitations of the "Ode to Evening" ', *TLS* (30 May 1929), p. 436.

1. *Oaten Stop*: the hole on a shepherd's pipe, hence pastoral music. Cf. *Comus*, l. 345: 'Or sound of pastoral reed with oaten stops'.

3. *Springs*: B. A. Wright, 'Collins's Use of the Word "Springs" ', *NQ*, 203 (1958), 222, points out that the word means 'brooks' here, although it may have been derived from the usual meaning (the source of a well or river).

5. *bright-hair'd Sun*: cf. 'Ode on the Poetical Character', l. 39.

6. *Skirts*: the edge of a cloud.

7. *Brede*: braid. 'Applied by the poets to things that show or suggest

interweaving of colours, or embroidery, *esp.* to the prismatic colouring of the rainbow' (*OED* 3).

14. *Pilgrim*: 'A traveller; a wanderer' (*Dict.*).

21. *folding Star*: 'The Star that bids the Shepherd fold' (*Comus*, l. 93).

28. For the possible connections between this description, Thomson's 'Summer' (ll. 113–29), and Guido Reni's fresco 'Aurora', see Jean Hagstrum, *The Sister Arts* (Chicago: Univ. of Chicago Press, 1958), p. 278.

29. *sheety*: the first example recorded in the *OED*.

32. *it's*: for a discussion of the syntax here, see H. W. Garrod, 'Errors in the Text of Collins', *TLS* (15 Mar. 1928), p. 188, and subsequent replies: pp. 221, 243, 272. The emendation of 'or' (l. 30) to 'and' or 'o'er' has been suggested, as well as the emendation of 'it's' to 'thy' (which would conform to the earlier version in the *Odes*). But 'it's' may refer either to 'some sheety Lake' (whose 'last cool Gleam' would be reflected by the ancient pile or upland fallows) or, as Lonsdale suggests, to 'thy shadowy Car' (l. 28).

42. *breathing*: giving off fragrance.

Ode to Peace

Although there is no specific evidence for dating this poem, it may be confidently assigned to the latter half of 1746, after the English victory over the Scots at Culloden (16 April) and before the publication of the *Odes* in December. The desire expressed in the poem for peace with honour, as Lonsdale suggests, more reasonably refers to the war of the Austrian succession against the French than to the rebellion of the Young Pretender. British forces returned to the Continent in June 1746, and peace talks continued in Breda until late in the autumn (see the *Gentleman's Magazine*, 16 (Sept.–Nov. 1746), 499, 559, 615). Also helpful in dating the ode is its similarity in places to the 'Ode to Mercy' (especially ll. 14–16 of that poem, describing the invasion of the '*Fiend of Nature*'), which was probably written in the late summer of 1746, and to the 'Ode to Liberty' (ll. 131–6, describing Concord's power over Anger and Rage), which seems to date from September or October.

1–6. Cf. Ovid, *Metamorphoses*, i. 89–150, for the myth of Astraea, goddess of justice, who took refuge in heaven with the passing of the Golden Age on earth.

1. *Turtles*: turtle-doves, emblems of peace.

4–5. Cf. 'Ode to Mercy', ll. 14–16. War was believed to have first made its appearance in the Iron Age (*Metamorphoses*, i. 141–3). The chariot of Mars, god of war, is drawn here by vultures, the voracious birds offered to him in Roman sacrifices.

7–9. 'It was a Roman custom to burn the arms collected on the battlefield, as an offering to Mars for victory. Collins imagines the English youth burning the shrines devoted to war' (Johnston, p. 192 n.).

9. *sullen*: 'Gloomy . . . dismal' (*Dict.*).

10–11. It was believed that the music of the spheres had not been heard by man since the Golden Age; cf. Milton's description of the 'meek-ey'd Peace' in 'On the Morning of Christ's Nativity', ll. 45–52.

15. *beamy*: 'Radiant; shining' (*Dict.*).

The Manners. An Ode

This poem has traditionally been considered the earliest of Collins's *Odes*, dating from the months in which he came to London a 'literary adventurer'. Thus Langhorne in his edition (1765), p. 174, argued that:

From the subject and sentiments of this ode, it seems not improbable that the author wrote it about the time when he left the University; when weary with the pursuit of academical studies, he no longer confined himself to the search of theoretical knowledge, but commenced the *scholar of humanity*, to study nature in her works, and man in society.

Gilbert White's description of Collins at Oxford provides the closest biographical background for this traditional interpretation and dating of the poem:

As he brought with him, for so the whole turn of his conversation discovered, too high an opinion of his school acquisitions, and a sovereign contempt for all academic studies and discipline, he never looked with any complacency on his situation in the University, but was always complaining of the dulness of a college life. (*GM*, 51 (1781), 11.)

'Everyone who has studied Collins has agreed', Oliver Sigworth states in *William Collins*, p. 128, 'that this poem must have been the earliest written in the 1746 volume, and that it probably somehow reflects his decision to throw up his Demyship at Magdalen College and go to London. There is only internal evidence for this supposition, but the evidence is fairly strong.' And yet the only real internal evidence in the poem—Collins's note to l. 67 telling (mistakenly) of the death of Le Sage in 1745—argues for a much later date, and ostensibly for a different origin for the poem (this discrepancy in dates is noted in Bronson's edition, p. 115). And although it is possible, as Bronson suggests, that these lines and the reference to Le Sage's death were a late addition to the poem, there is no evidence to prove that this poem is not contemporary with the other odes in the volume. As Lonsdale judiciously points out (p. 470), Collins is speaking primarily of his abandoning a kind of philosophical study which need not be specifically connected with his academic studies in the university. The argument of the poem is not necessarily a movement away from books in general, but towards an empirical study of the manners in nature and in the pages of Art's 'enchanted School'.

External evidence to substantiate this later dating is supplied by Joseph Warton. Collins's reference to Le Sage (ll. 67-70) apparently reflects the success of Thomson's *Tancred and Sigismunda* (first acted 18 March 1745), which had made the story of Blanche a popular one. Joseph Warton wrote to his brother Thomas in late March or early April 1745: 'Collins sent them [Akenside's *Odes*] to me with Tancred & Sigismunda: in which there are some moving Strokes. Yesterday I read the Story in the second Vol. of Gil Blas where it is inimitably related' (BL Add. MS. 42560, f. 3). The certainty that Collins knew Thomson's adaptation of Le Sage—and was interested in it to the point of sending a copy of the play to his friend—points to 1745 as the earliest possible date for the poem's composition.

Johnson defined the manners as our 'General way of life; morals; habits' in his *Dictionary*, but in Collins's ode the manners are spoken of in the specific context of artistic representation. Collins thus followed Dryden, in 'The Grounds of Criticism in Tragedy', prefixed to *Troilus and Cressida* (1679):

The manners in a poem are understood to be those inclinations, whether natural or acquired, which move and carry us to actions, good, bad, or indifferent, in a play; or which incline the persons to such or such actions. . . . The manners arise from many causes; and are either distinguished by complexion, as choleric and phlegmatic, or by the differences of age or sex, of climates, or quality of the persons, or their present condition: they are likewise to be gathered from the several virtues, vices, or passions, and many other commonplaces which a poet must be supposed to have learned from natural philosophy, ethics, and history; of all which whosoever is ignorant, does not deserve the name of poet. (Watson, i. 248.)

Similarly James Harris, in his *Three Treatises* (which Collins celebrated in Fragment 3), claimed that poetry excelled painting in its ability to 'lay open the *internal Constitution of Man*, and give us an Insight into (*b*) *Characters, Manners, Passions*, and *Sentiments*' (p. 84). Harris defined the manners by arguing that as 'a *certain System of them* makes a *Character*; and that as these Systems, by being *differently compounded*, make each a *different* Character, so is it that *one* Man *truly differs* from *another*' (p. 84 n.). And 'a just and decent Representation of *Human Manners*', Harris wrote, is important in producing 'that *Master-Knowledge* (*c*), without which, *all other* Knowledge will prove of little or no Utility' (pp. 86-7).

Lonsdale, moreover, points to a precedent in Shaftesbury's *Characteristicks* (5th edn., 1732), i. 286-7, for Collins's contrast between the manners and '*Philosophy* in some famous Schools':

There can be nothing more ridiculous than to expect that *Manners* or *Understanding* shou'd sprout from such a Stock. . . . had the craftiest of Men, for many Ages together, been imploy'd in finding out a method to confound *Reason*, and degrade the *Understanding* of Mankind; they cou'd not perhaps have succeeded better, than by the Establishment of such a *Mock-Science*.

4. *requir'd*: sought, demanded.

7-8. Collins is apparently referring to philosophical debate in general.

9. *round*: travel round, 'encircle' (*Dict.*).

10. *Spear and Shield*: a Spenserian formula, also used by Milton, and thus probably not an allusion to 'the heroes of the chap-books' (Blunden's edn., p. 174). See also Ovid's description of the spear and shield that enabled Perseus to slay Medusa (*Metamorphoses*, iv. 779–85).

13. *the Porch*: the portico in the agora of ancient Athens where the Stoic Zeno taught; often employed for Greek philosophy in general.

14. *Olive*: sacred to Athena, goddess of wisdom and patron deity of Athens.

15. *tissued*: 'Cloth interwoven with gold or silver' (*Dict.*, s.v. 'Tissue').

20. *Observance*: 'Observation' (*Dict.*).

33–4. i.e., alluring him away from the safe rule of Nature (l. 28) towards the 'enchanted School' of Art.

35–6. The emendation of 'Thou' and 'Hast' to 'Tho'' and 'Has' has been adopted in the Stone and Poole text (1937), but Collins's criticism of art (meddling, officious) can be read as affectionate.

39. *she*: presumably Art (l. 31).

40. *Mask*: masque.

44. In the *Spectator*, No. 514, Steele describes how '*Judgment*' corrects the inconsistencies of '*Fancy*' by 'showing them in his Mirror'.

45. *white-rob'd Maids*: numerous explanations have been offered: the virtues (Strutt, Johnston); the spiritual characteristics of men (Bronson, who also identifies the '*Satyrs*', l. 46, as men's earthly characteristics); the graces (Lonsdale, who quotes Parnell's 'To Mr. Pope', ll. 27–8: 'The Graces stand in sight; a *Satyr* Train / Peep o'er their Heads, and laugh behind the Scene').

49. *Thou*: Garrod (p. 47) suggested an emendation to 'Tho'' (adopted in the Stone and Poole text, 1937), arguing that 'It is not the Comedy of Humours, but Collins himself, who has been nursed by the Passions.' But Lonsdale is surely correct in maintaining that Collins's use of humour here 'involves an understanding of individual human "passions" or "humours"' (p. 474 n.). Dryden claimed that 'the soul of poesy . . . is imitation of humour and passions' (Watson, i. 56), and defined humour as 'some extravagant habit, passion, or affection, particular (as I said before) to some one person, by the oddness of which he is immediately distinguished from the rest of men; which being lively and naturally represented, most frequently begets that malicious pleasure in the audience which is testified by laughter' (Watson, i. 73).

50. *Sock*: 'The shoe of the ancient comick actors, taken in poems for comedy, and opposed to buskin or tragedy' (*Dict.*).

51–2. An eighteenth-century commonplace; cf. Sir William Temple, 'Of Poetry' (Spingarn, iii. 103), who spoke of humour as 'a Word peculiar to our Language', and Congreve's 'Concerning Humour in Comedy' (Spingarn, iii. 252).

54–8. 'The image of Wit is truly characterized. The mingled lustre of jewelry in his head-dress well describes the playful brilliancy of those ideas which receive advantages from proximity to each other' (Strutt, p. 3). Lonsdale points out that Collins may have been familiar with Corbyn Morris's recent *Essay towards Fixing the True Standards of Wit, Humour, Raillery, Satire, and Ridicule* (1744).

55. *crisped*: curled.

59–60 (59 n.). Miletus was the city in which the author Aristides (*c.*100 B.C.) wrote his tales, and not the name of the author himself. The stories, dealing with love (the 'Love-inwoven Song'), and often erotic, have not survived; cf. Sir William Temple, 'Of Poetry' (Spingarn, iii. 90): 'The next Succession of Poetry in Prose seems to have been in the *Miletian* Tales, which were a sort of little Pastoral Romances; and though much in request in old *Greece* and *Rome*, yet we have no Examples that I know of them.' See also Warburton's supplementary note to Charles Jarvis's translation of *Don Quixote* (1742), vol. i, and, in the same edition, the life of Cervantes by Don Gregorio Mayans y Siscar (i. 9).

61. *you*: apparently Giovanni Boccaccio (1313–75), author of the *Decameron*, who lived much of his life in Florence (in Tuscany).

62. *chang'd Italia*: cf. *An Epistle: Addrest to Sir Thomas Hanmer*, ll. 35–44, and 'Ode to Simplicity', ll. 31–42.

63–6. Cervantes wrote the first part of *Don Quixote* at Valladolid, in Castile, but the name of the province may stand here for Spain itself, which had been conquered by the Moors in the Middle Ages. Collins accepts the contemporary view that Cervantes intended to ridicule chivalry (and not the chivalric romances); cf. Sir William Temple, 'An Essay upon the Ancient and Modern Learning' (Spingarn, iii. 71–2), and Charles Jarvis's preface to his translation of *Don Quixote* (1742), i. iii–xxiii.

67–70 (67 n.). Alain-René Le Sage (1668–1747) in fact died in Boulogne two years later than Collins indicates in his note. H. O. White, 'William Collins', *TLS* (14 Feb. 1929), p. 118, suggests that 'The mistake may have been due to confusion with the death of the novelist's son [René André Le Sage, an actor], who died in Paris in 1743.' Blanche, the 'sad *Sicilian* Maid' of *Gil Blas* (IV. iv), was compelled by her father to marry another even though she loved and was loved by the King of Sicily; her jealous husband, mortally wounded by the king, stabbed her as she held him in her arms. Mrs Barbauld (p. xxxvi) believed that 'LE SAGE should not have been characterized by the story of *Blanche*, which, though beautiful, is not in his peculiar stile of excellence, and has more to do with the high passions than with *Manners*.' But, as Dyce points out, the success of Thomson's tragedy *Tancred and Sigismunda* (first acted 18 March 1745) had probably made the story of Blanche a popular one. A letter from Joseph Warton to his brother Thomas (BL Add. MS. 42560, f. 3) indicates that Collins sent Joseph a copy of the play *c.* April 1745.

68. *watchet*: 'pale blue' (*Dict.*), although Michael Gearin-Tosh, 'Obscurity in William Collins', *Studia Neophilologica*, 42 (1970), 26–7, argues for a 'light blue which was radiant rather than pastel or soft', citing the *Spectator*, No. 265 ('*Ovid* himself . . . tells us that the blue Water Nymphs are dressed in Sky-coloured Garments').

71. *boon*: bounteous.

73. Cf. 'Ode to Fear', l. 69.

75. *retreating Cynic*: a philosophical sect advocating retirement from the world.

77. *The Sports*: 'diversion . . . frolick' (*Dict.*).

78. *Scene-full*: the only example of the word recorded in the *OED*.

The Passions. An Ode for Music

This poem was first published in Collins's *Odes* (1747); there is no evidence for dating its composition differently from that of the other odes in 1745–6. The poem was, as Collins indicated in its title, expressly written with music in mind, and in fact was performed at the Oxford Encaenia on 2 July 1750, with a musical setting by the University's Professor of Music, Dr William Hayes (1705–77). An account of the performance and the ceremony commemorating the benefactors of the University appeared in the *Gentleman's Magazine*, 20 (July 1750), 328 (see also the *London Magazine*, 19 (July 1750), 330). The reasons behind the choice of Collins's ode for the performance are unknown, but it may have been through the agency of his friend Thomas Warton whose own 'Ode for Music', also with a setting by Hayes, was performed at the Encaenia in 1751. Hayes's score for Collins's ode is in the Bodleian Library (MS. Mus. d. 120–1). William Seward, in his *Supplement to the Anecdotes of Some Distinguished Persons* (1797), p. 123, wrote that 'The music . . . was excellently well adapted to the words. The chorusses were very full and majestic, and the airs gave completely the spirit of the Passions which they were intended to imitate.'

Collins wrote to Hayes on 8 November 1750 asking for a copy of the setting and communicating his thanks to the composer:

Mr Blackstone of Winchester some time since inform'd Me of the Honour You had done me at Oxford last Summer for which I return You my sincere thanks. I have another more perfect Copy of the Ode, which, had I known of your obliging design, I *would* have communicated to You. Inform me by a Line, If You should think one of my better Judgment acceptable; In such Case I could send you one written on a Nobler Subject, and which, tho' I have been persuaded to bring it forth in London, I think more calculated for an Audience in the University. The Subject is the Music of the Græcian Theatre. (This letter was first published in Seward's *Supplement*, and is reproduced in full in this edition.)

A 'more perfect Copy of the Ode' has not survived, nor has a major ode on 'the Music of the Græcian Theatre' (but see Fragment 11, which is clearly associated with this ode).

Collins apparently did not realize that Hayes's version of the poem contained a completely rewritten conclusion (ll. 93 ff.) when it was performed in Oxford and subsequently printed there (in ten pages) as *The Passions, An Ode. Written by Mr. Collins. Set to Musick by Dr. Hayes. Performed At the Theatre in Oxford, July 2, 1750* (cited here as *Hayes A*). A note added to one version of the poem (*Hayes D*; see below) points out that 'The Lines which conclude this Poem as it is here set to Music . . . were written for the Composer by the Earl of Litchfield Chancellor of the University of Oxford: the latter part of the original Ode not being calculated for musical expression' (p. [iii n.]). This printing of the ode (*Hayes A*) contains only one substantive variant in the opening ninety-two lines.

There is an eight-page issue of this pamphlet which contains different variants; another issue in this eight-page format, again with different variants, was printed at Winchester, apparently for a performance of the ode there (see the head-note to Collins's letter to Hayes). The poem was also printed by H. Hardy (no place, no date, but probably late in the century), and in 1760 by R. Bond in Gloucester as a result of another performance (see Daniel Lysons, *History of the Origin and Progress of the Meeting of the Three Choirs of Gloucester, Worcester, and Hereford* (Gloucester, 1812), p. 190, and A. D. McKillop, 'Collins's "Ode to the Passions"', *TLS* (7 Mar. 1936), p. 204).

There is no reason to believe that any of the variants occurring in these printings of the ode is authoritative. The present edition follows *Odes* (1747) as copy, and notes these and other substantive variants in the textual apparatus (but not the conclusion written by the Earl of Litchfield). The printing of the poem in the *Odes* presents some textual difficulties in determining the separation of stanzas, especially when these appear to occur at the foot of a page. The principle followed here, to assign a separate stanza to each major personification, is consistent with the presentation of the poem in the copy-text. The formats of the later editions are as follows:

> *Hayes A*: *The Passions, An Ode. Written by Mr. Collins. Set to Musick By Dr. Hayes. Performed At the Theatre in Oxford, July 2, 1750.* [Oxford? 1750?] 4°: A¹ B⁴ C¹; *1–2 3–10 11–12*; *1* title *2* blank *3–10* text *11–12* blank. Rothschild 660; Foxon C295. Foxon notes: 'A1 and C1 have been seen to be conjugate. The Rothschild copy is described as large paper; there is no watermark in the copies seen.' There is also no watermark in the Rothschild copy.
>
> *Hayes B*: *The Passions, An Ode. Written by Mr. Collins. Set to Musick by Doctor Hayes.* [London? 1750?] 8°: A⁴; *1–2 3–8*; *1* title *2* blank *3–8* text. Foxon C297. Foxon notes: 'Title in half-title form, with woodcut headpiece above and below.'

Hayes C: *The Passions, An Ode. Written by Mr. Collins. Set to Musick By Dr. Hayes.* ('Winchester: Printed by W. Greenville'; 1750–1?). 4⁰: A^8 B^2 (A2 as 'B'); *1–3* 4–8; *1* title *2* blank *3* 4–8 text. Williams, p. 111; Foxon C296.

Hayes D: *The Passions, An Ode Written by W. Collins, and Composed by Dr William Hayes, Professor of Music, in the University of Oxford* ('Printed by H. Hardy'; no place, no date). Contains a portrait of Hayes by J. Cornish (J. K. Sherwin, sculp.) and Hayes's musical score. 178 pages: *i–iv* 1 2–174; *i* title *ii* blank *iii* index *iv* blank *1* 2–174 text and score. Apparently published by Henry Hardy, in Oxford, *c.* 1790–1805; see Charles Humphries and William C. Smith, *Music Publishing in the British Isles* (London: Cassell, 1954; 2nd edn., Oxford: B. Blackwell, 1970), p. 170.

Hayes E: *The Passions, An Ode. Written by Mr. Collins, and set to Musick by Dr. Hayes.* ('Gloucester, Printed by R[.] Bond, 1760. Price Six-Pence'). Printed with an 'Ode To the Memory of Mr. Handel. Set to Musick by Dr. Hayes.' 4⁰: A^4 B^2; *1–3* 4–8 *9–11* 12; *1* title *2* blank *3* 4–8 text *9* title ('Ode to . . . Handel') *10* blank *11* 12 text.

Copies of each of these editions are rare; the following have been located:

Hayes *A*: O, OM, OW, MH, Rothschild.
Hayes *B*: L.
Hayes *C*: LVA-D.
Hayes *D*: OM, WcW.
Hayes *E*: WcW.

Collins's ode was set to music at least twice later in the century, in 1784 by Benjamin Cooke (1734–93) and in 1789 by James Sanderson (1769–1841). Of Cooke's setting, a reviewer in the *European Magazine*, 7 (Jan. 1785), 13, said: 'In this elaborate production of Dr. Cooke, though Genius does not unremittingly preside, nor Judgment, her Prime Minister, always lend her salutary counsel, yet we find much effect of the reigning principle of the former, and many happy regulations of the latter' (see also the discussion of Cooke's unusual setting in *Grove's Dictionary of Music and Musicians* (London, 1954), ii. 419–20). The *Gentleman's Magazine*, 52 (Jan. 1782), 22, noted that the poem was often publicly recited, 'a mark of its universally-acknowledged excellence' (cf. Dickens's use of this in Mr Wopsle's melodramatic performance in *Great Expectations*, ch. vii).

In grouping together his poems 'The Manners' and 'The Passions' at the end of his volume, Collins may have been thinking of the relationship between them described by Dryden in 'The Grounds of Criticism in Tragedy', prefixed to *Troilus and Cressida* (1679):

Under this general head of manners, the passions are naturally included as belonging to the characters. I speak not of pity and of terror, which are to be moved in the audience by the plot; but of anger, hatred, love, ambition, jealousy, revenge, etc., as they are shown in this or that person of the play. To describe these naturally, and to move them artfully, is one of the greatest commendations which can be given to a poet. (Watson, i. 253–4.)

And in his 'Preface' to the *Fables* (1700), Dryden spoke of both Ovid and Chaucer understanding 'the manners; under which name I comprehend the passions' (ii. 278).

As an ode written in praise of the power of music to stimulate and soothe the passions, Collins's poem should be viewed in the context of musical odes written for the annual festival of St. Cecilia. Collins's greatest debt is to Dryden's 'Alexander's Feast' and 'A Song for St. Cecilia's Day' ('What Passion cannot MUSICK raise and quell!' l. 16), and Pope's 'Ode for Musick on St. Cecilia's Day'. For a discussion of this genre see Robert M. Myers, 'Neo–Classical Criticism of the Ode for Music', *PMLA*, 62 (1947), 399–421; James Kinsley, 'Dryden and the *Encomium Musicae*', *RES*, n.s., 4 (1953), 263–7; Brewster Rogerson, 'The Art of Painting the Passions', *Journal of the History of Ideas*, 14 (1953), 68–94; and D. T. Mace, 'Musical Humanism, the Doctrine of Rhythmus, and the Saint Cecilia Odes of Dryden', *Journal of the Warburg and Courtauld Institutes*, 27 (1964), 251–92.

Thomas Warton noted in his edition of Milton's *Poems upon Several Occasions* (1785), p. 369 n., that 'Dr. J. WARTON might have added, that . . . a Poem of his, entitled the ASSEMBLY OF THE PASSIONS, [was written] before Collins's favourite Ode on that subject.' No such poem has been found, but J. S. Cunningham, 'Thomas Warton and William Collins: A Footnote', *Durham University Journal*, 46 (1953), 23, points out that among the Warton manuscripts at Trinity College, Oxford, there are some verses by Joseph Warton dated 1740 which allude to his design of writing 'The *Assembly* of Passions'. John Wooll, *Biographical Memoirs of the late Revd. Joseph Warton, D. D.* (1806), pp. 10–13, prints a prose sketch answering Thomas's description of Joseph's poem which was written when Joseph was 18 (i.e. in 1740) and 'laid out by him as a subject for verse'. In Warton's sketch the subjects of Reason, 'lately rebelled against him', are made to pay their obedience 'whilst he sits on his throne, attended by the Virtues, his handmaids'. Wooll (p. 13 n.) suggested that 'When the intimacy between Collins and Warton is recollected, it is no improbable surmise that the above sketch furnished the former with the idea of writing an Ode on the Passions.' Bronson has summarized the similarities:

at a few points the resemblance is striking enough to make it probable that he had seen the prose sketch and took one or two hints from it. In both poem and sketch Fear is the first passion mentioned and Anger the second; Joy is masculine, is crowned with ivy, is attended by Mirth and another figure (Pleasure in the sketch, Love in the poem), and is associated with the dance; Love and Hate are both mentioned in connection with Jealousy. (p. 119.)

3. Cf. 'Ode to Pity', l. 42 n.

10. *Fury*: 'Inspired frenzy, as of one possessed by a god or demon; esp. poetic "rage" ' (*OED* 4).

16. *expressive Pow'r*: 'Having the power of utterance or representation' (*Dict.*).

21. Spenser's Wrath and Furor have burning eyes; cf. *Faerie Queene*, I. iv. 33. 5 and II. iv. 15. 5–6.

26. 'sounds is either in apposition with *measures* (l. 25), or is governed by "with" understood' (Bronson, p. 119 n.).

43. *denouncing*: announcing.

45. This line, like l. 85, is unrhymed.

43–7. For similar details in the characterization of Revenge, see Dryden's 'A Song for St. Cecilia's Day', ll. 25–30, and 'Alexander's Feast', ll. 69–74.

50. *Soul-subduing*: the only earlier use cited in the *OED* is J. Beaumont, *Psyche* (1648), XVIII. cxl.

70–2. Chearfulness is modelled on Diana, the goddess of chastity (cf. the 'chast-eye'd *Queen*', l. 75).

75. *Oak-crown'd Sisters*: the Dryads (l. 74) are tree-nymphs, deriving their names from δρῦς (tree, especially the oak).

83. *awak'ning Viol*: cf. 'thy awak'ning Bards' ('Ode to Fear', l. 55).

85. Garrod (p. 97) points out that this line is unrhymed and suggests that a line may be missing, but the sense here (as in the unrhymed l. 45) is not impaired.

86. *Tempe*: a valley in northern Thessaly lying between Mts. Olympus and Ossa, recently celebrated in Akenside's *The Pleasures of Imagination*, i. 299–305.

92. *HE*: Love (l. 90).

95. 'Music is *Sphere-descended* because the basic harmony of the universe is the music made by the revolving of the spheres' (Johnston, p. 205 n.).

99. *Athenian Bow'r*: cf. ll. 1–16.

101. *mimic*: capable of imitation.

103. Cf. 'The Manners', l. 26.

104. *Devote*: devoted.

106. *Energic*: 'strenuous, forcible, vigorous' (*OED* 2).

108. *thy recording Sister*: Clio, the Muse of History.

111. *Rage*: cf. 'Fury', l. 10, and *An Epistle: Addrest to Sir Thomas Hanmer*, l. 19.

114. *Cæcilia*: St. Cecilia, patron saint of music, and the reputed inventor of the organ.

115–18. Cf. *An Epistle: Addrest to Sir Thomas Hanmer*, ll. 111–12, and 'Ode to Simplicity'.

ODE OCCASION'D BY THE DEATH OF MR. THOMSON

The poet James Thomson died at Richmond on 27 August 1748. Collins, who may have lived there temporarily as early as 1744–5, had settled there by 1747 and became a member of Thomson's circle of friends. His ode was published in June 1749 by R. Manby and H. S. Cox (*GM*, 19 (June 1749), 288), and sold for sixpence. (Manby was the Ludgate-Hill bookseller to whom Collins was supposed to contribute lives for the *Biographia Britannica*; see *The Reaper*, No. 26.) In the biography of Thomson prefixed to his edition of Thomson's *Works* (1762), i. xvi, Patrick Murdock wrote that 'Only one gentleman, Mr. *Collins*, who had lived some time at *Richmond*, but forsook it when Mr. *Thomson* died, wrote an Ode to his memory.' But Thomson was in fact the subject of several elegies: Shenstone's; Robert Shiels's *Musidorus: A Poem, Sacred to the Memory of Mr. James Thomson* (1748); two anonymous poems in the *Scots Magazine*, 10 (Sept.–Oct. 1748), 441, 486; and an unpublished 'Monody' by Thomas Warton (in an incomplete manuscript among the Warton papers, Trinity College, Oxford, dated 27 October 1748). According to John Ragsdale, who also lived in Richmond, David Garrick, James Quin, Dr John Armstrong, and the bookseller Andrew Millar were mutual friends of Collins and Thomson (*The Reaper*, No. 26). Joseph Warton mentions two conversations between Collins and Thomson, one of which he heard: 'Thomson was well acquainted with the Greek Tragedies, on which I heard him talk learnedly, when I was once introduced to him by my friend Mr. W. Colling [*sic*]' (*Works of Pope* (1797), iv. 10 n.; see also i. 61 n.).

Collins's ode was reprinted in *The Union: Or Select Scots and English Poems*, ed. Thomas Warton (1753), pp. 108–10, (2nd edn., 1759), pp. 116–18; in *The Art of Poetry on a New Plan*, ed. John Newbery (1762), ii. 68–9; and in Murdock's memoir of Thomson, *Works*, i. xxi–xxiii. Wordsworth echoed the poem in his own 'Remembrance of Collins, composed upon the Thames near Richmond' (1789). The text followed here is from the folio of 1749, whose format is:

2°: A^2 B^2; *1–4* 5–8; *1* title *2* blank *3* dedication *4* advertisement 5–8 text. Williams, pp. 110–11; Rothschild 659; Foxon C294.

Copies of this folio are rare; only the following have been located: L, LVA-D, Rothschild.

As in his earlier dirges, Collins seems here to be indebted to Pope's 'Elegy to the Memory of an Unfortunate Lady' and to James Hammond's *Love Elegies* (1743), especially Elegy III. The ode was set to music by Callcott (pre-1800?).

Motto. Virgil, *Eclogues*, v. 74–5 and v. 52: 'These rites shall be thine for ever, both when we pay our yearly vows to the Nymphs, and when we purify our fields', and 'me, too, Daphnis loved.'

Dedication. George Lyttelton, later first Baron Lyttelton (1709–73), was a patron of the arts and a minor poet and essayist. He had been secretary to the Prince of Wales (1737–44) and in 1744 was made a Lord of the Treasury. Lyttelton (often spelled Lyttleton) had been a generous friend and patron of Thomson and was one of his executors; in 1749 he was also the dedicatee of Fielding's *Tom Jones*. Thomson describes him in *The Castle of Indolence*, I. lxv–lxvi.

Advertisement. Langhorne added in his notes that 'The ode on the death of Thomson seems to have been written in an excursion to Richmond by water' (p. 184), but there is no other external authority for this assertion.

1. *Grave*: the emendation to 'grove' in the *Poetical Calendar* has no authority, attractive as it is. R. A. Wilmott accepted it in his edition (1854), pp. 68–9, arguing that Thomson's grave could not in fact be viewed from the river (see also *GM*, n.s., 19, Pt. 1 (1843), 494, 603). Groves were associated with druids, and 'grave' is repeated in l. 4, but the parallel opening and closing of the poem clearly indicate that Collins intended the word to read 'Grave'.

DRUID: Mrs Barbauld (p. xliii) objected that 'there is no propriety in calling THOMSON a Druid or a pilgrim, characters totally foreign to his own. To the sanguinary and superstitious Druid, whose rites were wrapped up in mystery, it was peculiarly improper to compare a Poet whose religion was simple as truth, sublime as nature, and liberal as the spirit of philosophy.' Johnson, however, had defined druids as 'The priests and philosophers of the antient Britons' (*Dict.*), and Collins was probably only evoking traditional associations of druids with nature, natural philosophy, and patriotism; see J. M. S. Tompkins, 'In Yonder Grave a Druid Lies', *RES*, 22 (1946), 1–16, and A. D. McKillop, *PQ*, 26 (1947), 113–14, who suggests that William King's *Templum Libertatis* (1742) may have supplied the image for Collins's temple. For Collins's own use of the druids, see 'Ode to Liberty', ll. 89–112; for Thomson's, see *The Castle of Indolence*, II. xxxiii (discussed by A. L. Owen, *The Famous Druids* (Oxford: Clarendon Press, 1962), pp. 172–8).

3–4. Thomson is 'The *Year*'s . . . POET' because of his descriptions of the changing aspects of nature during the year in *The Seasons*.

6 (n.). The Aeolian harp is a stringed instrument which will produce musical sounds when placed in a current of air. Thomson had mentioned it in *The Castle of Indolence*, I. xl–xli, and had written 'An Ode on Aeolus's Harp', printed in Dodsley's *Collection* (1748). For the re-invention of the harp by the Scottish musician James Oswald (perhaps with Thomson's assistance), see *The Castle of Indolence*, ed. A. D. McKillop (Lawrence, Kans.: Univ. of Kansas Press, 1961), pp. 206–9, and Roger Lonsdale, *Dr. Charles Burney* (Oxford: Clarendon Press, 1965), p. 29.

9. Cf. 'A Song from Shakespear's *Cymbelyne*', ll. 1–2.

10. *it's*: the harp's.

19 (n.). 'the church of Richmond is not white nor a spire, nor can it be seen from the river; and as to the monument erected in the last verse to this great Poet, it must be looked upon in the light of a prophecy which is not yet fulfilled' (Mrs Barbauld, pp. xliii–xliv). Thomson was buried in the church of St. Mary Magdalene, Richmond, on 29 August 1748. In his memoir of Thomson, Murdock wrote that 'Mr. *Thomson*'s remains were deposited in the church of *Richmond*, under a plain stone, without any inscription' (xvi). Douglas Grant has noted that 'It is uncertain whether any stone or monument was immediately erected over the vault where he was buried. Richard Crisp, the historian of Richmond, imagined that such a stone or monument had been erected soon after his burial, but that it had been destroyed later in the century when it became necessary to increase the pew accommodation. The phrase Collins used in his *Ode*, "thy pale shrine glimm'ring near", would suggest that some memorial had been erected in the church, but there is no other evidence that it ever existed' (*James Thomson: Poet of 'The Seasons'* (London: Cresset Press, 1951), p. 277). It is possible that in adapting the Richmond landscape here and in the last stanza Collins was drawing upon legends of druid groves and shrines (the druid circle is imitated in the structure of the ode). Cf. the engraving of groves and shrines in Henry Rowland's *Mona Antiqua Restaurata* (Dublin, 1723), facing p. 91, a probable source for details in the 'Ode to Liberty'.

20. *Landschape*: a spelling (from the Dutch) still occasionally used in the 1740s.

25–8. Collins is echoing Thomson's own boast in 'A Hymn on the Seasons', ll. 94–9: 'For me, when I forget the darling theme, / Whether the blossom blows, the summer-ray / Russets the plain, inspiring autumn gleams, / Or winter rises in the blackening east, / Be my tongue mute, may fancy paint no more, / And, dead to joy, forget my heart to beat!'

29. *lorn*: forlorn, 'Forsaken; lost' (*Dict.*).

30. Bronson (p. 121) takes 'now' to mean 'nowadays', in contrast with the 'poetical days of old'; but Lonsdale is surely right in suggesting that 'since the death of Thomson, the "sedge-crowned Sisters" or Naiads have deserted the Thames' (p. 490 n.). The Naiads had recently been celebrated in Akenside's 'Hymn to the Naiads', dated 1746 when it appeared in Dodsley's *Collection*, vi. 3–15.

39–40. Cf. 'A Song from Shakespear's *Cymbelyne*', ll. 1–4, 15–16.

41. *pointed Clay*: several explanations have been offered: 'pointed out' (E. M. W. Tillyard, 'William Collins's "Ode on the Death of Thomson" ', *A Review of English Literature*, 1, no. 3 (1960), 34–5); 'the simple head-stone and the clay thrown into a ridge over the grave' (Johnston, p. 209 n.); the brickwork of Thomson's tomb, with 'point' used in its technical sense of inserting mortar between the courses of bricks (Alexander Henderson, *A Review of English Literature*, 1, no. 4 (1960), 65); 'the shape of Thomson's

monument as visualized by C.' (Lonsdale, p. 491 n.). Each interpretation is possible, although Collins twice earlier used 'point' in the sense of 'pointing out' (cf. *An Epistle: Addrest to Sir Thomas Hanmer*, l. 120, and 'Ode, to a Lady', l. 12).

ODE TO A FRIEND ON HIS RETURN &c [AN ODE ON THE POPULAR SUPERSTITIONS OF THE HIGHLANDS OF SCOTLAND, CONSIDERED AS THE SUBJECT OF POETRY]

This poem has enjoyed an extraordinary textual history, sustained most recently by the unexpected rediscovery of the unfinished manuscript by Claire Lamont. In his 'Life of Collins', Samuel Johnson recounted a visit the Wartons made to Collins in Chichester in 1754. Collins showed them 'an ode inscribed to Mr. John Hume on the superstitions of the Highlands, which they thought superior to his other works, but which no search has yet found' (*Lives*, iii. 340). Thomas Warton, in his brief account of Collins in *The Reaper*, No. 26, recalled that the poet had shown them

an *Ode to Mr. John Hume, on his leaving England for Scotland*, in the Octave Stanza, very long, and beginning thus:—

Hume, thou return'st from Thames!

I remember there was a beautiful description of the Spectre of a Man drowned in the Night, or in the language of the old Scotch Superstitions—*seized by the angry Spirit of the Waters*, appearing to his wife *with pale blue cheek, &c.* Mr. Hume has no copy of it.

Collins had apparently met the clergyman and aspiring playwright John Home (1722–1808) in the autumn of 1749 when Home was trying unsuccessfully to persuade David Garrick to accept his *Agis* for performance on the London stage. Alexander Carlyle, in his *Anecdotes and Characters of the Times*, ed. James Kinsley (London: Oxford Univ. Press, 1973), p. 118, wrote that

In Winter 1749 it was that John Home went to London with his Tragedy of Agis, to try to bring it on the Stage, in which he fail'd; which was the Cause of his turning his Thoughts on the Tragedy of Douglas, after his Return. . . . I had given him a letter to Smollet, with whom he Contracted a Sincere Friendship, and he Consol'd himself for the Neglect he met with by the warm Approbation of the D[r.] and of John Blair, and his Friend Barrow an English Physician, who had escap'd with him from the Castle of Down: and who made him acquainted with Collins the Poet, with whom he Grew very Intimate.

Thomas Barrow (d. 1781), who had been a medical student at Edinburgh, was living in Chichester when Home arrived in London on 6 November 1749. Home apparently looked up his friend Barrow (whom he had known in the Rebellion), and it was Barrow, perhaps because of his residence in Chichester, who introduced the two writers to each other. Home and Collins later visited their friend in Chichester (not in Winchester as stated by Carlyle, below), and apparently on this occasion Collins presented Home with an ode on his return to Scotland. The poem has traditionally been dated from late 1749, but Lonsdale has pointed out that three incompletely dated letters from Home to Carlyle indicate that he may still have been in London early in 1750 (see the *Works of John Home*, ed. Henry Mackenzie (Edinburgh, 1822), i. 133, 136–7, and L. M. Knapp, *Tobias Smollett* (Princeton: Princeton Univ. Press, 1949), pp. 77, 89 n.). There is no evidence to suggest that Collins and Home ever saw each other again. When Collins's editor Alexander Dyce wrote to Home's friend, Henry Mackenzie, asking for anecdotes about the poet, the ageing 'man of feeling' replied that he did 'not recollect hearing any anecdotes from Mr. Home, or having any communication with him or any one else, regarding Collins, the close of whose life made the subject rather a distressing one' (*The Reminiscences of Alexander Dyce*, ed. Richard Schrader (Columbus, Ohio: Ohio State Univ. Press, 1972), p. 233; see also Mackenzie's *Anecdotes and Egotisms*, ed. H. W. Thompson (London: Oxford Univ. Press, 1927), p. 166).

Johnson's account of the poem was indirectly responsible for its first publication in 1788. Dr Alexander Carlyle (1722–1805), a Scottish minister and friend of Home, recalled while reading Johnson's 'Life of Collins' that he had once had a manuscript of the ode in his possession. Carlyle discovered the manuscript, unfinished and lacking a leaf, and eventually read it to the Literary Class of the recently established Royal Society of Edinburgh (19 April 1784). He later sent the manuscript to the Society to be published in the first volume of the *Transactions of the Royal Society of Edinburgh* (Mar. 1788), Pt. ii, pp. 63–75, as 'An Ode on the Popular Superstitions of the Highlands of Scotland, considered as the Subject of Poetry'. The poem was accompanied by the following information from Carlyle:

THE manuscript is in Mr COLLINS's handwriting, and fell into my hands among the papers of a friend of mine and Mr JOHN HOME's, who died as long ago as the year 1754. Soon after I found the poem, I shewed it to Mr HOME, who told me that it had been addressed to him by Mr COLLINS, on his leaving London in the year 1749: That it was hastily composed and incorrect; but that he would one day find leisure to look it over with care. Mr COLLINS and Mr HOME had been made acquainted by Mr JOHN [*sic*] BARROW (the *cordial youth* mentioned in the first stanza), who had been, for some time, at the university of Edinburgh; had been a volunteer, along with Mr HOME, in the year 1746; had been taken prisoner with him at the battle of Falkirk, and had escaped, together with him and five or six other gentlemen, from the castle of Down. Mr BARROW resided in 1749 at Winchester, where Mr COLLINS and Mr HOME were, for a week or two, together on a visit. Mr BARROW was paymaster in America, in the war that commenced in 1756, and died in that country.

I THOUGHT no more of the poem, till a few years ago, when, on reading Dr JOHNSON's life of COLLINS, I conjectured that it might be the very copy of verses which he mentions, which he says was much prized by some of his friends, and for the loss of which he expresses regret. I sought for it among my papers; and perceiving that a stanza and a half were wanting, I made the most diligent search I could for them, but in vain. Whether or not this great chasm was in the poem when it first came into my hands, is more than I can remember, at this distance of time.

As a curious and valuable fragment, I thought it could not appear with more advantage than in the Collection of the Royal Society. (Pt. ii, pp. 65–6.)

A similar letter by Carlyle, of which two copies survive, corroborates this account and makes it clear that the ode was 'hastily wrote on John Home's leaving Chichester', and not Winchester (see P. L. Carver, *NQ*, 177 (1939), 258–9, and W. Forbes Gray, 'The John Lee Collection—II', *TLS* (26 June 1943), p. 312).

Alexander Fraser Tytler (1747–1813), later Lord Woodhouselee, was charged by the Society to obtain from Carlyle 'every degree of information which he could give' concerning the ode. Tytler enclosed his findings in a letter addressed to John Robison, General Secretary of the Society, published with Carlyle's letter as a preface to the ode:

It is evidently the *prima cura* of the poem, as you will perceive from the alterations made in the manuscript, by deleting many lines and words, and substituting others, which are written above them. In particular, the greatest part of the twelfth stanza is new-modelled in that manner. These variations I have marked in notes on the copy which is inclosed, and I think they should be printed: For literary people are not indifferent to information of this kind, which shews the progressive improvement of a thought in the mind of a man of genius.

THIS ode is, beyond all doubt, the poem alluded to in the life of COLLINS by JOHNSON, who, mentioning a visit made by Dr WARTON and his brother to the poet in his last illness, says, 'He shewed them, at the same time, an ode, inscribed to Mr JOHN HOME, on the superstitions of the Highlands, which they thought superior to his other works, but which no search has yet found.' COLLINS himself, it appears from this passage, had kept a copy of the poem, which, considering the unhappy circumstances that attended his last illness, it is no wonder was mislaid or lost; and, but for that fortunate hint given by JOHNSON, it appears from DR CARLYLE'S letter, that the original manuscript would, in all probability, have undergone the same fate. (Pt. ii, pp. 63–4.)

Collins's other copy of the poem, which Tytler assumes the Wartons must have seen in their 1754 visit to Chichester, has never been found. Tytler attempted to remedy the small defects and larger gaps in the surviving manuscript by having Carlyle supply several 'hemistichs, and words left blank', and by having Henry Mackenzie contribute verses remedying 'the fifth stanza, and the half of the sixth, which were entirely lost'. Mackenzie described his attempt to fill the chasm in the ode as 'an almost extempore production' (*Anecdotes and Egotisms*, p. 166), and in a letter to Tytler stated that 'I have endeavoured to keep up a congenial Wildness of Imagery, with which indeed I have, from my Infancy, been well acqainted. I send it to you in the Moment of Composition, because, if I kept it longer, it is probable I should not venture to send it. Cancel, alter, or suppress it as you see proper' (quoted by Claire Lamont, 'William Collins's "Ode on the Popular Superstitions of the Highlands of Scotland"—A Newly Recovered Manuscript', *RES*, n.s., 19 (1968), 138).

The publication of the ode stimulated much interest, Collins having gained a considerable reputation by 1788. The poem was reprinted in numerous periodicals, included in the first American edition of Collins's poems, and published with supplementary stanzas by William Erskine, who described Scottish superstitions overlooked by Collins. By far the most interesting notice of the poem appeared in a letter signed 'Verax' published in the *St. James's Chronicle* (12–15 Apr. 1788), which argued that the text in the *Transactions* 'appears to have been taken from a mutilated and incorrect Copy' and 'is nothing more than a foul and early Draught of this Composition'. 'Verax' wrote that Thomas Warton had seen a manuscript of the poem which 'had every Appearance of the Authour's last Revisal, and of a Copy carefully and completely finished for the Press' which Warton had described in a letter to John [*sic*] Hymers, who had proposed an edition of Collins's poems. These remarks are not to be found, however, in the version of Warton's letter printed in *The Reaper* (quoted above), and therefore appear to be an interpolation in the letter which 'Verax' had somehow seen.

This suspicion is strengthened by the appearance in May 1788 of another version of the ode, published by J. Bell as *An Ode on the Popular Superstitions of the Highlands of Scotland; Considered as the Subject of Poetry. Inscribed to Mr. Home, Author of Douglas. . . . Never before printed* (a second edition appeared in 1789). An anonymous introduction claimed that this was the complete version seen by the Wartons in 1754, and the edition was in fact dedicated to them: '*Your mentioning it to* Dr. JOHNSON, *as it was the means that led to the imperfect first draught, so it likewise was the happy means of bringing this* PERFECT *copy to light.*' Bell's edition was treated with immediate suspicion when it appeared, and has been generally considered a forgery by Collins's modern editors (although Blunden accepted this text in his edition of 1929). The additional lines themselves do not bear close examination. Arthur Murphy, in the *Monthly Review*, 79 (Dec. 1788), 555, wrote that 'The lines that supply the chasm in the whole of the 5th and half of the 6th stanza, introduce the execution of Charles the First, the rebellion in 1745, the battles of Preston-Pans, Falkirk, and Culloden; but the style does not seem, to us, to be in the manner of Collins', and it is unlikely that these events would have interested Collins as late as 1749–50.

There is also external evidence which sheds light on this elaborate forgery. In the *Memoirs and Correspondence of Francis Horner, M.P.*, ed. Leonard Horner (1843), ii. 276, a letter from Horner to Thomas Thomson in 1815 records information which he received from Sir James Mackintosh, the distinguished historian:

I have made out the history of those supplementary stanzas in Collins's Ode on the Superstitions of the Highlands, which puzzled us. They are a mere fabrication. Mackintosh, who told me the story, would not mention the man's name; but it was a very low northern littérateur, who, about five and twenty years ago, published at Cadell's [*sic*] shop a new edition of that ode, as from another manuscript, with all the blanks and vacancies supplied. The additions were one and all a forgery of his own, of which he boasted to Mackintosh. The man is dead. This piece of literary history ought to be made known; for the forgery has not only crept into the edition of Collins which I shewed you, and that is part of a general collection, but also into the large body of the English poets published by Chalmers.

For a full analysis of the Bell forgery, see Roger Lonsdale's excellent discussion in his edition, pp. 495–9. Additional evidence supporting the case of a forgery is included below in the discussion of the manuscript.

The rediscovery of the defective manuscript in the summer of 1967 yields yet another perspective on the poem's textual history. After its publication in 1788, the manuscript remained in the possession of Alexander Fraser Tytler and his descendants, undiscovered in spite of a series of investigations. The manuscript is now owned by Colonel A. E. Cameron of Aldourie Castle, who has deposited it in the Bodleian Library (MS. Dep. e. 87). The rediscovery was announced and the manuscript poem printed by Claire Lamont in her article, cited above.

The manuscript originally consisted of twelve leaves, one of which (the fourth) is missing. The leaves measure 19·9 × 15·9 cm, and were apparently part of an unpaginated quarto notebook. The text is written on both sides of the leaves. The last leaves are blank (f. 10^v and ff. 11–12), except for the following note in Tytler's hand on 12^v: 'Original MS of Mr Collins's poem in his own handwriting Received from Dr Carlyle by AFT'. Miss Lamont has noted that the paper bears a 'Pro Patria' Vryheyt watermark, similar to figs. 3148–9 in E. Heawood, *Watermarks Mainly of the 17th and 18th Centuries* (Hilversum: The Paper Publications Society, 1950). For similar watermarks in Collins's other manuscripts, see the head-note to the Drafts and Fragments.

A collation of the manuscript text with Tytler's in the *Transactions* reveals that the version published by the Society was generally accurate. Tytler insisted upon marking passages and words added to the manuscript text with inverted commas, and the collation shows that this was usually done. Collins's two notes to his poem were elaborated in the *Transactions*, and several others added. In addition to changes in spelling, punctuation, and capitalization, the Edinburgh text also introduced twelve substantive changes of its own and a new title.

These substantive changes are interesting because they confirm the view that the anonymous editor of Bell's edition was indeed a forger. Bell's text follows its Scottish predecessor very closely except where a gap appears in the text, where Tytler suggests a line has been dropped, and in the notes. The only other differences between the two texts are occasional variants in Bell's edition, perhaps inserted solely for the appearance of authenticity. Collation with the Aldouri manuscript clearly demonstrates that where the *Transactions* text introduces a substantive variant, this is usually reprinted in Bell's edition. Thus of the twelve substantive variants in the Scottish edition, all but one are reproduced by Bell, and this exception involves only a slight change in the *Transactions* text (produced perhaps by simple misprinting) which Bell's editor chose not to follow: 'bank' for 'Banks' (l. 111; Bell also 'corrects' a misprint involving an accidental in l. 152: 'monarch's' for 'Monarchs'). And, significantly, where the Edinburgh text fails to suggest a missing line in stanza 12, Bell's edition also fails to supply one. The eleven variants (and one unmarked interpolation in l. 170) which are reproduced in Bell's edition suggest that the editor was relying on the *Transactions* text alone for his authority, and unwittingly reproducing variants in his text which had not appeared in Collins's 'defective' manuscript and which had only the Edinburgh edition as their authority. Similarly, the variants introduced into Bell's edition independently of the *Transactions* text derive no authority from the Aldouri manuscript.

Some of the variants in the *Transactions* seem to be attempts to 'improve' the poem or to tone down Collins's 'Scottish' diction; others are probably misprints. The substitution of a new title is more difficult to explain. The title of the Aldouri manuscript simply reads 'Ode to a Friend on his Return &c', and is possibly an abbreviated version of the title Thomas Warton recorded in his letter to Hymers: 'an *Ode to Mr. John Hume, on his leaving England for Scotland*' (although Miss Lamont interestingly notes that the unreliable version of this letter which appeared in the *St. James's Chronicle* in April 1788 referred to the poem as 'an Ode to Mr. Home, on his Return from England to Scotland in 1749'). It may be concluded, however, that the title which appeared in the *Transactions* was probably supplied by Carlyle and Tytler, who had seen Johnson's description (derived from the Wartons) of a poem on the 'superstitions of the Highlands'.

The present edition follows the Aldouri manuscript as its copy, including the abbreviated title (on the grounds that Collins wrote it, whereas the 'Superstitions' title is at least three times removed from the poet). Substantive variants from the Edinburgh text (1788, cited as *Transactions*) and from Bell's edition (1788, cited as *Bell*) are included in the textual notes, but not the interpolations by Mackenzie, Carlyle, or Bell's anonymous editor. Also noted are substantive variants occurring in the first collected edition to include the poem, *The Poetical Works of William Collins*, published in Philadelphia by Thomas Dobson (1788, cited here as *Dobson*). For details concerning the presentation of the manuscript, see the general textual introduction. It should be noted here, however, that ll. 133–7 are preceded by what appear to be question marks. Collins introduced similar marks preceding ll. 53–6 of Fragment 10, where they seem to query lines in a heavily reworked passage. In the present poem (as in Fragment 2 and Collins's transcription of Swift's 'On the Day of Judgement') the marks appear to indicate direct speech, and have been reproduced as quotation marks in the text.

The stanzaic pattern and rhyme scheme present particular problems of their own. Warton, who had only a brief glimpse of the manuscript, described it as written in 'the Octave Stanza'. Carlyle, in a letter already noted, wrote that he did not like its 'Spencerian stanza'. And apparently the transition in stanza 11 disturbed the editor of *The Poets of Great Britain* (1807), liii. 170, for there (and in Blunden's edition of 1929) stanzas 9 and 10 are interchanged. The recovery of the Aldouri manuscript makes it clear, however, that Carlyle did not assign a mistaken order to the stanzas, and that the stanzas themselves do not comprise a pair of 8- or 9-line segments, as Warton and Carlyle seem to have thought. The stanzas are, nevertheless, irregular: the normal length is 17 lines, but the second stanza contains 18, and the last three stanzas only 16. The Edinburgh editors surmised that the missing and deficient stanzas also had 17 lines, and their calculation has been followed in the present text (and notes added to point out the possible missing lines in the final stanzas).

Carlyle and Tytler did not reproduce Collins's inconsistent indentation, whose irregularity may have led him to add an extra line to stanza 2 and then to omit a line in the later stanzas. In the first stanza especially, Collins appears to have been working out a particular pattern of indentation to follow his rhyme scheme, but the unfinished and unrevised nature of the manuscript makes it difficult to determine his final intentions. For the sake of accuracy, Collins's own indentation in the manuscript is followed in the present text. From a textual viewpoint, the most important aspect of the manuscript's recovery may be that the poem must be considered an unfinished work whose printed editions lack any independent authority.

It should also be noted that the Aldouri manuscript provides us with our most sustained view of Collins's treatment of the accidentals of his text. Although the poem is neither finished nor revised for the press in this manuscript, some tentative conclusions may be drawn. It appears that Collins continued to employ a free use of capitals as late as 1749–50. Capitalization in the manuscript is often erratic—some adjectives are capitalized and some nouns often written in lower-case—but Collins's tendency is clear, especially with personifications and abstract nouns. The manuscript, while only partially punctuated, does indicate that Collins's fondness for the exclamation mark and semi-colon in the printed *Odes* was probably based on his own manuscript practice. It also seems that Collins intended to set off certain proper nouns by placing two short lines beneath them: 'Doric' and 'Solan's' (ll. 18, 166). Miss Lamont suggests that Collins meant 'perhaps to indicate to a printer that it should appear in capitals' (p. 140 n.), but this manuscript, at least, was intended only as a private copy for his friend Home. But even here, in a hurried copy where his practice is irregular, we can see that Collins intended to distinguish certain nouns from others in his text (this is also true of the Drafts and Fragments). These nouns have been placed in italics in the present edition. It might also be noted that the irregular spelling of the possessive 'its' in the *Odes* (printed 'it's') has a precedent in this manuscript poem (l. 111). Finally, it seems clear from the Aldouri manuscript and from the Drafts and Fragments that Collins appended his own notes to his poems, and that the notes printed with the published poems (for which we possess no manuscripts) are almost certainly his.

As early as in the *Transactions* it was pointed out that Collins's descriptions of Scotland and its superstitions were heavily indebted to the work of Martin Martin: 'COLLINS has taken all his information respecting the Western Isles from MARTIN; from whom he may likewise have derived his knowledge of the popular superstitions of the Highlanders, with which this ode shows so perfect an acquaintance' (Pt. ii, p. 72 n.). The initial stimulation for this subject may have come, as Collins seems to suggest in ll. 183–4, from Home himself, but Collins made free use of Martin's *A Description of the Western Islands of Scotland* (1703, corr. edn. 1716). A. S. P. Woodhouse, 'Collins and Martin Martin', *TLS* (20 Dec. 1928), p. 1011, pointed out that Collins, like his friend David Mallet (and, Lonsdale adds, James Thomson), was also indebted to Martin's earlier *A Late Voyage to St. Kilda* (1698), which had been republished as *A Voyage to St. Kilda* in March 1749. Woodhouse indicates that in his borrowings from Martin's *St. Kilda* Collins 'deliberately exaggerates the hardships suffered by the islanders, in order to intensify the impression of rugged courage and stoical endurance'.

1. *H—*: the playwright John Home, who was returning from London to his native Scotland; see head-note.

4. *thy Tragic Song*: Home's tragedy *Agis*, rejected by David Garrick for performance on the London stage. The play was finally acted in February 1758 in Drury Lane, following the success of Home's *Douglas* (first performed in Edinburgh in December 1756 and then in London in March 1757).

5. *cordial Youth*: Thomas Barrow, a mutual friend of Home and Collins whom they were visiting in Chichester when Collins apparently presented Home with this verse epistle.

6. 'Lavant' in Collins's cancelled line is a river running through Chichester.

8. Barrow married Mary Downer at Chichester on 2 April 1753 (see P. L. Carver, *The Life of a Poet*, pp. 151–3, and Mary Margaret Stewart, 'William Collins and Thomas Barrow', *PQ*, 48 (1969), 212–19).

14. *prompt*: to inspire; 'To incite' (*Dict.*).

16. *Pencil*: paintbrush.

18. *Doric Quill*: a rustic or pastoral reed; cf. the 'Oaten Stop' of 'Ode to Evening', l. 1.

21. *birken*: 'Made of birch' (*Dict.*, s.v. 'Birchen'); Lonsdale points out that 'birks' is included in the glossary of Allan Ramsay's *Poems* (1731).

22–5. Cf. Martin Martin, *A Description of the Western Islands of Scotland* (2nd edn., 1716), p. 391, who describes the work of the '*Browny*' in the Shetland Islands and the custom of rewarding him for his work by pouring 'some Milk and Wort through the Hole of a Stone, called *Browny*'s Stone' (cf. also Milton's 'L'Allegro', ll. 105–6). Martin mentions the spirit's music on p. 335.

26–9. *Elph-shot*: defined in a note in Ramsay's *Poems*, i. 139 n., as 'Bewitch'd, shot by fairies, country people tell odd tales of this distemper amongst cows. When elf-shot, the cow falls down suddenly dead, no part of the skin is pierced, but often a little triangular flat stone is found near the beast, as they report, which is call'd the elf's arrow.'

37. *Boreal*: 'Northern' (*Dict.*).

41. *Runic*: applied here to ancient Scottish poetry, the first such usage recorded in the *OED* (it usually denoted ancient Scandinavian literature). Sir William Temple had discussed Runic poetry in 'Of Poetry' (1690), Spingarn, iii. 93–6; Lonsdale points out that Temple's discussion was noted in the two 'Runic Odes' in Thomas Warton the Elder's *Poems* (1748), pp. 157–9.

42. *uncouth*: 'Odd; strange; unusual' (*Dict.*).

48 n. Collins's note on 'Shiel' is expanded in *Transactions* to: 'A kind of hut, built for a summer habitation to the herdsmen, when the cattle are sent to graze in distant pastures'.

52. *prove*: 'To make tryal' (*Dict.*).

53. *framing*: 'To make; to compose' (*Dict.*).

54–5. Martin, pp. 150–1, describes the caves on the Isle of Skye.

56. *Ust*: Uist. Martin, p. 85, describes the valley of Glenslyte on South Uist where 'The Natives who farm it . . . are possessed with a firm Belief that this Valley is haunted by Spirits, who by the Inhabitants are call'd the great Men.'

57–69. Martin speaks at length of 'second sight', pp. 300–35, defining it as 'a singular Faculty of Seeing an otherwise invisible Object. . . . the Vision makes such a lively impression upon the Seers, that they neither see nor think of any thing else, except the Vision, as long as it continues: and then they appear pensive or jovial, according to the Object which was represented to them' (p. 300).

58. *droop*: 'To faint; to grow weak; to be despirited' (*Dict.*).

59. *strath*: 'a plain on a river-side' (Glossary, Ramsay's *Poems* (1731)).
  Moss: 'bog, swamp, or morass' (*OED* 1).

61–4. Cf. Martin, pp. 320–1, for examples of these premonitions of the death of people in 'perfect health'.

65. *viewless*: 'Unseen; not discernible by the sight' (*Dict.*).

65–6. Martin, p. 309, specifies the passive nature of the seers, 'generally illiterate, and well-meaning People, and altogether void of design'.

68. *heartless*: dismayed; 'spiritless' (*Dict.*).

96. *excursive*: 'Rambling; wandering; deviating' (*Dict.*).

99. *unrustling*: the only usage recorded in the *OED*.

100. *mirk* (suggested reading): murky; 'dark' (Glossary, Ramsay's *Poems* (1731)).

wily Monster: the 'Kaelpie' (l. 137), or kelpie, described in Tytler's note as 'A name given in Scotland to a supposed spirit of the waters'. Cf. the *OED* definition, where Collins's usage is the first recorded: 'The Lowland Scottish name of a fabled water-spirit or demon assuming various shapes, but usually appearing in that of a horse; it is reputed to haunt lakes and rivers, and to take delight in, or even to bring about, the drowning of travellers and others.' Sir William Temple, 'Of Poetry' (Spingarn, iii. 97), mentions 'Old *Nicka*', a 'Sprite that came to strangle People who fell into the Water', in his discussion of Runic poetry (see the note to l. 41).

109. Cf. *An Epistle: Addrest to Sir Thomas Hanmer*, l. 25.

110. *Instant*: instantly.

111. *drown'd*: flooded.

119. *Fear-shook*: the only recorded example in the *OED*.

Youthly: youthful; 'Young; early in life. Obsolete' (*Dict.*).

121–4. Collins apparently modelled this scene on Thomson's 'Winter', ll. 311–17.

123. *To fall*: the close. This is the first recorded usage in the *OED*, although Arthur Johnston (p. 216 n.) points out that Collins was probably imitating its use in William Hamilton's 'The Braes of Yarrow', l. 79.

125–37. Mrs Barbauld (p. xlvii) compared this scene to Ovid's description of the dead Ceyx bending over the couch of Alcyone (*Metamorphoses*, xi. 652–62).

125. *Alone*: only.

126. *travell'd*: fatigued, travailed.

127. *Dropping*: dripping.

136. *weltring*: 'To roll in water or mire' (*Dict.*, s.v. 'Welter').

137. *Kaelpie*: see the note to l. 100.

142–5. Cf. Martin, p. 19, on 'The Island of *Pigmies*, or, as the Natives call it, *The Island of Little Men*' (the Flannan Islands), and p. 82, on the discovery of small bones in a stone vault at Bael-nin-Killach on Benbecula. Martin records the various conjectures about the bones: 'some said they were the Bones of Birds, others judg'd them rather to be the Bones of Pigmies.' See also *TLS* (10 Jan. 1929), p. 28.

146–7. Martin, p. 261, discusses the burial places of the kings of Scotland, Ireland, and Norway at St. Ouran's Church on Iona or Ocolmkill: 'On the South-side of the Church, mention'd above, is the Burial-place in which the Kings and Chiefs of Tribes are buried, and over them a Shrine; there was an Inscription, giving an account of each particular Tomb, but Time has worn them off.'

153. Cf. 'Ode to Simplicity', l. 9.

154. Cf. 'Ode, to a Lady', l. 20 (several versions).

155–71. Collins's description of this island is based on Martin's *A Late Voyage to St. Kilda* (1698; 2nd edn., 1749), in which he celebrated the rugged innocence of the primitive way of life there (see A. S. P. Woodhouse, 'Collins and Martin Martin', *TLS* (20 Dec. 1928), p. 1011). Martin also treats St. Kilda in *Western Islands*, pp. 280–99.

156, 161–2. Martin, *St. Kilda* (1749 edn.), p. 9, wrote that the island was fenced in by 'one continued Face of a Rock of great height, except a part of the Bay, which lies to the *South-East*, and is generally well fenced with a raging Sea'.

157–60, 167–9. David Mallet, in *Amyntor and Theodora* (1747), had earlier praised the virtues of these islanders, also taking his examples from Martin's *St. Kilda*. Martin described their world as a golden age founded on 'Innocency and Simplicity, Purity, mutual Love, and cordial Friendship, free from solicitous Cares, and anxious Covetousness; from Envy, Deceit, and Dissimulation; from Ambition and Pride, and the Consequences that attend them' (p. 68).

161. *ragged*: 'Rugged' (*Dict.*).

164. *Sainted Spring*: Martin describes many springs and wells, most notably '*the Well of Youth*' located upon a steep rock (*St. Kilda*, pp. 13–14).

165–6. Martin frequently mentions the islanders' attempts to steal eggs from the solan geese (gannets); cf. *St. Kilda*, pp. 20–1, 25–8, 55, and *Western Islands*, p. 293.

168–9. Martin mentions their 'frugal fare' in *St. Kilda*, pp. 58–9.

169. *Taste full*: as Lonsdale notes, a curious usage combining a sense of inducing appetite and of a task 'Mentally pleasant or agreeable' (*OED* 2b).

170. Based on Martin's description in *St. Kilda*, pp. 14–15, of the island as 'one hard Rock' covered by a thin layer of topsoil which is, however, 'very grateful to the Labourer'.

171. Cf. Martin, *St. Kilda*, p. 17: 'there is no Sort of Trees, no, not the least Shrub grows here, nor ever a Bee seen at any Time.'

172. *false Themes*: more appropriately the superstitions of the earlier stanzas than the simple life of the islanders described in the preceding stanza.

173. *gentle*: apparently 'Well born; well descended' (*Dict.*), in contrast to 'the Village Breast', l. 174.

177. *Wayward Sisters*: the witches in *Macbeth* ('Wayward' is a form of 'weird').

180–2. Cf. *Macbeth*, IV. i. This scene was illustrated in the frontispiece to the play in Pope's edition (9 vols., 1728), vol. vii.

188–91. Lonsdale and Arthur Johnston point out that Collins's defence of the supernatural closely imitates Dryden's 'Of Heroic Plays: An Essay' (Watson, i. 160–1), where Tasso's 'enchanted wood' is also mentioned: 'an heroic poet is not tied to a bare representation of what is true, or exceeding probable: but . . . may let himself loose to visionary objects, and to the representation of such things as depending not on sense, and therefore not to be comprehended by knowledge, may give him a freer scope for imagination.' Cf. also the *Spectator*, No. 419.

191–203. Collins refers to Tasso's *Gerusalemme Liberata* (1576–93), translated into English by Edward Fairfax in 1600 (and reissued in October 1749) as *Jerusalem Delivered: Or Godfrey of Bulloign* (see also Fragment 6, l. 14).

192–5. Cf. *Jerusalem Delivered*, XIII. xxxix–xlix, where Tasso describes Tancred's adventures in the enchanted wood, whose trees (masquerading as the souls of dead warriors) are inhabited by evil spirits.

202. *num'rous*: 'Harmonious' (*Dict.*).

205. *Firths*: 'A strait of the sea where the water being confined is rough' (*Dict.*, s.v. 'Frith').

206. *Annan . . . Tay*: the Annan flows into the firth of Solway; Perth is situated on the Tay.

207. *Don*: Aberdeen is located at the mouth of the Don.

212 (n.). 'BEN JOHNSON undertook a journey to Scotland a-foot in 1619, to visit the poet DRUMMOND, at his seat of Hawthornden, near Edinburgh. DRUMMOND has preserved in his works, some very curious heads of their conversation' (Tytler's note in *Transactions*, Pt. ii, p. 75 n.). Drummond's notes were first published in his *Works* (Edinburgh, 1711), pp. 224–7.

213. *Tiviot's dale*: the valley of the river Teviot in Roxburghshire.

214. *Yarrow Banks*: the river Yarrow in Selkirkshire; cf. William Hamilton's ballad 'The Braes of Yarrow', celebrating a young widow's lament for her husband on the banks of this river.

216. *Cordial Youth*: Collins clearly refers to Home in ll. 217, 219 ('he', 'my Absent Friend'), and 'Cordial Youth' seems to be the antecedent of these words. Home, moreover, was born in Midlothian and had been a minister in East Lothian. On the other hand, Collins had described Thomas Barrow with this phrase in l. 5; and Barrow, as Mary Margaret Stewart points out (in the article cited in the note to l. 8), had made his escape during the Rebellion across the plains of Lothian. Miss Stewart suggests that Collins may have meant Barrow in l. 216 and Home in the following lines, but she admits that this does not erase the syntactical confusion. Presumably Collins would have resolved this confusion in later revisions; as the text stands, the clearest reading remains Home.

217. *Muir*: moor.

219. *touch'd*: 'To affect; . . . To move . . . to melt' (*Dict.*, s.v. 'Touch').

DRAFTS AND FRAGMENTS

In his brief account of Collins in *The Reaper*, No. 26, Thomas Warton described several manuscript poems by Collins that he had seen and then mentioned that 'Doctor Warton, my brother, has a few fragments of some other Odes, but too loose and imperfect for publication, yet containing traces of high imagery.' These odes are almost certainly the manuscript poems discovered among Thomas Warton's papers at Trinity College, Oxford, and first published as *William Collins: Drafts & Fragments of Verse*, ed. J. S. Cunningham (Oxford: Clarendon Press, 1956). Cunningham suggests that Collins may have given Joseph Warton these poems during the Wartons' visit to Chichester in September 1754.

These fragments represent by far the largest amount of surviving manuscript material in Collins's hand, and increase the size of his poetic work by one quarter. Of the eleven poems (one of which is only partly in Collins's hand), six are verse epistles similar to *An Epistle: Addrest to Sir Thomas Hanmer* (1743–4), one is an elegy on an unknown (and probably fictitious) female painter, one is an autobiographical pastoral, two appear to be early versions of Collins's odes (or at least closely associated with them), and one is apparently a draft of Collins's undiscovered (and probably unfinished) ode on the music of the Grecian theatre.

A careful attempt to date and order the fragments has been made by Roger Lonsdale, and his judicious conclusions have been tested and accepted here. Although there is rarely substantial evidence for dating the poems, they do fall roughly into several groups. The verse epistles, written in heroic couplets and frequently echoing Pope, can be dated with some confidence from the time of Collins's arrival in London (probably early in 1744), and from the date of his one published epistle. These six fragments suggest a young writer's attempt to further his career, and are not inconsistent with Johnson's description, in his 'Life of Collins', of a 'literary adventurer, with many projects in his head, and very little money in his pocket' (*Lives*, iii. 335). The remaining poems are written in stanzas with more complicated rhyme schemes, and may be more closely associated with the published dirges and odes dating from 1744–6. Only Fragment 11 can be dated with some precision (in November 1750). Specific information for dating each poem is included in the individual head-notes.

An examination of the paper on which the poems are written helps verify dating which in some cases would otherwise rely on circumstantial evidence alone. There is a general similarity in watermarks throughout the manuscripts, and it is possible that Collins regularly bought his paper from a single source. Three separate pairs of poems, however, are written on paper which is identical, suggesting a greater probability that these poems may have similar dates of composition. The poems linked by this physical evidence are Fragments 3 and 4, both verse epistles which appear to have been written in 1744; Fragments 8 and 9, the early 'versions' of two of Collins's published odes, which probably date from 1745–6; and Fragments 10 and 11. This final pairing raises some problems: Fragment 10 has been thought to date from the time of the 'Ode, to a Lady' (in 1745), whereas the last fragment was probably written in 1750. It may be wiser to trust the circumstantial evidence in dating Fragment 10, the most clearly autobiographical of Collins's poems; but, as Lonsdale has warned, the association with Elizabeth Goddard and the 'Ode, to a Lady' may be too facile, and there remains a strong possibility that this fragment was also written later in the decade.

The references in the following description of the manuscripts are to E. Heawood, *Watermarks Mainly of the 17th and 18th Centuries* (Hilversum: The Paper Publication Society, 1950). It should be remembered that dating by watermark is at best an approximate form of analysis: here often the countermarks alone are known, and many of the manuscripts appear to predate Heawood's earliest examples.

Fragment 1: untraced.

Fragments 2, 10, 11: countermarks similar to Heawood 3696 ('Pro Patria', 1724–6) and Heawood 2745 (Gerrevink's 'Horn', 1755); Fragment 2 differs in size and texture of paper.

Fragments 3, 4: countermarks similar to Heawood 3148 (Vryheyt's 'Pro Patria', 1745), Heawood 3700 ('Pro Patria', 1747), Heawood 448 ('Coat of Arms', 1736), and Heawood 450 ('Coat of Arms', c.1760). The Aldouri MS. contains a watermark similar to Heawood 3148–9.

Fragment 5: watermark similar to Heawood 2745 (Gerrevink's 'Horn', 1755).

Fragments 6, 8, 9: watermarks similar to Heawood 448 ('Coat of Arms', 1736) and Heawood 450 ('Coat of Arms', c.1760); Fragment 6 differs in size of paper.

Fragment 7: countermark similar to Heawood 3696 ('Pro Patria', 1724–6).

'Oratio ad Portas': watermark similar to Heawood 3696 ('Pro Patria', 1724–6).

Cunningham's transcription of the manuscripts is generally accurate, and has been corrected at some points in Lonsdale's edition. It is currently possible, however, to provide a more exact transcription of the poems, both in the text itself and in the description of the precise nature of Collins's frequent revisions. The principles determining the presentation of the text are discussed in the textual introduction. It should be noted that these manuscripts, 'loose and imperfect' as Warton described them, do help corroborate the tentative conclusions drawn about the characteristics of Collins's manuscripts in the head-note to the 'Ode to a Friend on his Return &c', especially Collins's tendency to capitalize all nouns (and sometimes adjectives as well) and to annotate his own text.

Also included in Cunningham's edition are a transcription of Swift's 'On the Day of Judgement' in Collins's hand, Collins's 'Oratio ad Portas', and notes recorded by the Wartons concerning Collins and his library.

Cunningham's edition was reviewed by A. D. McKillop in *PQ*, 36 (1957), 352-4, and by John Butt in *RES*, n.s., 9 (1958), 220-2; both attempted to augment Cunningham's commentary on the fragments, and their reviews are cited by name in the individual head-notes.

FRAGMENT I

The similarities between this fragment and Collins's *An Epistle: Addrest to Sir Thomas Hanmer* (1743-4) have been noticed by Cunningham, McKillop, and Lonsdale. Like *An Epistle*, the fragment is written in heroic couplets and takes as its subject the history of English drama, extending its focus here to the Restoration stage, theatrical machinery, and (in Collins's view) the corrupt influence of the French theatre. These points of similarity—and the clear and frequent influence of Pope—argue for a probable date of 1744.

The poem is written on two sides of a folio leaf measuring 26·5 × 20 cm. Lines 1-18 are written on the recto, and the continuing lines (19-26) on the verso. Collins then returned to the recto side for lines 27-32 (written vertically in the right margin, and preceded by the numeral '2'), and back to the verso for the rest of the fragment (written upside-down from the foot of the page, and preceded by a '3'). The numerals appear to indicate the sequence of the lines and not formal stanzaic divisions in the text. Two words in the text also appear in the right margin: 'Thames', l. 2, and 'scented', l. 34. Their positioning, and the carets placed below 'scented' in both the text and margin, suggest that Collins was either clarifying his text or reminding himself of revisions to be made at a later time.

2. English theatres had been closed since 1642: patents for theatrical companies and playhouses were issued to Sir William Davenant (the Duke of York's Servants) and Thomas Killigrew (the King's Players) on 21 August 1660 by Charles II.

6. The references are to Raphael Holinshed's *Chronicles* (1577) and John Stow's *Summarie of Englyshe Chronicles* (1565) and *Chronicles of England* (1580; later issued as *Annales of England*, 1592). Although these names are asterisked in the text, Collins's note refers to l. 16. Some of the detail in these chronicles was considered trivial; cf. Pope, *Satires of Dr. John Donne*, iv. 130-1: 'Meer *Houshold Trash*! of Birth-Nights, Balls and Shows, / More than ten *Holingsheds*, or *Halls*, or *Stows*'.

8. Cf. Pope, *Imitations of Horace*, Epistle II. i. 140: 'and *Luxury* with *Charles* restor'd'.

lights: 'Illumination of mind; instruction; knowledge' (*Dict.*, s.v. 'Light').

13. Cf. Pope, 'Epilogue to the Satires', ii. 171: 'Let Courtly Wits to Wits afford supply.'

16 (6 n.). Monimia is the heroine of Thomas Otway's *The Orphan* (1680).

For Otway, cf. 'Ode to Pity', ll. 16–24 (and notes), and Fragment 10, ll. 25–30.

18. *Augustus*: Charles II (and London), corresponding to the court of Louis XIV at Versailles.

19. *His Hand*: Louis's.

22. *Richelieu*: Cardinal Richelieu (1585–1642), the chief minister of Louis XIII, engaged dramatists (including Corneille) to write plays under his direction. The hall of the Palais Royal was specifically built for the production of his own tragi-comedy *Mirame*, and was afterwards used by Moliere's company. Cf. Richard Flecknoe, *A Short Discourse of the English Stage* (1664): 'Cardinal *Richlieu* being the first that brought them [plays] into Vouge and Esteem as now they are, well knowing how much the Acting noble and heroick Plays conferr'd to the instilling a noble and heroick Spirit into the Nation' (Spingarn, ii. 91).

23–6. The Hôtel de Bourgogne, formerly the residence of the Dukes of Burgundy in Paris, became the theatre of the *Confrérie de la Passion* in 1548. The building was occasionally used by this acting company until 1588, and afterwards by professional companies (the actors were not 'heirs' to this residence in the seventeenth century alone, as Collins implies). The Hôtel is discussed in Warburton's supplementary note to Charles Jarvis's translation of *Don Quixote* (1742), vol. i.

31–3. Davenant's company in particular was responsible for elaborate scenery and mechanical effects unknown to London audiences. Cf. Pope, *Imitations of Horace*, Epistle II. i. 314–15, 324–7, on theatrical spectacle in the eighteenth century: 'The Play stands still; damn action and discourse, / Back fly the scenes, and enter foot and horse; / . . . / Ah luckless Poet! stretch thy lungs and roar, / That Bear or Elephant shall heed thee more; / While all its throats the Gallery extends, / And all the Thunder of the Pit ascends.'

39. *Betterton*: Thomas Betterton (1635–1710), one of the best-known Restoration actors and an original member of Davenant's company in 1661.

39–40. Cf. Pope, *Imitations of Horace*, Epistle II. i. 330–1, 336–7: 'Such is the shout, the long-applauding note, / At Quin's high plume, or Oldfield's petticoat, / . . . / "What shook the stage, and made the people stare?" / Cato's long Wig, flower'd gown, and lacquer'd chair.'

43. *Ask you*: a formula derived from Pope, *Epistles to Several Persons*, i. 206 and iii. 121.

FRAGMENT 2

This fragment was printed by Cunningham in an appendix as 'Lines of Composite Authorship' (ll. 1–24 are in an unidentified hand; only ll. 25–40 are written by Collins). Cunningham noted that its occasion is obscure and that it 'probably belongs to Collins's days at Winchester College'. But, as

Lonsdale has pointed out, the poem 'clearly concerns the cost of theatrical production and scenery, a topic which is more likely to have concerned C. during his early years in London, 1744-45, when he himself entertained theatrical ambitions' (p. 527). Like the preceding fragment (also written in heroic couplets), this poem can be associated with *An Epistle: Addrest to Sir Thomas Hanmer* (1743-4). The discussion of theatrical scenery is particularly similar to a passage in *An Epistle* where Collins had described the 'fair Design' (later 'free Design') of pictorial representation of scenes in Shakespeare (ll. 111-14). According to John Ragsdale (*The Reaper*, No. 26), Collins's friendship with Garrick procured him 'the liberty of the Scenes and Greenroom, where he made diverting observations on the vanity and false consequence of that class of people, and his manner of relating them to his particulars was extremely entertaining'. A probable date for this fragment is therefore 1744-5.

The poem is written on one quarto leaf measuring 23 × 21·3 cm, with two pages of text. The first twenty lines (which are not in Collins's hand) are each preceded by what appears to be a question mark, and ll. 17-20 are also concluded with this mark. Although Collins himself used a similar mark to query lines in Fragment 10, he used it in the Aldouri MS. ('Ode to a Friend on his Return &c') and in his transcription of Swift's 'On the Day of Judgement' as a quotation mark to point out direct speech. This seems to be its use here, the first twenty lines comprising a paraphrase of the objections which a financial backer might make ('But why you'll Say to me . . .'), and the following lines offering a reasoned reply ('Yes the Proud Cost allows some short Suspence / I grant the Terrors of that Word Expence'). These marks have been presented as quotation marks in the text.

33-4. Cf. *An Epistle: Addrest to Sir Thomas Hanmer*, ll. 111-14.

34. Collins probably alludes to Addison's popular *Cato* (1713) and Ambrose Philips's *The Distrest Mother* (1712), an adaptation of *Andromaque*.

FRAGMENT 3

This fragment was probably written shortly after May 1744. A note at the close of the manuscript in Joseph Warton's hand reads: 'This addrest by *Collins* to Mr Harris of Sarum'. James Harris (1709-80), a native of Salisbury, was the author of *Hermes: Or, A Philosophical Inquiry Concerning Language and Universal Grammar* (1751). There is no evidence to suggest that Collins himself was familiar with Harris, who was a patron of music in Salisbury and later a successful statesman. The work which Collins clearly reflects in his poem, however, is Harris's *Three Treatises. The First Concerning Art. The Second Concerning Music, Painting, and Poetry. The Third Concerning Happiness. By J. H.*, published in May 1744 (*GM*, 14 (1744), 288), several months after

Collins had arrived in London. Like Collins's *An Epistle: Addrest to Sir Thomas Hanmer*, issued in May 1744, this fragment is a verse epistle cast in heroic couplets which celebrates the sister arts and their encouragement in England.

The poem is written on one folio sheet measuring 32 × 20·5 cm, with two pages of text. Because the fragment begins one-third of the way down the recto side, it is possible that Collins left blank several lines which were meant to precede the opening of the poem as it now stands: 'These would I sing—'. A much shorter gap follows a deleted couplet further down the recto (preceding l. 11), and here it is difficult to determine whether the following lines were meant to replace those Collins cancelled, whether another couplet was to be inserted later, or whether a new stanza was to begin. Because the unfinished state of the fragment makes it impossible to read Collins's intentions exactly, this lacuna has been retained in the present text, but is ignored in numbering the lines.

1. *Art*: music.

3–5. Cf. 'Ode to Evening', ll. 15–16.

7–8. Cf. *An Epistle: Addrest to Sir Thomas Hanmer*, ll. 133–6.

7–10. In the second of his treatises, Harris argues for the supremacy of poetry over its sister arts, but elaborates each art's particular powers. He concludes by describing the combined effect of poetry and music: 'FROM what has been said it is evident, that these two Arts can never be so powerful *singly*, as when they are *properly united*' (p. 102).

11–12. Harris was the nephew of Anthony Ashley Cooper, third Earl of Shaftesbury (1671–1713), author of *Characteristicks of Men, Manners, Opinions, Times* (1711).

13. In his first and third treatises, Harris, like Shaftesbury, made use of the Platonic dialogue.

14. *careless*: 'unconcerned . . . neglectful' (*Dict.*).

15. *Wilton*: Harris's dialogue in the first treatise is occasioned by a visit to Wilton House, seat of the Earl of Pembroke.

22. *her*: music again.

24. Cf. 'The Passions', l. 105.

25. Cf. 'The Passions', l. 110.

31. *Adria*: apparently Venice, on the Adriatic Sea; cf. 'Ode to Liberty', l. 45.

FRAGMENT 4

This fragment was almost certainly written in 1744, probably late in the year if Collins meant 'the wintry gloom' of the opening line to be taken literally. An advertisement in the *Daily Advertiser*, pointed out by Mary

Margaret Stewart, may date this poem even more closely. On 14 November 1744 the Tonson firm announced the forthcoming publication of two works, with a new edition of Waller boldly emphasized (Collins refers to Waller's poetry in ll. 11–12). On 6 December, however, the final announcement for these publications appeared with the emphasis reversed; and it is possible that Collins, incited by the first advertisement, was then discouraged from finishing his poem by the second notice. The poem's implicit request for literary patronage, its formal characteristics (a verse epistle in heroic couplets with clear echoes of Pope), and its praise of Waller also suggest that it be considered, like the previous three fragments, an early production by Collins shortly after he arrived in London. The paper on which the fragment is written, moreover, is a quarto sheet measuring 20·8 × 16·2 cm, which represents exactly half (in size and countermark) the full folio sheet on which Fragment 3 is written (and that poem can be dated mid-1744 with some certainty).

The poem is addressed to Jacob Tonson (d. 1767), great-nephew of the Jacob Tonson (1656?–1736) who founded the successful publishing firm at Shakespeare's Head. After the founder's retirement in 1720, his nephew Jacob Tonson the Younger had directed the firm, and since 1735 the management had rested in the hands of a third Jacob, the addressee of Collins's poem. That Collins was not also addressing Richard Tonson (d. 1772), another great-nephew, has been demonstrated by Lonsdale: Richard had little to do with the actual management of the firm, and did not possess the famous Kit-Cat portraits (mentioned in ll. 3–4) until his brother's death in 1767 (see Nichols, i. 297–8). Henry M. Geduld, *Prince of Publishers: A Study of the Work and Career of Jacob Tonson* (Bloomington: Indiana Univ. Press, 1969), p. 232 n., claims that the portraits passed directly to Richard Tonson at Water Oakley in 1736, but this seems unlikely: Richard did not build his own room for the portraits there until shortly after his brother's death.

'Jovial Jacob', the founder of the firm, had been secretary of the Kit-Cat Club, a group of writers, wits, and Whig politicians who met at a tavern in London run by the publican Christopher Cat (see Robert J. Allen, *The Clubs of Augustan London* (Cambridge, Mass.: Harvard Univ. Press, 1933), pp. 35–54). In 1703 Tonson moved the group to a clubroom in his house at Barn Elms in Surrey, where the club continued to meet until 1717. A collection of paintings celebrating his fellow club members, comprising at least forty-two Kneller portraits, was commissioned by the Duke of Somerset. The portraits are now in the National Portrait Gallery; see David Piper, *Catalogue of Seventeenth-Century Portraits in the National Portrait Gallery* (Cambridge: Cambridge Univ. Press, 1963), pp. 398–403. Jacob Tonson the Younger apparently had a gallery contructed for these portraits at Barn Elms (Sarah Clapp, *Jacob Tonson in Ten Letters By and About Him* (Austin, Texas: Univ. of

Texas Press, 1948), p. 20). Engravings of the portraits were published by
Tonson in 1723 and republished by John Faber in 1735 as *The Kit-Cat Club,
Done from the Original Paintings of Sir Godfrey Kneller*.

   1. *You*: the publisher, Jacob Tonson the Third (see head-note).

   2. *Jovial Jacob*: Jacob Tonson the Elder, described by Pope as 'genial Jacob'
(*Dunciad*, i. 57).

   academic Room: the clubroom in Tonson's house at Barn Elms which
originally housed the Kit-Cat portraits, or possibly the gallery later con-
structed for them by Jacob Tonson the Younger (see head-note).

   11. *Courtly Waller*: cf. 'Courtly Davenant' in Fragment 1, l. 2. Collins
quotes Waller in Fragment 5; cf. his later assessment of Waller's poetry in
'Ode on the Poetical Character', l. 69. Lonsdale points out that Collins's is
an orthodox view of Waller's achievement in refining English verse; cf.
Francis Atterbury's *Preface to The Second Part of Mr. Waller's Poems* (1690),
often reprinted in eighteenth-century editions.

   14. *nicer*: more 'Refined' (*Dict.*).

   17–20. Collins's references to specific publications by Tonson have been
documented by McKillop and Lonsdale: in 1690 Tonson published *The
Maid's Tragedy Altered. With Some Other Pieces. By Edmund Waller, Esq; Not
Before Printed in the several Editions of his Poems*; and his name was added to the
title-page of Waller's *Poems* (1694), issued by Henry Herringman, the chief
publisher of both Waller and Cowley in the late seventeenth century.
Tonson's name also appears on the title-pages of Herringman's eighth and
ninth editions of Cowley (in 1693 and 1700), as well as in editions of in-
dividual works in 1681 and 1693. Tonson was a frequent publisher of both
Cowley and Waller in the early eighteenth century, and it is likely that
Collins, who presumably read both these poets in Tonson's editions, wished
to emphasize the firm's long association with English poetry.

   18. *Sacharissa*: Lady Dorothea Sidney, in Waller's poetry.

   20. Cf. Pope, *Imitations of Horace*, Epistle II. i. 75–6: 'Who now reads
Cowley? if he pleases yet, / His moral pleases, not his pointed wit.'

   21–6. Apparently the Restoration poets collected in Tonson's six–part
Miscellany Poems (1684–1709, reissued in 1716 and 1727); see Geduld, *Prince
of Publishers*, pp. 87–109.

   21–2. Cf. Pope, *Imitations of Horace*, Epistle II. i. 107–8, on the 'twinkling
Stars' of the 'Miscellanies': 'the Wits of either Charles's days, / The Mob of
Gentlemen who wrote with Ease'.

   24. *careless*: cf. *An Epistle: Addrest to Sir Thomas Hanmer*, l. 138.

   27. *Barn Elms*: the Tonson house in Surrey (see head-note).

   29. *price*: 'Reward' (*Dict.*).

FRAGMENT 5

The grounds for dating this poem are similar to those for the previous four fragments: like *An Epistle: Address to Sir Thomas Hanmer* (1743–4), this poem is a verse epistle written in heroic couplets; like several of the other fragments, it expresses opinions on English poetry (especially on Waller and on original composition) which are not characteristic of his mature verse; and allusions to Dodsley—who helped publish his epistle in 1744— and to Hayman—who supplied the illustrations for Hanmer's edition celebrated in the epistle—help confirm an early dating. Lonsdale has suggested a *terminus a quo* of May 1743 when Roger de Piles's *The Principles of Painting*, to which Collins alludes in l. 14, was first translated into English. The probable date for this address to a 'correct' young critic is therefore in the months following Collins's arrival in London in 1744.

The poem is written on two quarto leaves measuring 22·8 × 18·5 cm, with three pages of text. Because there are several lines omitted in the manuscript, evidence pointing to the specific form of the poem is inconclusive. It does seem, however, that Collins intended at least two breaks in the epistle, following ll. 4 and 42. Similarly, small variations in the distance between lines suggest that Collins probably intended the poem to appear in quatrain form.

1–8. The parallel between painting and poetry ('ut pictura poesis') was a critical commonplace derived from Horace's *Ars Poetica* (referred to in l. 5).

1. *Angelo*: Michelangelo (1475–1564).

5. *Fresnoy*: Charles Alphonse Dufresnoy (1611–65), the French painter and poet, and author of *De Arte Graphica*, a Latin poem translated by Dryden in 1695 (with an influential essay) as *The Art of Painting*.

7–8. *Vinci*: Leonardo da Vinci (1452–1519), whose *Trattato della Pittura*, published in Paris in 1651, had been translated into English in 1721 as *A Treatise on Painting*. Lonsdale suggests that Collins's description of 'Searchfull Vinci' may be indebted to the translation of de Piles's *The Art of Painting* (2nd edn., 1744), p. 104: Leonardo was 'incessantly busy'd in reflections about his art, and spar'd for no care or study to arrive at perfection in it'.

8. *Pencils*: paintbrushes; cf. Pope, 'Epistle to Mr. Jervas, With Dryden's Translation of Fresnoy's Art of Painting', ll. 69–70: 'The kindred arts shall in their praise conspire, / One dip the pencil, and one string the lyre.'

12. *Addison or Boyle*: famous arbiters of taste in the arts. Richard Boyle, third Earl of Burlington (1695–1753), was an admirer of Palladio; the fourth of Pope's *Epistles to Several Persons* ('Of the Use of Riches') was dedicated to him.

14. *Despiles*: Roger de Piles (1635–1709), a commentator on Dufresnoy's *De Arte Graphica* and the author of numerous works on art history and theory. McKillop suggests that Collins's use of 'weigh' may be a reference to de

Piles's *Dissertation sur la balance des peintres* (1708), translated into English as *The Principles of Painting . . . To which is Added, The Balance of Painters* (May 1743), in which de Piles attemped to compute (in a table) their 'Degrees of Perfection in the Four principal Parts of their ART'.

16. *Thornhill*: Sir James Thornhill (1675–1734) had painted the cupola of St. Paul's and the Painted Hall at Greenwich Hospital.

18. *Rowe*: the Poet Laureate Nicholas Rowe (1674–1718) was the author of eight plays and some occasional verse, which Collins apparently thought an 'unfruitfull' production.

20. *Mannerist*: the first usage recorded in the *OED* is from Dryden's translation of Dufresnoy: 'Those [Painters] whom we may call Mannerists, and who repeat five or six times over in the same Picture the same Hairs of a Head'.

21. *Anna's age*: Queen Anne ruled from 1702–14.

22, 24. *nice*: 'Fastidious' and 'Formed with minute exactness' (*Dict.*).

29. *Dodsley*: Robert Dodsley (1703–64), the London bookseller who was co-publisher of Collins's *An Epistle: Addrest to Sir Thomas Hanmer* (May 1744).

31. *Hayman*: Francis Hayman (1708–76), the painter who had provided the illustrations for Hanmer's edition of Shakespeare.

34–6 (n.). The passage Collins alludes to (and quotes from in his note) is Waller's 'To My Young Lady Lucy Sidney', ll. 1–6: 'Why came I so untimely forth / Into a world, which wanting thee, / Could entertain us with no worth, / Or shadow of felicity? / That time should me so far remove / From that which I was born to love!'

36. *Originals*: i.e., works of art which are not imitations.

38. *Carlo*: Carlo Maratta or Maratti (1625–1713), the Italian painter.

41. *Candid*: 'Without malice; . . . fair; open' (*Dict.*).

43–4. Cf. Pope's *Essay on Criticism*, ll. 134–6: 'But when t'examine ev'ry Part he came, / *Nature* and *Homer* were, he found, the *same*: / Convinc'd, amaz'd, he checks the bold Design.'

45. *Blackhall*: Collins apparently meant Thomas Blackwell (1701–57), who had written *An Enquiry into the Life and Writings of Homer* (1735), which examined Homer's superiority in epic poetry.

FRAGMENT 6

There is no actual evidence by which to date this poem, but its formal characteristics—a verse epistle written in heroic couplets with distinct echoes of Pope—argue for an early date, probably following Collins's arrival in London in early 1744. Cunningham and Butt both associate this fragment with the missing 'An Epistle to the Editor of Fairfax his Translation of Tasso's Jerusalem' (see Lost Poems) and with the republication of Fairfax's translation of Tasso in the autumn of 1749. But, as Lonsdale has pointed out, Collins had shown interest in Fairfax's translation of Tasso earlier (in 1747): see Collins's letter to John Gilbert Cooper, printed in this edition. As the second stanza of the poem makes clear, Collins is addressing a friend who is about to visit Italy, an occasion which Thomas Warton also celebrated in a similar ode, 'To a Gentleman upon his Travels thro' Italy', included in Joseph Warton's *Odes* (1746). It is possible, as Lonsdale suggests, that Collins and Warton were addressing the same person.

The poem is written on one quarto sheet measuring 21·5 × 18·4 cm, with two pages of text.

1–10. These lines are based on Pope's 'To Mr. Addison, Occasioned by his Dialogues on Medals', especially ll. 31–4 and 55–8, and possibly on Addison's *Dialogues Upon the Usefulness of Ancient Medals* as well.

1. *Vertù*: although the defective line makes Collins's sense imperfect, his spelling and the context particularly suggest 'The possession or display of manly qualities; . . . manliness, courage' (*OED*, s.v. 'Virtue', 7).

3. *grav'd*: engraved.

10. *genial air*: cf. Fragment 4, l. 4.

13–14. For Collins's opinion of Tasso and Edward Fairfax, his English translator, see 'Ode to a Friend on his Return &c', ll. 197, 200–3.

17. *Cynthio*: Giraldi Cinthio's *Gli Hecatommithi* (1566) supplied the plot for *Othello* and parts of plots for several other plays by Shakespeare. This was pointed out by Dryden in his 'Preface' to *An Evening's Love* (1671; Watson, i. 154), and by Gerard Langbaine, *An Account of the English Dramatick Poets* (Oxford, 1691), p. 461.

18. Milton refers to the poet Giovanni Battista Marino in 'Mansus', ll. 9, 51.

FRAGMENT 7

The female painter who is the subject of this elegy has not been identified, and Lonsdale argues that the close resemblance of the fragment in structure, argument, and verbal allusion to Pope's 'Elegy to the Memory of an Unfortunate Lady' suggests that this lady may be fictitious as well. The echoes of Pope and the interest in painting would link this poem with the preceding fragments, early in the period 1744–6. While this dating is probably accurate, the poem differs from the other early fragments in some significant respects. It is not written in heroic couplets, nor in the verse-epistle form, and its elegiac mood may associate it with Collins's other dirges of this period: 'A Song from Shakespear's *Cymbelyne*' (early 1744) and 'Song. The Sentiments borrowed from Shakespear' (probably 1744). Like those two dirges, this poem employs the more complicated formal structure of quatrains with alternating rhymes. It also appears to be the first fragment to suggest the influence of Thomson (especially in the 'mild Æthereal radiance' of l. 2). And at several points Collins employs words which are closely associated with the later odes (especially 'imbrown'd', l. 36, and 'bloomy', l. 40). Thus while the poem probably dates from 1744–5, it may be characterized as a transitional piece between the early fragments and the odes.

The poem is written on two quarto sheets measuring 20 × 16·4 cm, with three pages of text. Lines 1–12 are written on 1ʳ; 1ᵛ is blank. Lines 13–40 are written on 2ʳ (with the last two quatrains written sideways in the right margin); lines 41 ff. are written on 2ᵛ.

3. *Paly*: cf. 'Ode to Evening', l. 22.

13–16. Collins is describing Lavinia Fontana (1552–1614), known as a portrait painter and as the daughter of Prospero Fontana (1512–97), also a painter. Lavinia is mentioned in Felibien's *Entretiens* (1705), iii. 91; see the note to ll. 24–8.

24–8. Marietta, daughter of Tintoretto, was herself a painter and musician who died at the age of 30. McKillop and Lonsdale point out that Collins's source for calling her 'Tintoretta' and for mentioning Philip and the 'envied Bride' is probably André Felibien, *Entretiens Sur Les Vies Et Sur Les Ouvrages Des Plus Excellens Peintres Anciens Et Modernes* (1705), iii. 129: Tintoretto 'avoit une fille nommée MARIETTA TINTORETTA qui peignit parfaitement bien, particulierement des portraits. L'Empereur Maximilien, Philippe II. Roi d'Espagne, & l'Archiduc Ferdinand, tâcherent de l'avoir auprés d'eux, parce qu'elle avoit beaucoup de bonnes qualitez. Mais son pere qui l'aimoit passionnément, ne voulut jamais consentir qu'elle s'éloignât de lui, aimant mieux la marier à Venise à un Joüaillier nommé Mario Augusta, que de la voir dans une meilleure fortune qui l'auroit privé de sa présence. Elle mourut dans la fleur de son âge l'an 1590. au grand déplaisir de son pere qui en souffrit une douleur extrême.' Her delight and proficiency in music are mentioned in the translation of Roger de Piles's *Art of Painting* (1744), p. 173, which lacks, however, some of Felibien's information.

29–32. Cf. a similar description of the decay of art in Pope, *Essay on Criticism*, ll. 484–93.

31. *timeless*: 'Untimely; . . . done before the proper time' (*Dict.*).

33. Cf. 'Ode to a Friend on his Return &c', ll. 201–2.

36. *imbrown'd*: cf. 'Ode on the Poetical Character', l. 60.

40. *bloomy*: cf. Fragment 10, l. 13, and 'blooming' in 'Ode, to a Lady', l. 30.

43. *Adria*: the Adriatic Sea; cf. Fragment 3, l. 31, and 'Ode to Liberty', l. 45.

49, 56. The rough outline of these last two stanzas closely parallels Pope's 'Elegy to the Memory of an Unfortunate Lady', ll. 55–61, 82.

FRAGMENT 8

The rationale for dating this fragment before the publication of Collins's *Odes* in December 1746 is based on the assumption that this poem, especially in ll. 33–48, represents an early version of the 'Ode to Evening'. For a full discussion of the relationship between these poems, see A. D. McKillop, 'Collins's *Ode to Evening*—Background and Structure', *Tennessee Studies in Literature*, 5 (1960), 73–83. Collins's scheme, as McKillop points out in his review of *Drafts and Fragments* (*PQ*, 36 (1957), 353), is actually more ambitious in this poem: he traces the poet's progress through 'the ideal day of *L'Allegro* and Thomson's *Summer*' and closes with a frustrated assertion (corroborated by several unfinished lines) that neither poetry nor painting is capable of capturing the effects of moonlight. The 'Ode to Evening' does seem to represent a development of part of this fragment, and the sustained use of quatrains suggests a date of composition following Fragments 1–6. Lonsdale, moreover, has suggested a possible *terminus a quo* of July 1744 for the poem, based on an echo of Thomson's 'Spring' in l. 24. For the probable relation of this poem to Fragment 9, 'To Simplicity', see the head-note to that poem.

The fragment is written on two quarto leaves measuring $18 \cdot 6 \times 15 \cdot 3$ cm, with four pages of text.

1. *Genii*: tutelary spirits, 'The protecting or ruling power of men, places, or things' (*Dict.*, s.v. 'Genius'). Addison described them as 'Allegorical Beings' in his *Dialogues Upon the Usefulness of Ancient Medals* (*Works*, ed. A. C. Guthkelch (London: Bell, 1914), ii. 285), a possible source for Fragment 6.

11–12. *Gradual*: ripening, 'Proceeding by degrees . . . from one stage to another' (*Dict.*); cf. 'Ode to Evening', l. 40.

17. *Springlets*: the first recorded usage in the *OED* in this sense (a small spring) is Scott's *Marmion* (1808).

20. *Druids*: cf. 'Ode to Liberty', l. 111, and *Ode Occasion'd by the Death of Mr. Thomson*, ll. 1, 44. The oak (l. 19) was sacred to the druids.

24. *roughen*: 'To grow rough' (*Dict.*), a rare usage of this intransitive verb found also in Thomson, 'Spring', ll. 643 and 960, passages added in the revised edition of *The Seasons* published in July 1744.

27, 43. *Lorrain*: the popular landscape painter Claude Lorrain (1600–82), famous for his handling of morning and evening light. Roger de Piles, *The Art of Painting* (1744), p. 344, pointed out that Claude was interested in discovering 'the causes of the diversity of the same view or prospect, explaining why it appeared sometimes after one fashion, and sometimes after another, with respect to colours, instancing in the morning dews and evening vapours'.

28. *orient*: 'Bright; shining' (*Dict.*).

31. *Plats*: plots, 'A small piece of ground' (*Dict.*).

32. *Rysdael*: Jacob van Ruisdael (*c*.1629–82), the great Dutch landscape painter.

33–48. Cf. 'Ode to Evening', ll. 29–40.

36. *Rosa*: Salvator Rosa (1615–73), known for his 'sublime' landscapes; see E. W. Manwaring, *Italian Landscape in Eighteenth Century England* (New York: Oxford Univ. Press, 1925), pp. 44–56.

39. *Wizzard*: magic; cf. 'The Manners', l. 11.

40. *Pencill*: paintbrush.

FRAGMENT 9

To Simplicity

This fragment, entitled 'To Simplicity' in the manuscript, is apparently an early version of the 'Ode to Simplicity' included in Collins's *Odes* (1747), with which it should be closely compared. John Butt, speaking of the major odes, argues that 'Collins's interest lay in discovering fit embodiment for his allegoric abstractions, implying their nature (for example) by the attitudes they strike, by the garb they wear, and by the places they haunt. In the draft of the "Ode to Simplicity", of which not a single line is carried over into the final version, there is but the faintest anticipation of this practice, and perhaps that is why the draft was discarded.' Although P. L. Carver, *The Life of a Poet*, pp. 168–71, has claimed that this fragment in fact resolves some of the obscurities of the 'Ode to Simplicity', the evidence clearly points to an earlier date of composition. The unfinished state of the fragment is indicated by several blanks in the manuscript, by an unusual amount of repetition of important words, and by an uncertain focus on the subject of the poem (first introduced as 'Fancy', but clearly Simplicity in the later stanzas). The dating of this fragment is tentative and based on the evidence available for the dating of the 'Ode to Simplicity' (see the head-note to that poem). A possible date is 1745, or at least some time between July 1744 (the first recorded usage of 'unboastful', in Thomson's *The Seasons*) and May 1746 (when Collins met Joseph Warton at the Guildford Races and presumably began work on his volume in earnest). It should also be noted that the paper on which this poem is written is the same—in size, texture, and watermark—as the manuscript of Fragment 8, 'Ye Genii who in secret state', which is also an anticipation of a later ode. This physical evidence may further serve to link these two 'drafts' together.

The poem is written on two quarto leaves measuring 19·7 × 14·8 cm, with three pages of text. Collins has numbered each stanza.

1–3. Cf. 'Ode to Simplicity', ll. 7–9.

15–18. Cf. 'Ode to Simplicity', ll. 13–15.

34–5. Cf. 'Ode to Simplicity', ll. 10–11.

36. Cf. 'Ode to Simplicity', ll. 47, 51.

37–8. Cf. 'Ode to Simplicity', ll. 52–3.

39. Cf. 'Ode to Simplicity', l. 28.

FRAGMENT 10

The dating of this pastoral fragment remains uncertain, although it has been linked with the 'Ode, to a Lady' (May 1745) for several reasons. In both poems Collins associates himself with a village in Sussex. In the 'Ode, to a Lady' it is the village of Harting, which lies between Chichester and Winchester; here it may also be Harting (a deleted version of l. 1 is 'Village Friends') or Trotton or Woolbedding, the villages associated with the dramatist Otway, whom Collins refers to in stanza 4. From his days at Winchester Collins may have had friends at Up-Park near Harting; Lonsdale points out that Charles Mill, a contemporary of Collins at Winchester, was a member of the Mill family which owned the manor house at Woolbedding at this time. It is possible that the visitor to Collins's 'Southern vale' in both this fragment and in the published ode was the same woman, and also possible (although not certain, as Cunningham suggests) that in both cases she was Elizabeth Goddard, with whom Collins was reported to be in love (see the head-note to 'Ode, to a Lady'). It is clear from l. 44 of this fragment that Collins associates 'Delia', at least, with the Medway in Kent.

Lonsdale has strengthened this tentative dating by suggesting that in stanza 5 Collins is specifically referring to James Hammond's *Love Elegies*, published in December 1742. This identification is perhaps substantiated by the fact that Collins often alluded to Hammond's elegies in the two Shakespearean dirges dating from 1744–5, especially in his 'Song. The Sentiments borrowed from Shakspeare', which is another 'Damon' lyric. Lonsdale's other identification (Elizabeth Carter as the poetess mentioned in the last three stanzas) suggests that Collins had seen her manuscript poems circulating in 1745–6 (see the note to l. 49). These indications as to date are complicated, however, by the manuscript itself: the poem is written on paper identical to that used by Collins in Fragment 11, 'Recitative Accompanied', which almost certainly dates from 1750. It is therefore possible that this fragment was also written later in the decade, and that 'Delia' was a member of Elizabeth Carter's circle of friends.

The poem is written on two quarto leaves measuring 22·6 × 18·6 cm, with four pages of text. This is the most heavily revised of Collins's surviving manuscripts: 1^r comprises ll. 1–20 (and numerous revisions) and ll. 65–72 (in the right margin); 1^v comprises ll. 21–36; 2^r comprises ll. 37–52; and 2^v comprises ll. 53–64 (with a deleted stanza and stanza 8 in the right margin). Each stanza is numbered in the manuscript.

9. *Delia*: cf. Laura and Amanda (l. 60, both versions).

17. Cf. Collins's description of Chichester 'on the Southern coast' ('Ode to a Friend on his Return &c', l. 11).

20. *youngling*: 'youthful; inexperienced' (*OED* 3a).

25. *Resnel*: the dramatist Thomas Otway was born at Trotton in Sussex. Cunningham writes of the Resnel that 'No stream of this name is now known in the area. Harting Brook joins the Rother at Trotton, and a small stream rising at Elsted flows into the brook just before its junction with the main stream' (p. 32 n.). Lonsdale points out that Collins may have been referring to nearby Woolbedding, where Otway's father had been vicar. For Collins's celebration of Otway, see 'Ode to Pity', ll. 16–24.

33–6. Lonsdale suggests that if this shepherd is not merely an invention, Collins may be referring to James Hammond (1710–42), whose *Love Elegies. Written in the Year 1732* (1743) Collins echoed in his two Shakespearean dirges. It was believed that Hammond died of unrequited love for Catherine Dashwood (later a woman of the bedchamber to Queen Charlotte), who first accepted and then rejected his suit. Lonsdale concludes that 'Hammond's fate as a lover and the nature of his poetry correspond precisely and uniquely with what C. says of his "shepherd" ' (p. 551 n.).

43 n. Collins's quotation is the beginning of the first of two riddles in Virgil's *Eclogues*, iii. 104–7: 'Tell me in what land—and you shall be my great Apollo—Heaven's space is but three ells broad.' The riddle probably refers 'to one looking up at the sky from the bottom of a well or cavern'.

44. *Medway*: Collins suggests that Delia lives somewhere in Kent along the Medway, which flows north-east from Forest Ridges in Sussex through Kent until it joins the Thames.

49–64. Lonsdale offers the tentative suggestion that Collins's poetess may be Elizabeth Carter (1717-1806), the friend of Johnson and Richardson whose poetry had been published since the late 1730s. As Collins indicates, this poetess was frequently a visitor to (but not a native of) the Medway, who wrote of a greenwood nymph's complaint, Melancholy's gloomy power, and 'joys from Wisdom gain'd' (ll. 54–6). Miss Carter often visited friends in Canterbury, but was a native of Deal. She was the author of an 'Ode to Melancholy' (*GM*, 9 (Nov. 1739), 599), and an 'Ode to Wisdom' (printed in Richardson's *Clarissa* and in the *GM*, 17 (Dec. 1747), 585), as well as a poem 'To Dr. Walwyn On his Design of Cutting Down a Shady Walk' in which a 'weeping Hamadryad' complains for her 'fate-devoted trees'. As Lonsdale concludes, the similarities between 'Carter and C.'s poetess may be coincidental but they remain striking'.

FRAGMENT 11

Recitative Accompanied

This fragment appears to be part of the ode on 'the Music of the Græcian Theatre' which Collins mentions in his letter of 8 November 1750 to William Hayes. Following the performance of 'The Passions' at the Oxford Encaenia in June 1750, Collins wrote an appreciative letter to Hayes, the Professor of Music at Oxford who had set the ode to music. After offering to send Hayes an improved version of the ode, Collins mentioned yet another project:

I could send you one written on a Nobler Subject, and which, tho' I have been per-suaded to bring it forth in London, I think more calculated for an Audience in the University. The Subject is the Music of the Græcian Theatre, in which I have, I hope, Naturally introduc'd the Various Characters with which the Chorus was con-cern'd, as Oedipus, Medæa, Electra, Orestes &c &c The Composition too is probably more correct, as I have chosen the ancient Tragedies for my Models, and onely copied the most affecting Passages in Them.

Although the present fragment represents only the opening of a major ode for music (it is headed 'Recitative Accompanied'), it appears to be associated with the subject of Collins's announced poem, a composition which has never been discovered. And it would be characteristic of Collins, as Lonsdale suggests, to describe his poem as complete if in fact it had only been begun. If, as seems probable, this is a draft of Collins's projected ode, it can be dated in or near November 1750. The poem itself, on the other hand, is written on paper which exactly matches that on which Collins wrote Fragment 10, 'No longer ask me Gentle Friends', thought to have been composed in 1745–6. It is possible, however, that Fragment 10 dates from later in the decade. The physical evidence here is, in any case, less substantial than the close similarity to the ode on 'the Music of the Græcian Theatre', which was clearly on Collins's mind in late 1750.

The poem is written on one quarto sheet, recto only, measuring 22·7 × 18·5 cm.

1. Cf. Dryden, 'Alexander's Feast', l. 1. The Ptolomy to whom Collins refers is either Ptolomy Soter (c. 367/6–283/2 B.C.), founder of the Macedonian dynasty in Egypt, or his son Philadelphus (308–246 B.C.). Both had been 'by Merit rais'd': Ptolomy Soter from among Alexander's ranks, and Phila-delphus by his father (even though he was not the eldest son). 'Successive' (l. 2), in the sense of 'Succeeding by inheritance' or 'Next in order of suc-cession' (OED 3b–c), seems only to suit Philadelphus; similarly, Philadelphus 'successively' ruled in the sense that he first ruled jointly with his father and later alone. His friendship with Theocritus and Callimachus, moreover, may be referred to in l. 15. He was also celebrated in Joseph Warton's Essay on . . . Pope (1806 edn., i. 180–1). Collins's source for the setting of his poem

seems to have been the *Deipnosophistae* of Athenaeus, which he had already drawn upon in the 'Ode to Liberty.' Athenaeus' speaker describes an extraordinary procession staged by Philadelphus in Alexandria in which large choral groups were featured: 'There were other carts besides, which carried images of kings and of gods as well, many of them. After them marched a choral band of six hundred men; among them three hundred harp-players perfomed together, carrying harps gilded all over, and wearing gold crowns' (v. 201 f.). For another discussion of the Ptolomies, see Michael Gearin-Tosh, 'Obscurity in William Collins', *Studia Neophilologica*, 42 (1970), 27–9.

8. *Dome*: 'A building; . . . a fabrick' (*Dict.*).

10. *Obsequant*: the obsolete 'obsequent', meaning 'Compliant, yielding, obedient' (*OED*).

12 n. *The* Μουσειον: the great museum at Alexandria founded either by Ptolomy Soter or, as was widely believed in the seventeenth century, by his son Philadelphus, who was a patron of learning and literature in the third century B.C. (see Gearin-Tosh's article, cited above). The museum, separate from the famous library, housed a hundred research scholars drawn from the Mediterranean area. '*Μουσειον*' originally denoted a place connected with the Muses or the arts inspired by them (see ll. 9, 12).

LETTERS

To John Gilbert Cooper. 10–17 November 1747

The only manuscript letter of Collins's to survive is addressed to the poet and critic John Gilbert Cooper (1723–69), portrayed here as Collins's collaborator on a literary journal which the two friends were planning to edit together. Cooper, educated at Westminster and Trinity College, Cambridge, had been a steady contributor to Dodsley's *Museum* under the pseudonym 'Philaretes' (see Charles Ryskamp, 'John Gilbert Cooper and Dodsley's "Museum"', *NQ*, 203 (1958), 210–11). In 1745 he published *The Power of Harmony*, a poem; he later published *Letters on Taste* (1754), in which he twice paid tribute to Collins's 'Ode to Evening'. Collins, who had apparently received a letter from Cooper which included a proposed essay for the journal, is here characteristically intent on formulating the title, format, and mottoes for his enterprise almost at the expense of his friend's contribution. In a postscript he adds a compressed account of recent entertainment on the London stage.

No trace has been found of Cooper's and Collins's projected journal, although it may be the same publication which Thomas Warton reports Collins was considering three years later: 'He then told me of his intended History of the *Revival of Learning*, and proposed a scheme of a *Review*, to be called the *Clarendon Review*, and to be printed at the University Press, under the conduct and authority of the University' (*The Reaper*, No. 26). Collins's postscript, on the other hand, corroborates Ragsdale's remark that his friends included

Mess. Quin, Garrick, and Foot, who frequently took his opinion on their Pieces before they were seen by the Public.— . . . From his knowledge of Garrick he had the liberty of the Scenes and Greenroom, where he made diverting observations on the vanity and false consequence of that class of people, and his manner of relating them to his particulars was extremely entertaining.— (*The Reaper*, No. 26.)

Gilbert White also testified that Collins was 'a man of the town, spending his time in all the dissipation of Ranelagh, Vauxhall, and the playhouses' (*GM*, 51 (1781), 11).

Based on the theatrical information with which Collins provides Cooper in the postscript to the letter, Mary Margaret Stewart, 'Collins's Letter to Cooper', *NQ*, 212 (1967), 412–14, has argued that Collins is mistaken in dating the letter, that it was actually written on 17 November 1747 instead of on 10 November. An examination of the theatrical schedules in *The London Stage 1660–1800: A Calendar of Plays, Entertainments & Afterpieces, Part 4: 1747–1776*, ed. George Winchester Stone, Jr. (Carbondale, Ill.: Univ. of Southern Illinois Press, 1962), upon which Miss Stewart draws, reveals that the postscript was indeed written on 17 November, and her evidence is corroborated by the letter's postmark, which clearly reads '17/NO.' These facts suggest that either Collins was mistaken in dating the letter or that he added his postscript a week later. Miss Stewart rejects this second suggestion because 'it seems likely that Collins wrote the entire piece at one time. There are certain consistencies about the whole', most significantly Collins's enthusiasm and carelessness. Yet if Collins is occasionally careless in the execution of his letter, his theatrical information is certainly correct. The ink, as Miss Stewart points out, appears to be the same in both the body of the letter and in the postscript, but whereas the handwriting is of normal size in the letter itself (even in Collins's final notice of Cooper's essay), it is small and crowded in the postscript. The cramped style may simply be a consequence of the small space allotted the postscript, but it may also be interpreted as Collins's attempt to inform his friend of all the theatrical news he had gathered during a week in which the letter itself had been laid aside. Without further evidence the letter cannot be given a definite date, but there appears to be no reason for doubting the evidence available now, which suggests that the letter was written at two different times.

The manuscript of the letter is BL Add. MS. 41178, ff. 35–6. It was first printed as 'A Hitherto Unpublished Letter of William Collins' by E. H. W. Meyerstein, the *London Mercury*, 11 (Dec. 1924), 169–74, and reprinted with fuller annotation by H. O. White, 'The Letters of William Collins', *RES*, 3 (1927), 12–21. The text of the present edition follows the author's manuscript (for a description of editorial principles, see the textual introduction). The letter is written on a sheet, folded lengthwise, measuring 22·5 × 18·2 cm.

Collins filled the first three pages (1^r–2^r), and then added a postscript on the fourth page (2^v) perpendicular to his address in the centre of the page. The corresponding area on the other side of the fourth page is blank except for the following remark in a different hand (possibly Cooper's): 'The famous Wm. Collins 1747'.

   9. *Polémon*: H. O. White, 'The Letters of William Collins', p. 17, suggests either the Greek grammarian and geographer Polemon or Antonius Polemon, the 'well-known rhetorician'. The former is frequently quoted by Athenaeus (whom Collins mentions in l. 31). It seems more likely, however, that Collins is referring to Polemon of Athens (d. 270 B.C.), head of the Academy, who is also mentioned by Athenaeus. Horace, *Satires*, II. iii. 253–7, alludes to Polemon's famous conversion from a dissolute to a pious life following a lecture by Xenocrates, whom he later succeeded as head of the Academy. Polemon's association with the Academy and his sudden conversion to a serious calling may explain why Collins chose him to grace 'the more literary papers'. White notes a French edition of Athenaeus (Paris, 1680), which may explain Collins's use of an accent in his spelling of the name.

   10. *Philèthus*: literally, 'loving *ethics*, ethics being *ratio vitae* and comedy the representation of *vita*' (White, p. 17).

   11. *the Clar——*: the *Clarendon Review*, a rejected title for their journal; see head-note.

nimis fastuosum: excessively haughty.

   11–12. *Le Sage's Salzedo*: Salzedo is a character in Alain René Le Sage's *Le Bachelier de Salamanque* (Paris, 1736): 'Don Juan de Salzedo . . . ne manquoit pas d'esprit; mais il avoit le défaut d'aimer trop le Latin, & de citer à tous propos des passages d'Horace, d'Ovide, ou de Petrone. Toutes les fois qu'il me voyoit, il me parloit en Latin, & je lui répondois dans la même langue pour m'accommoder à son foible' (i. 96). Collins refers to Le Sage's *Gil Blas* in 'The Manners', ll. 67–70.

   26. *Duo turba sumus*: Collins takes this motto from Ovid's story of Deucalion and Pyrrha, *Metamorphoses*, i. 354–5: 'terrarum, quascumque vident occasus et ortus, / nos duo turba sumus; possedit cetera pontus' ('of all the lands which the rising and the setting sun behold, we two are the throng. The sea holds all the rest').

   27. *Idonea dicere vitæ*: quoted from Horace, *Ars Poetica*, ll. 333–4: 'Aut prodesse volunt aut delectare poetae / aut simul et iucunda et idonea dicere vitae' ('Poets aim either to benefit, or to amuse, or to utter words at once both pleasing and helpful to life').

   28. *illustrans commoda vitæ*: quoted from Lucretius' address to Epicurus, *De Rerum Natura*, iii. 1–3: 'E tenebris tantis tam clarum extollere lumen / qui primus potuisti inlustrans commoda vitae, / te sequor' ('O thou who first from so great a darkness wert able to raise aloft a light so clear, illumining the blessings of life, thee I follow').

29–30. *Usus vetusto genere, sed rebus novis. Phædr*: quoted from Phaedrus, *Fabularum Aesopiarum*, iv, Prol. 11–13: '(quas Aesopias, non Aesopi, nomino, / quia paucas ille ostendit, ego plures sero, / usus vetusto genere sed rebus novis)' ('fables which I call Aesopic rather than Aesop's, since he brought out only a few, and I compose a larger number using the old form but treating new themes').

30. *Plus operis quanto veniæ minus*: incorrectly quoted from Horace, *Epistles*, II. i. 168–70: 'Creditur, ex medio quia res accersit, habere / sudoris minimum, sed habet Comoedia tanto / plus oneris, quanto veniae minus' (' 'Tis thought that Comedy, drawing its themes from daily life, calls for less labour; but in truth it carries a heavier burden, as the indulgence allowed is less').

32. *Athenæus*: compiler of the *Deipnosophistae*, from which Collins quotes a fragment in the 'Ode to Liberty', l. 7 n.

33. *Fairfax*: Edward Fairfax (d. 1635) was primarily known for his translation of Tasso's *Gerusalemme Liberata* in 1600. Collins refers to him in his 'Ode to a Friend on his Return &c', l. 197, and Fragment 6, l. 14.

37. *the Essay*: Meyerstein, 'A Hitherto Unpublished Letter of William Collins', p. 173, suggests that Cooper's 'Picturesque' and 'forcible Allegory' may later have been appended to the third edition of his *Letters Concerning Taste* (1757). White specifically suggests either No. IV, 'On Self-Love. A Fable', or No. IX, 'On Contentment. A Fable', but both had already appeared in Dodsley's *Museum* (see James E. Tierney, '*Museum* Attributions in John Cooper's Unpublished Letters', *SB*, 27 (1974), 232–5).

46. Samuel Foote presented *Tea* on Saturday 14 November 1747 at Covent Garden, having given it twice earlier there (11 and 13 November) and numerous times at the Haymarket (Stone, i. 14–15).

47–9. *The Sailor's Rendezvous at Portsmouth* had been sung at Drury Lane on Tuesday 17 November. The previous day it had been billed as 'New *Sailor's Song* and Chorus, call'd *Tit for Tat*' (Stone, i. 15–16). Collins's commentary strengthens Stone's attribution of the song to Cibber.

49. *Rich*: John Rich (*c.*1692–1761), actor, and manager of Covent Garden.

50–1. John Sowden was apparently the 'Gentleman who never appear'd on any stage before' who played Pierre in Otway's *Venice Preserved* at Covent Garden, 4 December 1747 (Stone, i. 18). Sowden was under contract to Rich during the 1747–8 season.

51–2. Stone (i. 5) characterizes the opera season as 'not successful'.

52–3. Giulia Frasi was a principal singer in the 1747–8 opera season and later sang at Ranelagh in 1751–2 (*Grove's Dictionary of Music and Musicians* (1954), iii. 488). Collins's comment suggests that she either had an earlier engagement at Ranelagh or had made plans for one. John Beard (*c.*1716–91) was a well-known actor and singer who appeared both at Ranelagh and on the stage. In November 1747 he was appearing as Macheath in Gay's *The Beggar's Opera* at Covent Garden, to which Foote's *Tea* served as an afterpiece (Stone, i. 13, 15). Frasi and Beard apparently sang William Hayes's version of Collins's 'The Passions' at Gloucester in 1760; see Daniel Lysons, *History of the Origin and Progress of the Meeting of the Three Choirs of Gloucester, Worcester, and Hereford* (Gloucester, 1812), p. 190.

To William Hayes. 8 November 1750

Collins's only other surviving letter is addressed to Dr William Hayes (1705–77), Professor of Music at Oxford, who had set Collins's 'The Passions' to music for a performance at the Oxford Encaenia on 2 July 1750. In his letter Collins extends his appreciation to Hayes and offers the composer both an improved version of 'The Passions' and another, more correct ode dealing with the music of the Grecian theatre. Neither of the poems Collins mentions has survived, although Fragment 11 is probably associated with, and is perhaps an early draft of, the ode on the Grecian theatre. In return Collins asks Hayes for copies of *The Passions*, which had been printed in Oxford in conjunction with the Encaenia performance, and for a transcription of Hayes's setting of the piece. Collins was apparently unaware that Hayes had substituted lines by the Chancellor of the University, the Earl of Litchfield, for his own conclusion to the poem. H. O. White, 'The Letters of William Collins', *RES*, 3 (1927), 21, suggests that Collins 'wrote to Dr. Hayes for copies of the music and of the printed ode, because his friends were contemplating a public performance of the ode at Winchester. That such a performance took place we may safely infer from the fact that the ode with the new termination was specially printed at Winchester, evidently for distribution among the audience.' White's suggestion is plausible: the reprinting of the Hayes text in the Winchester edition (including the substituted conclusion) is best explained if these materials had been posted directly to Collins's friends in Winchester and not to the poet himself.

The manuscript of Collins's letter apparently passed from William Hayes to his son Philip, also Professor of Music at Oxford; Philip in turn showed the letter to William Hymers, a fellow of Queen's College, Oxford, who was preparing an edition of Collins's poetry in the 1780s. In his annotated copy of Langhorne's edition (1781), now in the Osborn Collection at Yale, Hymers reproduced the letter with this explanation: 'Accurately copied Nov. 30. 1782 from the manuscript of Collins, communicated to me by Dr· Philip Hayes, in whose possession it remains / WH.' Hymers's text is followed here, with substantive variants noted from the letter's first printing in William Seward's *Supplement to Anecdotes of Some Distinguished Persons* (1797), pp. 123–4. The manuscript itself has not been traced.

1. *Mr Blackstone of Winchester*: apparently Charles Blackstone, a scholar at Winchester and New College, Oxford, later a fellow of New College and,

in 1748, a fellow of Winchester (T. F. Kirby, *Winchester Scholars* (1888), p. 236). Charles's brother Henry was an exact contemporary of Collins at Winchester and Oxford, and as a fellow of New College from 1740–68 would have been in a position to inform his brother of the performance of 'The Passions' at the Oxford Encaenia in 1750.

3–4. *another more perfect Copy of the Ode*: i.e., of 'The Passions' (see head-note); this copy has not been found.

7. *one written on a Nobler Subject*: see the head-note, and Fragment 11.

17. *the Score of the last*: Hayes's musical arrangement of the ode is Bodleian MS. Mus. d. 120–1.

18–19. The text of *The Passions* printed at Oxford is described in the head-note to the ode.

19 (and Postscript). *M*^{r}*· Clarke at Winchester*: Mary Margaret Stewart, 'Mr. Clarke of William Collins's Letter', *NQ*, 213 (1968), 214–15, has cogently argued that this is Jasper Clarke, a Winchester composer who had renounced a Winchester College scholarship in 1738, and who was later an organist or lay clerk at Durham Cathedral. 'Mr. Jasper Clarke of Winchester' was a subscriber to William Hayes's *Six Cantatas*; Hayes, his son Philip, Joseph Warton, and the Musical Society of Winchester were among the subscribers to Clarke's *A Cantata*, and *Five English Songs* (1760?). Another of Clarke's publications, 'The Invitation. Set by Mr. Jasper Clarke, of Winchester', appeared in *The Universal Magazine of Knowledge and Pleasure* (Dec. 1754). Jasper Clarke thus fits the suggestions in the letter that Clarke was a resident of Winchester and a composer (known to Dr Hayes) eager in 1750 to gain 'some Advantage' from Mr Worgan, whom Collins mentions in his post-script.

26 (Postscript). *M*^{r}*· Worgan*: either James Worgan (1715–53), organist at Vauxhall Gardens, or his younger brother John (1724–90), who had graduated Mus.B. from Cambridge in 1748, was organist at the Church of St. Andrew Undershaft in 1749, and succeeded his brother at Vauxhall *c*. 1751. H. O. White, 'The Letters of William Collins', p. 21, suggests that Collins is probably referring to the younger brother, who was a well-known composer of songs for the theatre and for Vauxhall and Ranelagh. A 'Memoir of the Life and Works of John Worgan, Mus.D.', *The Quarterly Musical Magazine and Review*, 5 (1823), 122, corroborates this suggestion:

That his [Worgan's] mind's eye turned frequently to the antients cannot be denied, and it is not improbable that his youthful intimacy with poor COLLINS inspired the couplet—

> 'Arise as in that elder time!
> Warm, energetic [*sic*], chaste, sublime.'
> *Ode on the Passions.*

Both Worgan brothers could have been known to Collins, whom Gilbert White described as 'passionately fond of music' and 'a man of the town, spending his time in all the dissipation of Ranelagh, Vauxhall, and the play-houses' (*GM*, 51 (Jan. 1781), 11).

ORATIO AD PORTAS

Surviving with Collins's Drafts and Fragments in the Warton collection at Trinity College, Oxford, is a Latin oration in Collins's hand entitled (by another hand) 'Declamatio ad portas by Collins'. At Winchester College distinguished visitors are traditionally welcomed in a Latin address delivered by the senior scholar. The speeches, Cunningham notes, are usually 'the work of the Headmaster or some other adult classical scholar, not of the boys. The present example was probably written by Collins as a school exercise. Similar exercises by other Winchester boys are to be found among the Trinity College Warton papers' (p. 39).

P. L. Carver, *The Life of a Poet*, pp. 13–15, has demonstrated that the oration probably dates from the summer of 1740. The deceased Warden of the College whom Collins mentions in the address was Henry Bigg, who died between 28 June and 11 August 1740. His successor was John Coxed, who had previously been Warden of New College, Oxford. Thus the New College electors who visited Winchester in the summer of 1740 were headed by the Sub-Warden of New College, Thomas Coker. The two electors accompanying him were Richard Eyre and Lancelot Mitchell, both formerly scholars of Winchester and currently fellows of New College. Collins addresses himself first to Coker, then to Eyre (who had travelled in Italy), and finally to Mitchell. Carver apparently thought that Coxed was the first person to be addressed and that Coker was not mentioned; but Collins is clearly referring to the College's guest, who (it is hoped) will repeat his visit next year.

The oration comprises two folio leaves measuring 33·1 × 21 cm, with three pages of text.

1. Collins alludes to *Aeneid*, ii. 650–1: 'Talia perstabat memorans fixusque manebat. / nos contra effusi lacrimis' ('So he [Anchises] continued in his speech and remained unshaken. But we were dissolved in tears').

6. 'penuria' and 'humanitate' (ll. 35–6) are ablatives where accusatives seem required, and perhaps were caused by omission of a line over the final vowel representing a final 'm'.

12–13. Cf. *Aeneid*, vi. 143–4: 'primo avolso non deficit alter / aureus, et simili frondescit virga metallo' ('When the first is torn away, a second fails not, golden too, and the spray bears leaf of the selfsame ore').

16–17. Cf. Cicero, *Tusculan Disputations*, i. 49. 119: 'Quo utinam velis passis perhevi liceat!' ('Would that we might be wafted there under full sail!'). Collins refers to this work in l. 29.

LOST POEMS

A Battle of the School Books at Winchester

William Seward contributed a brief notice to the *European Magazine*, 28 (Dec. 1795), 377, which mentioned a lost poem by Collins:

A SINGULAR line of this great Poet, in a juvenile Poem which he made when he was twelve years old, on a Battle of the School Books at Winchester, is remembered,

'And every Gradus flapped his leathern wing.'

This is the earliest date suggested for a poem by Collins. If Seward's information is accurate, this poem would have been written in 1734 during Collins's first year at Winchester (he was admitted a scholar on 23 February 1734). Seward's source has not been identified, but it could have been Joseph Warton, Collins's close friend at school. The poem appears to have been inspired by Swift's *Battle of the Books*. The phrase 'leathern wing', commonly associated with the bat, occurs again in the 'Ode to Evening', l. 10. 'Gradus' is an abbreviation of the *Gradus ad Parnassum*, a 'dictionary of prosody until recently used in English public schools, intended as an aid in Latin versification, both by giving the "quantities" of words and by suggesting poetical epithets and phraseology' (*OED*).

The Bell of Arragon

Thomas Warton, in his account of a visit with his brother Joseph to Collins at Chichester in September 1754 (*The Reaper*, No. 26), described Collins's 'Ode to a Friend on his Return &c' as well as a poem which has not been traced:

He also shewed us another Ode, of two or three-four-lined Stanzas, called *The Bell of Arragon*, on a tradition that, anciently, just before a King of Spain died, the great bell of the Cathedral of Sarragossa, in Arragon, tolled spontaneously. It began thus:

> The Bell of Arragon, they say
> Spontaneous speaks the fatal day, &c.

Soon afterwards were these lines:—

> Whatever dark aerial Power,
> Commission'd haunts the gloomy Tower.

The last Stanza consisted of a moral transition to his own Death and *Knell*, which he called *some simpler Bell*.

Nothing else is known of this poem. Nathan Drake, who reprinted Warton's account in *The Gleaner* (1811), iv. 476–7, attempted to complete the poem in *Mornings in Spring* (1828), ii. 337–8.

An Epistle to the Editor of Fairfax his Translation of Tasso's Jerusalem

The *Whitehall Evening Post* (1–3 Feb. 1750) announced that '*In a few Days*' would be published 'AN EPISTLE to the EDITOR of FAIRFAX his TRANSLATION of TASSO. By Mr. WILLIAM COLLINS' by R. Manby and H. S. Cox, publishers of Collins's *Ode Occasion'd by the Death of Mr. Thomson* the previous year. The poem was later given a definite date of publication in the *General Advertiser* for 27 March 1750 (Tuesday): '*On Saturday next will be published*, Price 1*s*., AN Epistle to the Editor of Fairfax his Translation of Tasso's Jerusalem. By WILLIAM COLLINS.' These advertisements were first noticed by A. D. McKillop, 'A Lost Poem By Collins', *TLS* (6 Dec. 1928), p. 965. The poem has not been traced, and was probably not published. In a note in his copy of Langhorne's edition (1781, p. xiii), William Hymers wrote that 'Mr Collins some time before his death advertised a letter to the Editor of Fairfax's Tasso but never published it.'

A new edition of Fairfax's translation of Tasso, which had originally been published in 1600, was issued in October 1749: *Tasso's Jerusalem Delivered: Or Godfrey of Bulloign. An Heroic Poem. Done into English, In the Reign of Queen Elizabeth, By Edward Fairfax, Gent.* The editor of this edition has not been identified. Collins had often expressed his admiration for Tasso and Fairfax prior to the date of these announcements: see his letter of 10–17 November 1747 to John Gilbert Cooper which mentions 'some MSS of Fairfax which I can procure'; Fragment 6, ll. 13–14; and his 'Ode to a Friend on his Return &c', ll. 188–203, written soon before these intended publication dates for his epistle. McKillop suggests that the lines on Tasso in the parodic 'Ode to Horror' may refer specifically to this poem, known in manuscript form to the anonymous author (probably Thomas Warton). But, as Lonsdale points out, the Wartons also alluded to Tasso in their poetry: see, for example, the ode 'To a Gentleman upon his Travels thro' Italy', l. 57 (by Thomas, according to David Fairer, 'The Poems of Thomas Warton the Elder?' *RES*, n.s., 26 (1975), 298–9.

MISSING LETTERS

Missing Letters

Although only two of Collins's letters appear to survive, information concerning several others has been preserved by his friends:

I. John Mulso to Gilbert White, 1 August 1746: 'I have just reciev'd a Letter from Collin's, dated Antwerp. He gives me a very descriptive Journal of his Travells thro' Holland to that Place, which He is in Raptures about, & promises a more particular Account of: He is in high Spirits, tho' near ye French. He was just setting out for ye Army, which He says are in a poor way, & He met many wounded & sick Countrymen as He travell'd from Helvoet-Sluys.' (*Letters to Gilbert White of Selborne from . . . the Rev. John Mulso*, ed. R. Holt-White [1907], p. 15.)

II. Gilbert White mentions other letters written by Collins in Flanders during the war: 'While on this tour he wrote several entertaining letters to his Oxford friends, some of which I saw.' (*GM*, 51 (Jan. 1781), 11.)

III. Collins's letter to Cooper (10–17 Nov. 1747) suggests that the two friends carried on a steady correspondence while planning their *Clarendon Review*. Collins specifically states that 'You found by my last [letter]. . . .'

IV. John Ragsdale, July 1793: 'I have a few of his letters, the subjects of which are chiefly on business, but I think there are in them some flights which strongly mark his character, for which reason I preserved them.' (*The Reaper*, No. 26.)

V. Thomas Warton: 'in the summer he sent me a letter on some private business, which I have now by me, dated Chichester, June 9th, 1751, written in a fine hand, and without the least symptom of a disordered or debilitated understanding.' (*The Reaper*, No. 26.)

UNFINISHED PROJECTS

Galeomyomachia

A previously unknown project of Collins's, perhaps his first enterprise as a 'literary adventurer' in London, is noted in William Hymers's copy of Langhorne's edition (1781) in the Osborn Collection, Yale University Library:

He transcribed Galeomuomachia from a manuscript in the Bodleian Library [and prevailed with M$^{r\cdot}$ Davies to print it] . . . He designed to translate and comment upon it and was fond of supposing it a relic of Aristophanes—The text was well printed in 4$^{to\cdot}$ without accent but the comment and translation never executed—a dramatic bawble 32 pages—. (p. vii.)

The only copy known is in the Bodleian Library (Vet. A5 d. 221), presented to the Library in 1930 by James P. R. Lyell; it was once in the collection of Richard Prime. Collins probably transcribed the manuscript before leaving Oxford for London in late 1743 or early 1744, but it was not printed until 1768, at the Clarendon Press (see Harry Carter, *A History of the Oxford University Press* (Oxford: Clarendon Press, 1975), p. 586). A transcription of the manuscript in Collins's hand apparently has not survived, but the printed copy—a 32-page quarto printed without accent—exactly matches Hymers's description of the project.

Although Collins supposed the *Galeomyomachia* to be 'a relic of Aristophanes', it was in fact written by Theodorus Prodromus (12th c.); see Wolfram Hörandner, *Theodoros Prodromus: Historische Gedichte* (Vienna: Verlag der Österreichischen Akademie der Wissenschaften, 1974). As a 'battle of cats and mice', Theodorus' poem lies in the tradition of the pseudo-Homeric *Batrachomyomachia*, the 'battle of frogs and mice' which was often imitated in the early eighteenth century: Foxon cites poems by Parnell (1717; P73), Samuel Wesley the Younger (1726; W342), and Henry Price (1736; P1039). The Bodleian manuscript is Codices Barocciani 64, f. 18: 'Poema, quod dicitur Galeomyomachia, cum scholiis nonnullis glossulisque, prævio argumento'; see H. O. Coxe, *Bodleian Library*

Quarto Catalogues: I. *Greek Manuscripts* (1853; rpt. Oxford: Bodleian Library, 1969).

A History of the Revival of Learning

Collins's most ambitious project, and one which he apparently intended to complete even after receiving a portion of his uncle's inheritance in 1749, was described by his friends as 'A History of the Revival of Learning'. James Hampton reported that after arriving in London, Collins 'soon dissipated his small fortune, to compensate for which, he projected the history of the revival of learning in Italy, under the pontificates of Julius II. and Leo X. His subscription for this work not answering his expectations, he engaged with a bookseller, to translate Aristotle's Poetics' (*Poetical Calendar*, xii. 109). Scant attention was paid to the project by Langhorne (who implied that the work was only projected), but Johnson, in his 'Life of Collins', claimed that the poet 'published proposals for a *History of the Revival of Learning*, and I have heard him speak with great kindness of Leo the Tenth, and with keen resentment of his tasteless successor [Adrian VI]' (*Lives*, iii. 335).

John Ragsdale singled out this history as the first of Collins's projects: his cousin Payne's refusal to supply him with funds 'forced him to set about some work, of which his History of the Revival of Learning was the first, and for which he printed proposals (one of which I have) and took the first subscription money from many of his particular friends. The Work was begun, but soon stood still' (*The Reaper*, No. 26). Similarly Thomas Warton, in a postscript to his letter to William Hymers published in *The Reaper*, wrote that 'I have just been informed, from undoubted authority, that Collins had finished a Preliminary Dissertation to be prefixed to his History of the Restoration of Learning, and that it was written with great judgment, precision, and knowledge of the subject.' And Gilbert White, in his memoir of Collins, remembered his friend 'always planning schemes for elaborate publications, which were carried no farther than the drawing-up proposals for subscriptions, some of which were published; and in particular, as far as I remember, one for "A History of the darker Ages" ' (*GM*, 51 (1781), 11).

This formidable project appears to have been on Collins's mind at least by early 1744, when, in the revised edition of his *An Epistle: Addrest to Sir Thomas Hanmer*, he wrote:

> As Arts expir'd, resistless Dulness rose;
> *Goths*, *Priests*, or *Vandals*, - - - - all were Learning's Foes.
> Till *Julius* first recall'd each exil'd Maid,
> And *Cosmo* own'd them in th' *Etrurian* Shade. (ll. 35–8)

(Julius II, he added in a note, was the immediate predecessor of Leo X.) On 18 July 1744 his friend John Mulso wrote that Collins was 'entirely an Author, & hardly speaks out of Rule: I hope his Subscriptions go on well in Oxford' (*Letters to Gilbert White of Selborne from . . . the Rev. John Mulso*, ed. R. Holt-White [1907], p. 3). These subscriptions probably refer to Collins's history. In the October–December 1744 issue of *A Literary Journal*, 1, Pt. i (Dublin), 226, appeared the following notice under the heading 'The following Books [published in London] deserve also to be mentioned': '*A Review of the Advancement of Learning, from* 1300. *to* 1521. *by* Wm. Collins, 4to.' Attention was first drawn to this announcement by H. O. White, 'The Letters of William Collins', *RES*, 3 (1927), 16 n. No trace of this volume has been found, and later comments by the Wartons indicate that the history had not been completed by the end of 1744.

Thomas Warton reported that Collins told him of his 'intended History of the *Revival of Learning*' in 1750. In his *Essay on the Writings and Genius of Pope* (1756), Joseph Warton wrote that 'Concerning the particular encouragement given by Leo X. to polite literature, and the fine arts, I forbear to enlarge; because a friend of mine is at present engaged in writing, THE HISTORY OF THE AGE OF LEO X.' (1806 edn., i. 182). Similarly Thomas, in his *History of English Poetry*, recalled that Collins had shown him Skelton's '*Nigramansir*'

not many months before his death: and he pointed it out as a very rare and valuable curiosity. He intended to write the HISTORY OF THE RESTORATION OF LEARNING UNDER LEO THE TENTH, and with a view to that design, had collected many scarce books. Some few of these fell into my hands at his death. The rest . . . were dispersed. (1824 edn., iii. 185 n.)

It may be safe to conclude that Collins's history, pursued for most of his adult life, was never realized. The attraction of the project, however, may be easily understood: Joseph Warton claimed in his *Essay on . . . Pope* that 'History has recorded five ages of the world, in which the human mind has exerted itself in an extra-ordinary manner; and in which its productions in literature and the fine arts, have arrived at a perfection not equalled in other periods.' The fourth age was that of 'Julius II. and Leo X. which produced Ariosto, Tasso, Fracastorius, Sannazarius, Vida, Bembo, Sadolet, Machiavel, Guicciardin, Michael Angelo, Raphael, Titian', many of whom Collins had celebrated in his poetry. 'It is a noble period,' Warton continued, 'and full of those most important events which have had the greatest influence on human affairs. Such is the discovery of the West-Indies, by the Spaniards; and of a passage to the East, by the Portugueze: the invention of printing; the reforma-tion of religion; with many others' (1806 edn., i. 180–2). For the specific dates mentioned in the announcement of 1744, H. O. White suggests the famous centennial Jubilee festival held in Rome under Boniface VIII in 1300, and the death of Leo X in 1521.

A Translation of Aristotle's *Poetics*

According to James Hampton's memoir of Collins in the *Poetical Calendar* (xii. 109), the poet's subscriptions for his *History of the Revival of Learning* 'not answering his expectations, he engaged with a bookseller, to translate Aristotle's Poetics, and to illustrate it with a large and regular comment'. Samuel Johnson enlarged this notice in his 'Life of Collins':

One day [I] was admitted to him when he was immured by a bailiff that was prowling in the street. On this occasion recourse was had to the booksellers, who, on the credit of a translation of Aristotle's *Poeticks*, which he engaged to write with a large commentary, advanced as much money as enabled him to escape into the country.

He shewed me the guineas safe in his hand. Soon afterwards his uncle, Mr. Martin, a lieutenant-colonel, left him about two thousand pounds; a sum which Collins could scarcely think exhaustible, and which he did not live to exhaust. The guineas were then repaid, and the translation neglected. (*Lives*, iii. 336–7.)

According to Langhorne (p. ix), Collins was capable of performing this project, but became a critic only 'in idea'. Ragsdale, however, claimed that

Both Dr. Johnson and Mr. Langhorne are mistaken, when they say the Translation of Aristotle was never begun; I know to the contrary, for some progress was made in both [the history and the translation], but most in the latter. From the freedom subsisting between us, we took the liberty of saying any thing to each other: I one day reproached him with idleness; when to convince me my censure was unjust, he shewed me many sheets of his Translation of Aristotle, which he said he had fully employed himself about, to prevent him calling on any of his friends so frequently as he used to do. (*The Reaper*, No. 26.)

In his preface to Dodsley's *Preceptor* (published 7 April 1748), Johnson wrote that 'a more accurate and Philosophical Account [of rhetoric and poetry] is expected from a Commentary upon *Aristotle*'s Art of Poetry, with which the Literature of this Nation will be in a short Time augmented' (*Samuel Johnson's Prefaces & Dedications*, ed. Allen T. Hazen (New Haven: Yale Univ. Press, 1937), p. 184). Although Johnson's allusion is generally thought to be to Collins's project, it is almost certain the project was never completed.

The date of Collins's work on his translation and commentary has been a matter of dispute, but something like the following explanation is likely: the project appears to have been one of several 'plans to raise a general subsistence' which Collins undertook upon his arrival in London. The most probable date for it is thus 1745 or early 1746 (following his unsuccessful subscriptions for the *History of the Revival of Learning*), but his work on the translation may have been sporadic at this time. Johnson does not date his account of Collins's immurement at Miss Bundy's, but he almost certainly is describing the same situation mentioned in John Mulso's letter of 28 May 1746 (quoted in the head-note to 'Ode to

Pity'). Johnson was apparently Collins's middleman with the pub-lishers (as he was later to be with Goldsmith's *The Vicar of Wakefield*), and it is likely that Collins agreed to a project which he had at least contemplated, if not begun. The poet's 'escape into the country' may have been directly to Chichester, although he probably settled in Richmond as early as 1747. And it would be in Richmond that John Ragsdale would have had easy access to Collins. How long Collins continued his work on the translation is not known, but Johnson's note in *The Preceptor* and his claim that the project was left unfinished after the death of Colonel Martin suggest that Collins at least 'intended' to produce the work until 1749, when he became free of financial worries.

Biographia Britannica

According to John Ragsdale (*The Reaper*, No. 26), Collins was to have been a contributor to the *Biographia Britannica*: 'Soon after this [the translation of Aristotle's *Poetics*] he engaged with Mr. Manby, a bookseller on Ludgate Hill, to furnish him with some lives for the *Biographia Britannica*, which Manby was then publishing. He shewed me some of the Lives in embryo, but I do not recollect that any of them came to maturity.' The *Biographia* was published in six volumes (1747–66); it first appeared in instalments in 1745, the probable date of Collins's work on these lives. One of the publishers was Mary Cooper (who had issued Collins's *Verses Humbly Address'd to Sir Thomas Hanmer* in 1743, and who was co-publisher of the revised version in 1744), and it may have been through her that Collins was offered several of the biographies. It is also possible that Collins was introduced to this project by the antiquarian William Oldys, whose letter mentioning 'Mr Collins' and his 'Subscription' is dated 22 February 1744 (see the head-note to *An Epistle: Addrest to Sir Thomas Hanmer*). Oldys himself contributed twenty-two articles to the *Biographia*: see Bolton Corney, *Curiosities of Literature Illustrated* (1838), p. 177. Both Carver, *The Life of a Poet*, p. 67, and Sigworth, p. 35, mention the possibility that Collins may have been responsible for lives in the first volume of the *Biographia*, but this seems unlikely. There is no other evidence concerning Collins's contributions to this project, and it appears that Collins's sketches remained in their embryonic state.

The Clarendon Review

According to Collins's letter of 10–17 November 1747 to John Gilbert Cooper, he and his friend planned to edit a literary periodical to be called *The Clarendon Review*. The review was to comprise 'literary' and 'Comic' papers, apparently in the manner of Dodsley's *Museum*, to which Cooper had been a steady contributor. (For details of their plans, see Collins's letter, printed above.) Thomas Warton wrote that Collins mentioned his plans to him in 1750: 'He then told me of his intended History of the *Revival of Learning*, and proposed a scheme of a *Review*, to be called the *Clarendon Review*, and to be printed at the University Press, under the conduct and authority of the University' (*The Reaper*, No. 26). In his letter to Cooper, Collins offered 'more modest' but 'equally comprehensive' titles for the review: 'The Friendly Examiner, or Letters of Polémon and Philèthus; or, the Plain Dealer'. A copy of Collins's and Cooper's periodical has never been located under any of its names, and presumably the review was never published. Bronson, in his edition, pointed out the originality of their plans: 'When it is remembered that the reviews of the eighteenth century were booksellers' organs, written by literary hacks, Collins's idea is seen to be original and bold. . . . in 1750 the project probably was not practicable' (p. xxiii).

POEMS
FORMERLY ATTRIBUTED
TO COLLINS

A Poem Humbly Address'd to His Highness The Prince of Orange, And The Princess Royal of Great Britain

In a supplementary note to Dyce's edition of Collins (1827), p. 42*, Thomas Park first pointed out a notice of newly-published books and pamphlets appearing in the *Gentleman's Magazine*, 4 (Mar. 1734), 167, which mentioned an unknown poem by Collins:

> 18. On the Royal Nuptials. An Irregular Ode. By Mr *Philips*, price 1 *s*.
> 19. A Poem on the same Occasion. By *Wm Collins*. Printed for *J. Roberts*, pr. 6 *d*.

Dyce remarked that 'For a copy of this poem I have sought in vain. As our poet in 1734 was only in his fourteenth [*sic*] year, I incline to believe that it must have been written by another William Collins.' And yet Dyce did admit that Collins was known to have written poetry at age 12 (the lost 'Battle of the School Books at Winchester'), and that Roberts was the publisher of his *Persian Eclogues* in 1742, a work written while Collins was still in school. Scepticism was also expressed by Moy Thomas and Bronson in their editions, and Iolo A. Williams, *Seven XVIIIth Century Bibliographies*, p. 107, suggested that 'Collins' might be a misprint for William Collier, whose *A Congratulatory Poem on His Majesty's Happy Return to England* Roberts had published in 1732 (Foxon C292).

Although the existence of the poems by Edward Philips and 'Collins' advertised in the *Gentleman's* has been questioned, both poems have been located by Charles Ryskamp, 'William Collins's *Poem to the Prince of Orange*', *The Book Collector*, 21 (1972), 40–9. The Philips poem is a 14-page folio; the only known copy is located in the Yale University Library: *On The Nuptials Of His Highness The Prince of Orange, To Her Highness The Princess Royal of England. An Irregular Ode. . . . By Mr. Edward Phillips*' (the Yale copy is signed 'EDWARD PHILLIPS'). The only copy of the poem by 'Collins' yet discovered is Bodleian Pamph. 401 (10): *A Poem Humbly*

Address'd to His Highness The Prince of Orange, And The Princess Royal of Great Britain. The collation of this pamphlet is:

2°: *A*² B²; *1–3* 4–8; *1* title *2* blank *3* 4–8 text. Foxon P527.

An advertisement for this poem, announcing it to be published 'This Day', appeared in the *Daily Journal*, Nos. 4104–5 (13–14 Mar. 1734). The advertisement exactly reproduced the poem's title and also supplied the titles of its four parts:

I. An Epistle to NASSAU, presented to the PRINCE soon after his coming to England. II. On that PRINCE's Sickness. III. On his Recovery. IV. LIBERTY and RELIGION flourishing; the hoped for Consequence of the Marriage of this Prince with the illustrious ANNE, Princess Royal of Great Britain.

Anne (1709–59), the second child of George II and Queen Caroline, was married to William, Prince of Orange, on 14 March 1734. The nuptials elicited numerous poems addressed to the prince and princess, most of them published in 1733 or in March 1734. Among the congratulatory authors were David Mallet and Stephen Duck.

The only basis for attributing this poem to Collins is the advertisement in the *Gentleman's Magazine*. Neither the poem nor the notice in the *Daily Journal* mentions Collins's name. It is possible, however, that at age 12 Collins was capable of writing a lengthy poem on an important occasion. Among the Warton papers in Trinity College, Oxford, moreover, is a poem by Collins's school-fellow Joseph Warton entitled 'Mamon's Plea. A Tale', dated '1737. Repeated by me at Winchester School in the Easter time' (for notice of Warton's translations at age 9, see Nichols, vi. 175 n.). And short poems written at Winchester by both Warton and Collins were published in the *Gentleman's Magazine* in 1739. It may also be doubted whether William Collier is the author of this poem. Although Collier's *A Congratulatory Poem on His Majesty's Happy Return to England* contains some parallels to the poem addressed to the Prince of Orange—notably in its subject, in the poet's hesitations, and in the image of 'fame's magnetic tube', which surveys past history—Collier's poem, written two years earlier, appears to be clearer, more learned, and more mature than the poem in question. It is also difficult to explain why Collier's name would appear on a poem published in 1732, but not on a longer, more ambitious poem issued by the same publisher in 1734.

The text of the poem itself, printed in Ryskamp's article, does little to confirm or deny the attribution to the 12-year-old Collins. The first and third sections are written in (clanging) heroic couplets, the other sections in blank verse. There are occasional passages suggesting the pictorial and allegorical effects Collins was later to pursue, as in the opening lines of the second section:

> Serene as Light, I saw BRITANNIA sit,
> With peaceful Olive Wreath about her Head;
> She sat unmov'd, as Fav'rite of high Heav'n!
> No surging Billows dar'd to lash her Shores,
> Nor fiery Meteors tinge her Silver Zones.

And there are passages, like those opening and concluding the fourth section, which anticipate the maturer Collins's consciousness of the burden of the past:

> Oh! could I equal every antient Bard,
> With eager hast I'd make a fond Attempt
> To paint the Glories of the op'ning Scenes,
> And by strong Images somewhat assist
> Mens lab'ring Minds at fault.
>
> . . . .
>
> But here I stop; each great *Idea* swells
> Beyond the utmost Strength of all my Powers!
> I sink beneath the Task.——

But the epistle as a whole is not characteristic of Collins, nor of the kind of poetry he first attempted: lyric and pastoral. The most telling objection to the attribution, however, is the disparity between his contemporaries' remembrance of one line from a poem written while he was 12 and their complete ignorance of an entire poem of 230 lines, presumably written at the same time. Surely a poem written at this precocious age, and published by a major London bookseller, would have provoked commentary from some of Collins's friends, and Joseph Warton in particular. Thus while the missing poem on the royal nuptials has at last been discovered, the attribution to Collins is still doubtful.

On Hercules

This short, humorous poem was first attributed to Collins in *The Crypt, Or, Receptacle for Things Past: An Antiquarian, Literary, and Miscellaneous Journal* (Ringwood, 1828), ii. 56–8, probably by the journal's editor, Peter Hall, a Wykehamist:

The M.S. of the following Poem (on a subject of most interesting applicability to certain braggadocios) was formerly in the possession of the great Thomas Warton, to whom it probably passed from his brother, the school-fellow and friend of Collins. In that family, we understand, it has always passed as a youthful production of the 'Cicestrian Bard;' it bears the appearance of a school exercise, written out for the Master's inspection. If such it be, however, and the date of 1747 be that of the original composition, all claim to it on the part of *the* poet Collins must give way, as he quitted Winchester for Oxford, in 1740. Under this difficulty, an application was lately made to the Bishop of Hereford, the present Warden of Winchester College, by whose kindness we have obtained a list of every boy of that name admitted into the School within seventeen years of the above date; and we do not hesitate to decide, that to none of them is there any reasonable probability for attributing the verses in question. Whether, therefore, it be, or be not, a school performance, the date must be rather assigned to the time when the transcript was made, and the tradition in favour of William Collins be permitted, in lack of more substantial authority, to predominate.

Printed below this account is the text of the poem, signed 'COLLINS, JUN. 1747'. The article itself is entitled 'W. Collins's Unpublished Poetry', but, as pointed out by P. L. Carver, *NQ*, 177 (1939), 272, the poem was first published in the *Gentleman's Magazine*, 8 (Jan. 1738), 45, in an identical text but with the title '*On* HERCULES'. Carver argued that the publication date of 1738, when Collins was still at Winchester, strengthened the attribution made in *The Crypt*; and in *The Life of a Poet*, pp. 15–17, he speculated that the satirical attack on Walpole may even have been inspired by Thomson's *Liberty*.

There is nothing in the poem, however, to suggest a specific attack on Walpole, and the attribution to Collins has been questioned on poetic grounds by Sigworth (p. 24) and seriously challenged by Lonsdale (p. 560), who argues that 'further evidence is surely needed to demonstrate that C., at the age of just sixteen, could or would have written this dull satirical poem.' Collins appears to have written his *Persian Eclogues* just a year later, and 1739 is also the date of his 'Sonnet' and 'To Miss Aurelia C——r', much more polished (and characteristic) works. On the other hand, the description in *The Crypt* of a signed manuscript in the possession of Thomas Warton makes it difficult to dismiss the possibility that 'On Hercules' is in fact the work of the 16-year-old Collins.

On Our Late Taste in Musick

This 88-line attack on the popularity of foreign music was first attributed to Collins by Sir Harris Nicolas in Brydges's edition (1830), p. xxxviii:

From the coincidence between Collins's love of, and addresses to, Music, his residence at Oxford, and from internal evidence, Some Verses on Our Late Taste in Music, which appeared in the Gentleman's Magazine for 1740 [10 (Oct.), 520], and there said to be 'by a Gentleman of Oxford,' are printed in this edition of Collins's works, not, however, as positively his, but as being so likely to be written by him, as to justify their being brought to the notice of his readers.

This poem was reprinted in several later nineteenth-century editions, but there is no evidence—external or internal—to support an attribution to Collins.

On a Quack Doctor of Chichester

This short poem was first published by William Seward in the *Whitehall Evening Post* for 8–10 July 1794 (see *The Journal of the Rev. William Bagshaw Stevens*, ed. G. Galbraith (Oxford: Clarendon Press, 1965), p. 166), and reprinted in Seward's account of Collins in his *Supplement to the Anecdotes of Some Distinguished Persons* (1797), p. 125:

This great Poet did not often wander into the gayer and lively scenes of his art. The following Verses by him, on a Quack Doctor of Chichester, are still remembered in that city:

> Seventh son of Doctor John,
> Physician and Chirurgeon,
> Who hath travelled wide and far,
> Man-Midwife to a Man of War,
> In Chichester hath ta'en a house,
> Hippocrates, Hippocratous.

In the *Whitehall Evening Post*, Collins was said to have written these lines on the doctor's window. These verses are mentioned by Dyce and Moy Thomas in their editions, but Blunden is the only editor to include them among Collins's collected works (p. 135).

In his remarks on Collins in *The Reaper*, No. 26, John Ragsdale mentions some humorous verses which suggest that Collins occasionally wrote in this vein:

I had formerly several scraps of his poetry, which were suddenly written on particular occasions, these I lent among our acquaintance, who were never civil enough to return them, and being then engaged in extensive business, I forgot to ask for them, and they are lost; all I have remaining of his are about twenty lines, which would require a little history to be understood, being written on trifling subjects.

There is no other evidence to substantiate this attribution. Moy Thomas (1858), p. lix n., elucidated the first line by pointing out that 'A popular proverb assigns, as an hereditary right to all seventh sons, the name of Septimus, and the profession of a surgeon.'

On the Use and Abuse of Poetry

This fragment was attributed to Collins by Blunden in his edition (1929), pp. 156–7, 179. The poem had appeared in Joseph Warton's *Essay on the Writings and Genius of Pope* (1756), i. 60–1, following Warton's discussion of Pope's 'Ode on St. Cecilia's Day':

I have lately seen a manuscript ode, entitled, 'On the Use and Abuse of Poetry,' in which Orpheus is considered in another, and a higher light, according to ancient mythology, as the first legislator and civilizer of mankind. I shall here insert a stanza of it, containing part of what relates to this subject.

ANTISTROPHE. II.

Such was wise Orpheus' moral song,
The lonely cliffs and caves among;
From hollow oak, or mountain-den,
He drew the naked, gazing men,
Or where in turf-built sheds, or rushy bowers,
They shiver'd in cold wintry showers,
Or sunk in heapy snows;
Then sudden, while his melting music stole
With powerful magic o'er each softening soul,
Society, and law, and sacred order rose.

EPODE II.

Father of peace and arts! he first the city built;
No more the neighbour's blood was by his neighbour spilt;
He taught to till, and separate the lands;
He fix'd the roving youths in Hymen's myrtle bands;
Whence dear domestic life began,
And all the charities that soften'd man:
The babes that in their father's faces smil'd,
With lisping blandishments their rage beguil'd,
And tender thoughts inspir'd!—&c.

I am not permitted to transcribe any more, and therefore return to POPE again.

Blunden's conclusion that 'it is all but certain that Collins is the author' is based on the assumption that this poem formed one of those 'fragments' which Collins presented to Joseph Warton in September 1754, and on the 'beautiful, sensitive, and imaginative style' of the piece, especially 'its metrical and expressional consonances with Collins's known work' (p. 179). This poem, however, is not one of those drafts and fragments discovered among the Warton papers at Trinity College, Oxford. And if the poem was in fact in Warton's possession, it is strange that he should claim that he was 'not permitted to transcribe any more'. It is also strange that Warton should not proclaim Collins's authorship of the piece (as he had done with other poems) if it was actually known to be his. It may be doubted as well whether the lines printed by Blunden are any more characteristic of Collins's odes than of much other mid-century poetry. Lonsdale is surely correct in believing that the poem is both clearer and less imaginative than Collins's known work. Finally, it should be pointed out that among the Warton papers there is a scheme of a poem by Joseph Warton entitled 'Of the Use & Abuse of Poetry', written on the verso of a quarto sheet of verses entitled 'Of the Usefulness of Poetry'. Although the printed fragment does not closely correspond with Warton's plan for his poem (which appears to be a progress poem ranging from Homer to the Restoration poets), it is at least possible that the fragment is by Warton himself and that it bears some relation to his manuscript jottings.

A Song. Imitated from the Midsummer-Night's Dream of Shakespeare. Act II. Scene V.

Collins's authorship of this Shakespearean imitation has been argued (in spite of strong contrary evidence) by Iolo A. Williams in the *London Mercury*, 8 (May 1923), 81–2, and in his *Seven XVIIIth Century Bibliographies* (1924), pp. 102–4, and by H. W. Garrod, *Collins*, pp. 113–15. The poem appeared anonymously in the *Museum* (16 Aug. 1746), i. 425. Williams's claim that this poem 'must almost certainly be the work of Collins' is based on 'the general similarity, both of style and of derivation of subject-matter from Shakespeare, to Collins's acknowledged poems', and on 'numerous particular similarities, of phrase and idea, to passages in his poems, especially the *Odes*'. Williams further speculates that the poem may have been 'rejected by him because he afterwards used so many of its phrases and thoughts in more important poems'.

But the poem had already been attributed to Thomas Warton by his brother Joseph, as Alexander Chalmers pointed out in his *British Poets* (1810), xviii. 76 n., where Warton's contributions to the periodical were listed as 'a song imitated from the Midsummer Night's Dream, and a prose essay on Snugness, written partly by him and partly by Dr. Vansittart. They are authenticated by Dr. Warton's autograph, in his copy of the Museum *penes me*' (Lonsdale suggests that Chalmers may have acquired his set of the *Museum* at the sale of Joseph Warton's books in 1801). Williams preferred, however, 'to think that Collins was the real author of the *Song*, more especially since none of Thomas Warton's acknowledged poems is in the least like it', and because, had Warton written the poem, he 'must have seen the manuscript of Collins's *Odes* and have had it pretty well by heart'. It makes more sense, on the other hand, to suppose that Collins's odes, many of which were apparently written later in 1746, may have been influenced by a poem published in August (and perhaps read in manuscript even earlier). Both Carver (pp. 186–8) and Lonsdale (p. 564), moreover, have demonstrated that similarities between this poem and Collins's 'Ode to Evening' are also characteristic of Milton (presumably a source for both poems) and of several authors whose work appeared in the *Museum* at this time. The only substantial evidence available to us, therefore, assigns this poem to Thomas Warton.

An Ode to the People of Great Britain

Blunden included this poem—'In Imitation of the Sixth Ode of the Third Book of Horace'—among the 'Poems of Doubtful Authenticity' in his edition (1929), pp. 145–50. The poem first appeared in the *Museum* (24 May 1746), i. 179–82. Blunden attributed the poem to the 'mind of Collins' on the strength of 'numerous phrases and symbols', but offered an alternative attribution to Robert Lowth (pp. 178–9). Lowth, as W. P. Courtney has demonstrated, was in fact the author of the poem (*Dodsley's Collection of Poetry: Its Contents & Contributors* (London: Humphreys, 1910), p. 25). See *Memoirs of the Life and Writings of the Late Right Reverend Robert Lowth* (1787), p. 18, and Lowth's *Sermons, and Other Remains*, ed. Peter Hall (1834), pp. 17, 472–6.

Prologue to *Venice Preserv'd*.
Acted by some Young Gentlemen at Winchester School

This prologue was attributed to Collins by Blunden (1929), p. 179, on the strength of 'The zeal that Collins had for Otway, joined with several characteristic epithets, adjectives, and images'. The poem first appeared anonymously in the *Museum* (10 May 1746), i. 133–4; Blunden added that the accompanying 'Epilogue reads like Joseph Warton'. The prologue is in fact by Robert Lowth, Collins's fellow-Wykehamist. It is included in his *Sermons, and Other Remains*, ed. Peter Hall (1834), pp. 486–7, where it is described as having been '*Communicated by Dr. Warton to the Hampshire Repository, in 1799, and there said to have been first published in the Oxford Student, about forty years before*'. In his communication to *The [Annual] Hampshire Repository*, 2, Pt. iii [Winchester, 1801], 100–1, Joseph Warton introduced the poem as 'a Prologue, written by Bishop Lowth, to a Play once acted at the College, which perhaps you have never met with, and which was but once printed, forty years ago, in The Oxford Student'. The poem did not, however, appear in *The Student, Or, The Oxford, and Cambridge Monthly Miscellany* (1750–1), and it seems probable that Warton was confusing this periodical with the *Museum*.

An Ode, To the Memory of Colonel Gardiner, In Imitation of Milton

An Ode to Evening, In Imitation of Milton

P. L. Carver, in 'Collins and Alexander Carlyle', *RES*, 15 (1939), 35–44, and later in *The Life of a Poet* (1967), pp. 78–84, suggested that these two poems were joint compositions of Collins and Carlyle, the Scottish minister responsible for publishing the 'Ode to a Friend on his Return &c' in 1788. The poems had appeared anonymously in the *British Magazine: or, the London and Edinburgh*

Intelligencer for February 1747. It is possible that Collins met Carlyle during the clergyman's stay in London in 1750, and possible that Carlyle wrote these pieces, but it is very unlikely that Collins was his collaborator or that these poems influenced his own odes, which had been published two months earlier. The poems in fact represent outright plagiarism of Collins's 'Ode, Written in the beginning of the Year 1746', 'Ode, to a Lady', and 'Ode to Evening'.

Prologue to Home's *Douglas*

Prologue to *Douglas*, Spoken at Edinburgh

Epilogue to *Douglas*

Collins's assistance in writing these three pieces has been claimed by Blunden (1929), p. 179, who argues that 'Collins's enthusiasm and knowledge of the stage suggest that he would have helped the young author, who was not a polished versifier, with these.' Blunden concludes, entirely on the basis of internal evidence, that several 'significances' may 'obtain me a licence to print them as possibly by Collins'. There is no evidence to substantiate Blunden's attribution of these poems, which are characteristic of much mid-eighteenth-century poetry. Collins apparently never saw John Home after presenting him with 'An Ode to a Friend on his Return &c' in late 1749 or early 1750. Henry Mackenzie, in his *Anecdotes and Egotisms*, ed. H. W. Thompson (London: Oxford Univ. Press, 1927), p. 166, wrote that he 'never . . . heard Mr. Home speak of Collins (probably from his thinking it an unpleasant subject), nor among Mr. Home's papers were any letters or notes from Collins or concerning him'. Similarly, Home's friend Alexander Carlyle, in his *Anecdotes and Characters of the Times*, ed. James Kinsley (London: Oxford Univ. Press, 1973), p. 152, reports that *Douglas* 'had Receiv'd all the Corrections and Improvements, that it needed, by many excellent Criticks who were Mr Homes Friends . . . with whom he Daily Liv'd', and Collins is not mentioned among this group. A presentation copy of the play (Edinburgh, 1798) in the Princeton University Library, marked by Home throughout, reveals no sign that the prologues and epilogue were not written by the playwright himself. Collins, moreover, was in relative seclusion after 1754, and was almost certainly not writing poetry in 1756–7, when these pieces were presumably written.

Tomorrow

The Mulberry Tree

The Despondent Negro

Despite the differences in their style, subject-matter, and dates of composition (as well as the more obvious difference in their authors' Christian names), the works of the poet William Collins and the actor and songster John Collins became confused in early-nineteenth-century poetical collections. Peter Hall, editor of *The Crypt*, who had attributed the poem 'Hercules' to William Collins in his February 1828 issue, later put the following question to his correspondents concerning the authorship of the song 'Tomorrow': ' "A. D." suggests to us, that in Ritson's Collection of Songs, there is one by *a* Collins, certainly not *the* Collins: Query, was this the author of the Verses in our Number for February?' (ii. 192). The answer, which *The Crypt* never published during its brief lifetime, is negative. 'Tomorrow' is in fact the work of John Collins (d. 1808), author of 'The Evening Brush' and *Scripscrapologia*. Similarly, two poems attributed to Collins in the Osborn Collection in the Yale University Library, 'The Mulberry Tree' and 'The Despondent Negro', are also by John Collins. For a full discussion of these three poems, see Richard Wendorf, 'William Collins and John Collins: A Problem in Attribution'. *NQ*, 222 (1977), 318–19.

ESSAYS
FORMERLY ATTRIBUTED
TO COLLINS

Of the Essential Excellencies in Poetry

Frederick Page, 'An Essay by Collins', *TLS* (11 July 1935), p. 448, attributed to Collins an essay entitled '*Of the Essential Excellencies in Poetry*', which appeared anonymously in the *Museum* (4 July 1747), iii. 281–6. Page contended that the 'argument of the essay is the argument of the Ode on the Poetical Character, with an incidental coincidence with the Ode to Fear', and he quoted the essayist's major premise: 'there is something in Poetry supernatural or divine. . . . There is nothing that gives us so clear a Notion of the Divinity, as his Power of Creating. . . . Yet this very Power of Creating, tho' in a very weak and remote Degree, seems to be communicated to the Poet' (pp. 281–2). Page pointed out illustrations from Spenser, Shakespeare, and Milton as further proof of the attribution, as well as the striking conclusion which celebrates David Mallet's *Amyntor and Theodora* and Martin Martin's *A Voyage to St. Kilda*, both sources for Collins's 'Ode to a Friend on his Return &c'. Edmund Blunden, *TLS* (8 Aug. 1935), p. 501, cautioned that 'the period which produced Dodsley's *Museum* was rather apt to dominate individuality, and critical positions and expressions then were shared by not a few writers. . . . Many other hands were concerned in the periodical.' But the tendency among most of the essay's readers has been to agree with Page's attribution; see, for instance, E. W. H. Meyerstein, *TLS* (25 July 1935), p. 477; P. L. Carver, *The Life of a Poet*, p. 137; and Sigworth, *William Collins*, pp. 46–7.

'If internal evidence could decide the question we should suppose that soon after this he was writing for Dodsley, who must, in that case, have liked his prose better than his poetry', Carver writes; but, strong as the internal evidence is, there is unfortunately no external evidence to authorize this essay's inclusion among Collins's works. Although Collins had contributed his 'Ode, to a Lady' to the *Museum* a year earlier, and although he was at this time engaged in plans for a literary periodical, there is no mention of this—or any other essay—in memoirs written by his friends. This seems

especially significant in light of the attention which friends be-
stowed on projects which were never finished.

An Enquiry into the Nature of the Passions

Milton's Muse

Theatrical Reviews

Blunden, in his edition of Collins (p. 174), mentions an essay in the
Museum (29 Aug. 1747), iii. 437–42, implying that it may have been
written by Collins. Similarly E. H. W. Meyerstein, 'An Essay by
Collins', *TLS* (25 July 1935), p. 477, suggests this essay for inspec-
tion, pointing out that one phrase in particular—'I wave all these
Considerations'—echoed the attributed 'Essay on the Essential
Excellencies of Poetry'. The essay is '*An Enquiry into the Nature of
the* PASSIONS, *and the Manner in which they are represented by the
Tragick Poets, particularly with respect to Jealousy; including some Ob-
servations on* SHAKESPEAR's OTHELLO'. Although the anonymous
author discusses Shakespeare's sources for his play, and mentions
Cinthio, Fletcher, and Rowe—authors referred to in Collins's poems
and fragments—there is little similarity between this essay and
Collins's 'The Passions. An Ode', written a year earlier. The essay
is unattributed in James E. Tierney's 'A Study of *The Museum: Or,
The Literary and Historical Register*', Diss., New York Univ., 1969,
pp. 182–3, and id., '*The Museum*, the "Super-Excellent Magazine"',
SEL, 13 (1973), 503–15.

Meyerstein also suggests that Collins may have been the author
of the unsigned essay on 'MILTON's *MUSE*' in the *Museum* (7
June 1746), i. 210–12, and of several theatrical letters as well (e.g.,
28 Feb. and 4 July 1747). Arthur Johnston points out, however,
that 'Milton's Muse' is the work of John Callender, whose 'com-
mentary on Book I of *Paradise Lost* was later published in Glasgow
in 1750' ('The Poetry of William Collins', *Proceedings of the British
Academy*, 59 (1973), 327 n.). There is no evidence to suggest that
Collins was in fact the author of the other essays, which could have
been written by many of the periodical's numerous contributors.

INDEX OF FIRST LINES